Humanity's Dark Side

Humanity's Dark Side

Evil, Destructive Experience, and Psychotherapy

Edited by **Arthur C. Bohart, Barbara S. Held, Edward Mendelowitz, and Kirk J. Schneider**

American Psychological Association • Washington, DC

Published by
American Psychological Association
750 First Street, NE
Washington, DC 20002
www.apa.org

To order
APA Order Department
P.O. Box 92984
Washington, DC 20090-2984
Tel: (800) 374-2721; Direct: (202) 336-5510
Fax: (202) 336-5502; TDD/TTY: (202) 336-6123
Online: www.apa.org/pubs/books
E-mail: order@apa.org

In the U.K., Europe, Africa, and the Middle East, copies may be ordered from
American Psychological Association
3 Henrietta Street
Covent Garden, London
WC2E 8LU England

Typeset in Goudy by Circle Graphics, Inc., Columbia, MD

Printer: Maple Press, York, PA
Cover Designer: Mercury Publishing Services, Rockville, MD

The opinions and statements published are the responsibility of the authors, and such opinions and statements do not necessarily represent the policies of the American Psychological Association.

Library of Congress Cataloging-in-Publication Data

Humanity's dark side : evil, destructive experience, and psychotherapy / edited by Arthur C. Bohart ... [et al.].
    p. cm.
  Includes index.
  ISBN 978-1-4338-1181-4—ISBN 1-4338-1181-2 1. Good and evil—Psychological aspects. 2. Psychotherapy. I. Bohart, Arthur C.
  BF789.E94H86 2013
  158.3—dc23
                                    2012023271

British Library Cataloguing-in-Publication Data

A CIP record is available from the British Library.

Printed in the United States of America
First Edition

DOI: 10.1037/13941-000

CONTENTS

CONTRIBUTORS

Arthur C. Bohart, PhD, California State University, Dominguez Hills

John Briere, PhD, Keck School of Medicine, University of Southern California, Los Angeles

Barbara S. Held, PhD, Bowdoin College, Brunswick, ME

James Hollis, PhD, private practice, Houston, TX

Arnold A. Lazarus, PhD, ABPP, Rutgers University, The State University of New Jersey, Piscataway; President, The Lazarus Institute, Skillman, NJ

Larry M. Leitner, PhD, Miami University, Oxford, OH

Edward Mendelowitz, PhD, private practice, Boston, MA

Ronald B. Miller, PhD, Saint Michael's College, Colchester, VT

Maureen O'Hara, PhD, National University, La Jolla, CA

Aftab Omer, PhD, Meridian University, Petaluma, CA

Peter F. Schmid, PhD, Sigmund Freud University, Vienna, Austria

Kirk J. Schneider, PhD, Saybrook University and the Existential–Humanistic Institute, San Francisco, CA

David Livingstone Smith, PhD, University of New England, Biddeford, ME

PREFACE

There are many forms of human destructiveness: war, rape, murder, slavery, the Holocaust, other manifestations of genocide, oppression, torture, theft, exploitation, child abuse, gang warfare, and extortion, to name just a few. There are also everyday "little" ways in which we hurt each other: malicious gossip, social exclusion, treating others with contempt, blaming others wrongfully, not listening to others, and imposing our ideologies on others. Human destructiveness, from everyday forms to extreme forms, can be thought of as comprising what is often metaphorically referred to as humanity's "dark side."

Humanity's dark side plays a role in psychotherapy. Many therapists may not have worked with perpetrators of seriously destructive behavior. However, most have worked with the victims of it—victims of physical or sexual abuse, emotional abuse, harmful parenting practices, oppression, racism, sexism, the vast range of abuses of social inequities and injustices, and so on. Furthermore, virtually all therapists have worked with clients who have inflicted at least some pain on others, at least in petty, insensitive, everyday ways. Yet at least in recent years, the dark side has not been a major focus in writings on psychotherapy. Although many books about human evil have been written (e.g., Baron-Cohen, 2010; Staub, 2011; Zimbardo, 2007), remarkably scant attention has been paid to how psychotherapists conceptualize and deal with the dark side of human nature in psychotherapy.

This trend may reflect the growth of a technological (i.e., technique-based) emphasis in psychotherapy. Owing to the proliferation of evidence-based interventions, therapists have been encouraged to understand their practice in terms of the techniques and procedures that have been claimed to work best for different disorders. Case conceptualizations are typically enacted in these terms. Concomitantly, there has been a corresponding decline in emphasis on theory (Carlson & Englar-Carlson, 2010; L'Abate, 2009)—so much so that the question of whether theory is still relevant to the practice of psychotherapy is now being raised (Carlson & Englar-Carlson, 2010).

Nonetheless, how therapists construe the dark side of humanity is highly relevant to how they practice—or so we believe. This belief forms the foundation for this book. Thus, we ask the following questions in this book: How do therapists understand the nature and existence of destructive human behavior, from profound evil to more mundane expressions of humanity's dark side? How does this understanding affect therapists' attempts to prevent and/or remediate either destructive behavior itself or its effects?

Humanity's Dark Side was conceived when Barbara Held, then president of the Society for Theoretical and Philosophical Psychology (Division 24 of the American Psychological Association [APA]), organized a symposium at the 2009 APA Annual Convention. The symposium focused on a famous debate between two humanistic psychotherapists, Rollo May and Carl Rogers, about evil, destructive behavior, and human nature—in particular, whether psychotherapists must confront the dark side with their clients to be fully effective.

The symposium naturally seemed to raise important questions for psychotherapists, and this book was born. Two of the presenters at the 2009 convention, Arthur C. Bohart and Kirk J. Schneider, joined with Barbara S. Held and Edward Mendelowitz to become coeditors of the book. Each of us wrote his or her own chapter. In addition, we invited well-known psychologists to contribute chapters. Five chapters came from authors associated with the humanistic–existential tradition: Kirk J. Schneider, Peter F. Schmid, Arthur C. Bohart, Edward Mendelowitz, and Maureen O'Hara and Aftab Omer. One chapter came from an author, Larry M. Leitner, who integrates humanistic ideas with George Kelly's (1963) personal construct theory. Two authors, James Hollis and David Livingstone Smith, work within the psychodynamic tradition. One author, Arnold A. Lazarus, works within an integrative cognitive–behavioral tradition, and another, John Briere, is a well-known trauma psychologist who works within an eclectic, evidence-based tradition. Two authors, Ronald B. Miller and Barbara S. Held, can best be thought of as philosophical psychologists.

All but two chapters focus on psychotherapy directly. Two chapters go beyond psychotherapy to focus on broader issues: The chapter by Barbara S. Held examines the relation between feeling bad and being bad, especially in the context of the positive psychology movement. The chapter by Maureen O'Hara and Aftab Omer examines how "virtue-driven" organizations may inadvertently perpetrate destructive behavior.

We wish to thank Susan Reynolds, who first suggested that we develop the ideas presented in the APA symposium into a book. She said that APA Books was interested in publishing "a book that dealt with how theoretical perspectives on evil affect psychotherapy practice." We appreciate Susan's editorial guidance in formulating this book: She has been a consistent source of information and support when the inevitable bumps in the road were encountered. We also wish to thank Beth Hatch, who served as our development editor: Beth helped us sharpen and shape the message of our book and its individual chapters. Finally, we give our heartfelt thanks to all our authors for their unique and outstanding contributions to this most daunting subject.

REFERENCES

Baron-Cohen, S. (2011). *The science of evil*. New York, NY: Basic Books.

Carlson, J., & Englar-Carlson, M. (2010). Series preface. In B. E. Wampold (Ed.), *The basics of psychotherapy* (pp. ix–xii). Washington, DC: American Psychological Association.

Kelly, G. (1963). *A theory of personality: The psychology of personal constructs*. New York, NY: Norton.

L'Abate, L. (2009). In search of a relational theory. *American Psychologist, 64*, 779–788.

Staub, E. (2011). *Overcoming evil: Genocide, violent conflict, and terrorism*. New York, NY: Oxford University Press.

Zimbardo, P. (2007). *The Lucifer effect: Understanding how good people turn evil*. New York, NY: Random House.

Humanity's
Dark Side

INTRODUCTION: THE DARK SIDE METAPHOR

ARTHUR C. BOHART

The idea that humans have a dark side, or that there is a dark side to life that can seduce them, goes back thousands of years. One can think of the serpent seducing Adam and Eve in the Garden of Eden. One can think of stories of people such as Faust making a pact with the devil to gain power. One prominent use of the dark side metaphor can be found in the well-known *Star Wars* film series. There, the "dark side of the Force" is a power that people use for evil, evil being a desire for illegitimate power, which leads to the murder and oppression of others. The protagonist of the films, Darth Vader, is a character who starts out fighting for the good but is seduced by the dark side and becomes a force for evil.

The dark side metaphor therefore deals with the human capacity for engaging in evil and other forms of destructive behavior. In this book, we define the *dark side* as that aspect of human nature that has the potential to lead people to behave in destructive ways, either toward themselves or

DOI: 10.1037/13941-013
Humanity's Dark Side: Evil, Destructive Experience, and Psychotherapy, A. C. Bohart, B. S. Held, E. Mendelowitz, and K. J. Schneider (Editors)

3

toward others. This can range from hurtful criticism to insensitive treatment, exploitation, treating people unjustly and unfairly, on up to actively vicious cruelty toward others. Individuals can also treat themselves harshly, cruelly, and insensitively. This potential for destructiveness can be associated with or result from negative emotions such as anger, disgust, contempt, shame, despair, pessimism, hopelessness, and fear. Other emotions, such as pride and guilt, may also, under certain circumstances, manifest themselves in destructive behavior. The dark side may also reside in certain attitudes, such as those of arrogance, superiority, egocentricity, ingroup–outgroup thinking, ideological blindness, or self-righteousness. Finally, it may reside in certain motives, such as the lust for power, desire for dominance, greed, the desire to fit in at any cost, and a motive to resist or rebel against authority. Many of these emotions, attitudes, and motives do not necessarily lead to destructive behavior. However, they have the potential to do so given the wrong circumstances.

This book is not about evil per se. The *dark side* is a broader and more inclusive concept of which evil is a subset. However, evil is an important subset and forms a large part of what several authors in this book focus on.

Many questions can be raised about the dark side. These have to do with the theoretical positions represented in this volume. Is there a dark side of human nature? Or are there merely destructive behaviors that can be learned and unlearned? The dark side metaphor usually incorporates something more than merely a set of behaviors—it can be conceptualized as an underlying dispositional aspect of human personality or nature that can manifest itself in destructive behavior. Therefore, if there is a dark side, are there ways in which humans relate to themselves and to others that incite, exacerbate, or perpetuate it coming out?

Additional questions arise: When people act destructively, how personally responsible are they? Are there "bad" people or only bad behaviors? If one has been hurt by the destructive actions of others, how important is forgiveness to recovery? Finally, how may society and larger organizations contribute to dark side behaviors or acts?

With regard to therapy, must therapists address the dark side of human nature to help people grow constructively? Or is it sufficient to work to change dark, destructive, and negative behaviors, thoughts, and feelings? That is, can therapists help people by working to develop their positive features without addressing dark sides at all? These many questions are important to therapists, who must decide how to help their clients develop in positive, prosocial, constructive directions and thus diminish destructive behaviors, whether those be destructive behaviors directed toward others or destructive behaviors directed toward themselves (e.g., excessive self-criticism, self-multilation, substance abuse, self-starvation, self-neglect).

This book does not focus on the causes or origins of human destructiveness per se, although several authors offer opinions on those. A comprehensive review of factors that have been studied would entail a book in itself (see Baron-Cohen, 2011; Shaver & Mikulincer, 2011; Staub, 2011; Zimbardo, 2007). Various factors that have been considered include evolution (Hawley, 2006; McCullough, Kurzban, & Tabak, 2011; Sell, 2011), genetic theories that implicate genetic predispositions (Baron-Cohen, 2011), neuropsychological theories (Baron-Cohen, 2011), and psychogenic developmental theories that emphasize such factors as attachment (Mikulincer & Shaver, 2010) and child abuse (Toth, Harris, Goodman, & Cicchetti, 2011). Other factors that have been studied include the emotions of guilt and shame (Tangney, 2001) and cognitive factors such as the way people construe or make sense of the events in their lives (Coie & Dodge, 1998; Huesmann & Reynolds, 2001). Socioenvironmental factors that have been implicated include various forms of social inequality and discrimination (Staub, 2011) and the media (Eron, 2001).

Zimbardo's (2007) work has emphasized the importance of such social psychological factors as pressures toward uniformity and deindividuation. Zimbardo (2007) also noted the importance of people's egocentric biases, which lead them to see themselves as special and unique, particularly in terms of self-integrity, in comparison with others. Albert Bandura (1986) explained how, by dehumanizing others, people can treat those so selected inhumanely and despicably, all the while maintaining compassion toward those whom people do not dehumanize (see also Smith, 2011). In that regard the phenomenon of ingroups and outgroups also plays a role in destructive behavior, "sanctioning" aggression toward outgroups (Hinde, 2001). There are also larger institutional forces that promote aggressive acts such as war (Hinde, 2001). Hinde, for instance, argued that human aggression does not produce war. Rather, war as a societal institution produces human aggression.

Conversely, there are theories and research that maintain that humans also have a propensity for prosocial behavior, with some of the same factors involved: evolutionary factors, genetic factors, the existence of mirror neurons, child-rearing practices, empathy, and prosocial environmental practices (Mikulincer & Shaver, 2010). Baron-Cohen (2011), Feshbach (1997), Eisenberg (2010), Hoffman (2001), and others have emphasized the importance of empathy in the promotion of prosocial and moral behavior.

Again, in this book we do not seek to answer the daunting question, what are the causes of human evil and other forms of destructiveness? As we have seen, there are many potential causes. Rather, we ask, how do therapists of different stripes use their theories to understand and conceptualize the dark side of human nature, and moreover, how do they use those conceptualizations to help their clients deal with their dark sides? Therapists do this in the service of (a) helping people reduce their tendencies to inflict destructive behavior on others, (b) helping people who have been victimized by the destructive behavior of others cope with such experiences, and (c) helping people who behave destructively toward themselves find more constructive ways of living.

At a broader level, two authors in the book ask, (a) how might certain psychological theories themselves contribute to the existence of self-destructive behavior, and (b) how may some of the factors that perpetuate destructive behavior in individuals also perpetuate it in organizations, particularly organizations that consider themselves to be "virtuous"?

THE ROLE OF THEORY IN PRACTICE
AND IN THE ROGERS–MAY DEBATE

On a more general level, this book is about the role of theory in psychotherapy practice. As both L'Abate (2009) and Carlson and Englar-Carlson (2010) have noted, in recent years the role of theory in practice has been minimized. This has been attributed to a focus on evidence-based intervention. Carlson and Englar-Carlson, who are currently editing a series of monographs on theories of psychotherapy for the American Psychological Association, have noted that "Some might argue that in the contemporary clinical practice of psychotherapy, evidence-based intervention and effective outcome have overshadowed theory in importance. Maybe. . . . We do know that psychotherapists adopt and practice according to one theory or another . . ." (Carlson & Englar-Carlson, 2010, p. ix). They go on to say that "Theory is the compass that allows psychotherapists to navigate the vast territory of clinical practice" (p. x). Wampold (2010) also argued that theory is necessary for therapeutic practice.

There is only equivocal evidence to support the claim that it is legitimate to place techniques center stage in psychotherapy. Those who favor an empirically supported treatment approach place primary emphasis on the idea that specific techniques are needed for specific problems or disorders (e.g., Chambless & Crits-Christoph, 2006). Others (e.g., Wampold, 2010) argue that there is little evidence that techniques play an important role and that all bona fide psychotherapies are roughly equally effective for virtually all disorders. Those who adopt this latter point of view place great emphasis on the therapeutic relationship (Norcross, 2011) or the therapist him- or herself (Wampold, 2010).

Whether or not techniques are of primary importance, the role of theory tends to be de-emphasized in current thinking about psychotherapy. Yet even if one is using an empirically supported intervention, there will be cases in which one cannot rely on empirically supported interventions alone. There will be cases in which clients either do not fit the populations on which the research was done or in which implementation of the procedures does not work with a particular client. There is reason to believe that in those cases therapists fall back on theory to guide their next steps (e.g., Westen, Novotny, & Thompson-Brenner, 2004). Finally, case formulation and treatment planning involve theory (Wampold, 2010). We therefore decided to ask therapists of different theoretical persuasions how they use theory to help determine their conceptualizations of and practical dealings with humanity's dark side. Although we know of no research to support our contention, we suspect that therapists are more theory guided than is apparent from the alleged focus on intervention.

The debate between Carl Rogers and Rollo May, two famous humanistic psychotherapists, illustrates how an emphasis on theory may affect how therapists practice. Rollo May (1982) criticized Carl Rogers for, in May's view, believing that human beings at core were fundamentally constructive. May said that Rogers failed to pay sufficient attention to the dark side of human nature. He criticized Rogers for blaming all evil on society and for failing to take seriously humans' potential for acting in negative and destructive ways. He argued that Rogers believed that negative and destructive behavior and affects derived from individuals' encounters with negative and unaccepting societal experiences, which had obviated their natural tendency to develop in positive directions. May argued that people had a much greater potential for evil behavior than what Rogers professed and that this potential could be enacted much more easily than what Rogers believed. May cited the Zimbardo Stanford Prison Experiment (Zimbardo, 2007) as an example of how easy it was to turn normal individuals toward the dark side.

The difference between Rogers and May was not merely academic. For May it also impacted on how Rogerians practiced psychotherapy. In 1967, Rogers and colleagues published the results of the Wisconsin Schizophrenia Project (Rogers, Gendlin, Kiesler, & Truax, 1967). Rogers had invited several prominent psychotherapists, including May, to listen to excerpts of tapes of Rogerian therapists working with schizophrenics. May was critical of the therapists he listened to. One criticism in particular consisted in his concern that the Rogerian manner of conducting therapy was so focused on warmth and empathy that it discouraged clients from accessing, expressing, and confronting anger. To be sure, anger is not necessarily identical to evil. However, anger can, if not effectively dealt with, emerge in destructive ways. For May it was crucial for therapists to actively support clients in confronting their anger.

The Rogers–May debate raises questions about how therapists theorize about the effects of the dark side on human behavior and how those presumed effects in turn impact the way they practice therapy. If humans are as constructive at their core as Rogers believed, perhaps it is sufficient for thera-pists to promote clients' constructive, growth-producing processes (see Chap-ters 2 and 3, this volume), that is, focus on promoting their growth potential. On the other hand, if May is correct, then perhaps therapists need to actively help individuals confront their neglected or disowned dark side so as to allow these to be fully integrated into their personality with the goal of diminishing their cause of or contribution to human destructiveness (see Chapters 1 and 4, this volume).

In this book we have a diversity of theoretical perspectives. The major-ity of the authors may loosely be said to come from the *depth psychological* point of view. These perspectives are more likely to find theoretical questions about the dark side compelling because they focus on how self-awareness and self-acceptance of thoughts and feelings relate to behaving in "healthy" ways. In this book depth psychological perspectives include the chapters from humanistic–existential writers like Kirk J. Schneider, Peter F. Schmid, Arthur C. Bohart, and Edward Mendelowitz; an integrative humanistic–constructivistic chapter from Larry M. Leitner; as well as chapters from two psychodynamic writers, David Livingstone Smith and James Hollis. We also have a chapter from two humanistic writers, Maureen O'Hara and Aftab Omer, who focus on how larger organizations can engage in destructive behavior all the while believing themselves to be virtuous.

Depth psychological perspectives assume that people's problems result primarily from how humans relate to themselves in terms of such dimen-sions as (a) what they allow into awareness, (b) what they disown or deny, (c) what they defend against, (d) what they take responsibility for, (e) how much they delude themselves, (f) how they construe and construct meaning in their lives, (g) how much they have worked through problems from the past, (h) how much they trust themselves, and (i) how much they are able to form good "internal working relationships" with themselves. Problems in these internal arrangements are, for most of the authors in this grouping, seen as resulting from dysfunctional or destructive relationships that individuals have experienced with others. The therapist's job is largely one of providing an atmosphere that allows individuals to (a) confront themselves; (b) work through issues that are blocking them from being more open to themselves and others; and (c) find ways of getting more deeply in touch with their potential to be more fully themselves—to "find their own voice"—and be more open, empathic, and trusting with others.

By contrast, we found it more difficult to locate cognitive–behavioral therapists who found questions about humanity's dark side in relationship to psychotherapy as compelling as depth psychological therapists. This is not to say that cognitive behaviorists have not worked extensively to remediate destructive behavior. Particularly at the level of conduct disorder problems in childhood and adolescence, cognitive behaviorists have been foremost in developing treatment strategies that work to modify destructive behaviors (e.g., Kazdin, 2008). Nonetheless, their theoretical point of view tends to make the question of the dark side less compelling. For them there is nothing really different about dark side or destructive human behaviors from any other behavior. Individuals engage in destructive behaviors when they have learned dysfunctional ways of interpreting events and of thinking about themselves and others. Additionally, they are more likely to act destructively if they have been rewarded or reinforced for behaving destructively and/or if they have not learned more effective coping devices. Therapy is less a matter of helping individuals rearrange how they relate to themselves and how they find themselves in the world and more a matter of learning better and more effective coping skills. Accordingly, in therapy cognitive–behavioral therapists tend to focus on three things: (a) learned emotional reactions that can be modified through various procedures; (b) unlearning of dysfunctional behavioral styles and learning new, more proactive skills; and (c) unlearning dysfunctional ways of thinking and developing new more constructive ways of thinking about their lives.

Nonetheless, we are honored to have one eminent writer, Arnold A. Lazarus, from the cognitive–behavioral/social learning tradition. Although Lazarus has transcended cognitive–behavioral therapy to create his own integrative "multimodal psychotherapy," one can nonetheless see the cognitive–behavioral way of theorizing in how Lazarus works with the case presented in Chapter 8. Even if there is a dark side (Lazarus believes humans are innately aggressive), Lazarus still focuses on helping his client learn better and more effective coping skills and on modifying beliefs that are causing her harm.

We invited John Briere to contribute a chapter because he is one of the world's leading experts on childhood sexual abuse and other forms of trauma. Briere can best be described as an evidence-based integrative therapist. *Treating Complex Trauma in Adolescents and Young Adults* (Briere & Lanktree, 2011) describes an empirically validated, multicomponent approach to the treatment of traumatized adolescents and young adults. Interventions include relationship building, psychoeducation, affect regulation training, trigger identification, cognitive processing, titrated emotional processing, mindfulness training, collateral treatments with parents and families, group therapy, and system-level advocacy. In Chapter 7, Briere describes how Buddhist ideas help him understand and work with both perpetrators and victims of human destructiveness.

Finally, two authors write from a philosophical perspective, perhaps what might best be called a *metatheoretical* perspective. Barbara S. Held is one of the foremost critics of certain unconstructive tendencies she finds in the positive psychology movement, namely, those that can increase the stigmatization and thus the harm of people who are not as positive as this movement suggests they ought to be to achieve optimum (mental) health (Held, 2002, 2004, 2005). In Chapter 12, she raises concerns about how positive psychology's claims could inadvertently contribute to negative and self-destructive beliefs about oneself. This leads her to consider how psychological theories themselves can inadvertently contribute to the dark side.

Ronald B. Miller similarly writes from a metatheoretical perspective. He has been at the forefront of scholars who have argued forcefully that there is a moral dimension to human suffering (Miller, 2004). In Chapter 11, he asks to what degree morality itself is involved in determining how therapists should work with the dark side. Even more broadly he asks to what degree the practice of psychotherapy in particular and clinical psychology in general are fundamentally moral enterprises.

We believe that one of the major virtues of this book is that it may induce thoughts about one's own theoretical perspective. In so doing, it may help to raise many important psychological and sociocultural questions. At least that was the case for us as editors. Here we briefly delineate some of the questions addressed in this book by various authors as they discuss their notions about psychotherapy and beyond. These include

- In what does evil or destructive behavior originate?
- Are humans intrinsically evil?
- Are there bad people or only bad behaviors?
- Is the dark side largely created through disowning or denying certain aspects of the self?
- To what degree does living an unactualized life, or an inauthentic life, lead to destructive behavior?
- To what degree is the dark side created by how people treat one another?
- In that regard, could larger social institutions have their own dark sides, and could institutions that have benevolent purposes act in ways that hurt and oppress people?
- Could psychology, which could be thought of as a profession dedicated to creating good, have its own dark side through its means of providing help and the theories it sanctions, either or both of which could inadvertently produce destructive effects?
- How much does morality play a role in psychotherapy and in clinical psychology?
- Is forgiveness a good thing and should it be fostered?
- Can clients grow without confronting their dark sides?
- How much does society contribute to destructive behavior, and in that regard, to what extent should therapists focus on the

broader sociocultural context and not merely on individual client's dynamics and experiences?

- To what degree does therapy actually promote the positive, or constructive, side of the human nature; to what extent does it actually counteract the potential for destructive behavior?
- To what degree is it possible to believe oneself to be so well-meaning and well-intentioned that one may not be aware of the dark side that one embodies, which can give rise to destructive features of one's own behavior?
- To what degree must therapists face their own dark sides?

CONCLUDING NOTE

The book consists of three parts. In Part I, Kirk J. Schneider, a former colleague of Rollo May's, and Peter F. Schmid and Arthur C. Bohart, both person-centered therapists, consider the May–Rogers debate. In Part II, theorists from different traditions consider clinical implications of their theoretical notions for working in therapy and for understanding the functioning of "virtuous organizations." In Part III, David Livingstone Smith, Ronald B. Miller, and Barbara S. Held examine the broader implications of certain current psychological theories and practices for their potential to do harm. An afterword integrates the chapters and highlights key issues that have been raised.

REFERENCES

Bandura, A. (1986). *Social foundations of thought and action: A social cognitive theory.* New York, NY: Prentice-Hall.

Baron-Cohen, S. (2011). *The science of evil.* New York, NY: Basic Books.

Briere, J. N., & Lanktree, C. B. (2011). *Treating complex trauma in adolescents and young adults.* Thousand Oaks, CA: Sage.

Carlson, J., & Englar-Carlson, M. (Series Eds.). (2010). Series preface. In B. E. Wampold, *The basics of psychotherapy: An introduction to theory and practice* (pp. ix–xii). Washington, DC: American Psychological Association.

Chambless, D. L., & Crits-Christoph, P. (2006). The treatment method. In J. C. Norcross, L. E. Beutler, & R. F. Levant (Eds.), *Evidence-based practices in mental health: Debate and dialogue on the fundamental questions* (pp. 191–256). Washington, DC: American Psychological Association. doi:10.1037/11265-005

Coie, J. D., & Dodge, K. A. (1998). Aggression and antisocial behavior. In W. Damon & N. Eisenberg (Eds.), *Handbook of child psychology: Vol. 3. Social, emotional, and personality development* (5th ed., pp. 779–862). New York, NY: Wiley.

Eisenberg, N. (2010). Empathy-related responding: Links with self-regulation, moral judgment, and moral behavior. In M. Mikulincer & P. R. Shaver (Eds.), *Prosocial motives, emotions, and behavior: The better angels of our nature* (pp. 129–148). Washington, DC: American Psychological Association. doi:10.1037/12061-007

Eron, L. D. (2001). Seeing is believing: How viewing violence alters attitudes and aggressive behavior. In A. C. Bohart & D. J. Stipek (Eds.), *Constructive and destructive behavior: Implications for family, school, & society* (pp. 49–60). Washington, DC: American Psychological Association. doi:10.1037/10433-002

Feshbach, N. D. (1997). Empathy—the formative years: Implications for clinical practice. In A. C. Bohart & L. S. Greenberg (Eds.), *Empathy reconsidered: New directions in psychotherapy* (pp. 33–59). Washington, DC: American Psychological Association. doi:10.1037/10226-001

Hawley, P. H. (2006). Evolution and personality: A new look at Machiavellianism. In D. K. Mroczek & T. D. Little (Eds.), *Handbook of personality development* (pp. 147–161). Mahwah, NJ: Erlbaum.

Held, B. S. (2002). The tyranny of the positive attitude in America: Observation and speculation. *Journal of Clinical Psychology, 58,* 965–992. doi:10.1002/jclp.10093

Held, B. S. (2004). The negative side of positive psychology. *Journal of Humanistic Psychology, 44,* 9–46. doi:10.1177/0022167803259645

Held, B. S. (2005). The "virtues" of positive psychology. *Journal of Theoretical and Philosophical Psychology, 25,* 1–34. doi:10.1037/h0091249

Hinde, R. A. (2001). Institutionalized aggression: Cultural and individual factors that support war. In A. C. Bohart & D. J. Stipek (Eds.), *Constructive and destructive behavior: Implications for family, school, & society* (pp. 87–93). Washington, DC: American Psychological Association. doi:10.1037/10433-004

Hoffman, M. L. (2001). Toward a comprehensive empathy-based theory of prosocial moral development. In A. C. Bohart & D. J. Stipek (Eds.), *Constructive and destructive behavior: Implications for family, school, & society* (pp. 61–86). Washington, DC: American Psychological Association. doi:10.1037/10433-003

Huesmann, R. L., & Reynolds, M. A. (2001). Cognitive processes and the development of aggression. In A. C. Bohart & D. J. Stipek (Eds.), *Constructive and destructive behavior: Implications for family, school, & society* (pp. 249–269). Washington, DC: American Psychological Association. doi:10.1037/10433-012

Kazdin, A. E. (2008). *Parent management training: Treatment for oppositional, aggressive, and antisocial behavior in children and adolescents.* New York, NY: Oxford University Press.

L'Abate, L. (2009). In search of a relational theory. *American Psychologist, 64,* 779–788. doi:10.1037/0003-066X.64.8.779

May, R. (1982). The problem of evil: An open letter to Carl Rogers. *Journal of Humanistic Psychology, 22*(3), 10–21. doi:10.1177/0022167882223003

McCullough, M. E., Kurzban, R., & Tabak, B. A. (2011). Evolved mechanisms for revenge and forgiveness. In P. R. Shaver & M. Mikulincer (Eds.), *Human aggression and violence: Causes, manifestations, and consequences* (pp. 221–239). Washington, DC: American Psychological Association. doi:10.1037/12346-012

Mikulincer, M., & Shaver, P. R. (Eds.). (2010). *Prosocial motives, emotions, and behavior: The better angels of our nature* (pp. 129–148). Washington, DC: American Psychological Association. doi:10.1037/12061-000

Miller, R. B. (2004). *Facing human suffering: Psychology and psychotherapy as moral engagement*. Washington, DC: American Psychological Association. doi:10.1037/10691-000

Norcross, J. C. (Ed.). (2011). *Psychotherapy relationships that work: Evidence-based responsiveness* (2nd ed.). New York, NY: Oxford University Press. doi:10.1093/acprof:oso/9780199737208.001.0001

Rogers, C. R., Gendlin, E. T., Kiesler, D., & Truax, C. (Eds.). (1967). *The therapeutic relationship and its impact*. Madison: University of Wisconsin Press.

Sell, A. (2011). Applying adaptationism to human anger: The recalibration theory. In P. R. Shaver & M. Mikulincer (Eds.), *Human aggression and violence: Causes, manifestations, and consequences* (pp. 53–70). Washington, DC: American Psychological Association. doi:10.1037/12346-003

Shaver, P. R., & Mikulincer, M. (Eds.). (2011). *Human aggression and violence: Causes, manifestations, and consequences*. Washington, DC: American Psychological Association. doi:10.1037/12346-000

Smith, D. L. (2011). *Less than human: Why we demean, enslave and exterminate others*. New York, NY: St. Martin's Press.

Staub, E. (2011). *Overcoming evil: Genocide, violent conflict, and terrorism*. New York, NY: Oxford University Press.

Tangney, J. P. (2001). Constructive and destructive aspects of shame and guilt. In A. C. Bohart & D. J. Stipek (Eds.), *Constructive and destructive behavior: Implications for family, school, & society* (pp. 127–146). Washington, DC: American Psychological Association.

Toth, S. L., Harris, L. S., Goodman, G. S., & Cicchetti, D. (2011). Influence of violence and aggression on children's psychological development: Trauma, attachment, and memory. In P. R. Shaver & M. Mikulincer (Eds.), *Human aggression and violence: Causes, manifestations, and consequences* (pp. 351–365). Washington, DC: American Psychological Association. doi:10.1037/12346-019

Wampold, B. E. (2010). *The basics of psychotherapy: An introduction to theory and practice*. Washington, DC: American Psychological Association.

Westen, D., Novotny, C. M., & Thompson-Brenner, H. (2004). The empirical status of empirically supported psychotherapies: Assumptions, findings, and reporting in controlled clinical trials. *Psychological Bulletin, 130,* 631–663. doi:10.1037/0033-2909.130.4.631

Zimbardo, P. (2007). *The Lucifer effect: Understanding how good people turn evil*. New York, NY: Random House.

I

JOURNEYS BEYOND THE CARL ROGERS–ROLLO MAY DEBATE

INTRODUCTION: JOURNEYS BEYOND THE CARL ROGERS–ROLLO MAY DEBATE

In this section, three authors from the humanistic tradition use the debate between Carl Rogers and Rollo May as a springboard to present their theoretical ideas on the dark side of human nature and its relationship to psychotherapy. For humanistic therapists, therapy is a process of self-discovery facilitated by the therapist. The focus is on uncovering new meanings and getting in touch with emotions and experience. The two perspectives in the Rogers–May debate, those of existential psychotherapy and person-centered therapy, share these general principles but differ in important ways regarding how therapy should proceed. The issues raised in this section resonate throughout the book with authors from the psychodynamic, cognitive–behavioral, integrative, and philosophical points of view.

Kirk J. Schneider (Chapter 1) discusses the relationship between psychological symptoms, negative emotions, and deeper issues concerning what it means for a human being to lead a meaningful life. He argues that in addressing negative emotions, existential therapists also address a deeper issue—what it is to be fundamentally human. In other words, negative emotions do not merely represent particular reactions to particular things; they are connected to deeper fundamental life stances as well. To give an example, if I have been traumatized, I may fear relationships. But at a more fundamental level, the fear raises issues about who I am as a self and how I fundamentally position myself in regard to threat and opportunity in life. Therapy needs to help clients address these deeper issues. For people to become more fully human, they must confront their darker sides. Schneider raises questions about approaches that may focus too narrowly on clients' "good" sides in that they close down on possibility. He raises questions about the Rogerian approach in this regard. Schneider concludes with a view of therapy as offering an expanded capacity to experience life fully, focusing on the capacity to experience awe.

Peter F. Schmid (Chapter 2) is both a philosopher and a psychologist. He briefly explores the history of the concept of evil and shows how two basic positions in Western history parallel the debate between Rogers and May: Is evil something in its own right, or is it the absence of the good? He argues that May misunderstood Rogers's view of the human potential for evil. He then elaborates on Rogers's belief that a facilitative relationship promotes clients growing in a "good" or "prosocial" direction. A human encounter is needed, but of a different sort than what May argued for. Schmid argues that in therapy we need to go from the general question of "What is the nature of the human being?" to "Who is this (specified) human being?" Schmid corrects the view held by many that Rogers focused on self-actualization to the detriment of positive relationships with others. He presents a new elaboration of person-centered theory and a new view of what it means to be a person in person-centered theory. Schmid then provides a rigorous philosophical analysis of evil and argues that evil arises from depersonalization. As with several other authors in this volume, Schmid notes that as therapists we must think more broadly than just about psychotherapy and that "psychotherapy is political or it is not psychotherapy."

Arthur C. Bohart (Chapter 3) is an integrative person-centered therapist who has focused in previous work on the idea of the client as active self-healer in psychotherapy. Here he uses the Rogers–May debate to extend his ideas by examining the nature of clients' capacities for self-generated growth through their potential for "self-organizing wisdom." He uses the story of Darth Vader in the *Star Wars* movies to explore the issue. He focuses on the idea that therapy works by mobilizing self-organizing wisdom and describes how that works, imagining a brief scenario of Darth Vader in person-centered therapy. Bohart then deals with the question of why, if there is self-organizing wisdom, people so often act unwisely and even evilly.

1

RADICAL OPENNESS TO RADICAL MYSTERY: ROLLO MAY AND THE AWE-BASED WAY

KIRK J. SCHNEIDER

Rollo May (1909–1994) was a romantic realist of the first order. Romantic realism is characterized by "big picture" thinking that is at the same time grounded in the practical realities of everyday life. As Paul Tillich (1963) so deftly intimated, romantic realism is the "awareness of the infinite in the finite."

Rollo May's philosophy of psychotherapy directly reflected his philosophy of life. Everything that happened in therapy took place within the vast backdrop of the mystery of existence and must be understood within the parameters of that backdrop. Hence anger, fear, or sadness, for Rollo,[1] did not simply relate to a conflict with some particular individual or social unit but to the inscrutable conditions of existence itself, the struggle with existence itself. To put it more concretely, when a client experiences fear, he does not simply experience it in, say, the context of his father's terrifying yell or his

---

[1] In keeping with the authenticity of my close relationship with Rollo May, I refer to him on a first-name basis throughout the balance of this chapter.

DOI: 10.1037/13941-001

Humanity's Dark Side: Evil, Destructive Experience, and Psychotherapy, A. C. Bohart, B. S. Held, E. Mendelowitz, and K. J. Schneider (Editors)

mother's agonizing rejection but also in the context of the daunting dimensions that surround and exceed these experiences, namely, creation itself. Similarly, when a client rages or self-inflates, the expression almost invariably contains an element of defiance toward the universe, not just toward a given individual or group (May, 1958, 1981, 1991).

Rollo also believed that to address such existential (or ontological) dimensions, the therapist needs to develop a stance of *radical* openness: not just openness to the moment-to-moment interactions between therapist and client but also to the implications of those interactions for the cultural, circumstantial, genetic, and cosmic "givens" within which they take place (May, 1981). Second, and following from this radically open view, the therapist needs to stand ready to encounter, acknowledge, or make a space for each of the givens as they arise. This means that the therapist brings a certain energy and activism to the therapeutic relationship that conveys "whatever you are struggling with, I will be with you in that struggle." It also means that the therapist allows for—and in most cases encounters—expressions of rage, irritability, and desperation as much as expressions of sorrow, melancholy, or timidity. There is no theoretical privileging from this point of view because there is no theoretical precondition (short of an emergency) set on what can be experienced. It also means that affect and gesture are attended to equally with content and words. The point here is to offer a relationship that can, if appropriate, bear the intensity of maximal self-attunement, maximal realization of the layers of that attunement, and maximal recognition of the freedom one has to respond to those layers.

One of Rollo's closest contemporaries, James Bugental (1967), put this approach in terms of the therapeutic commitment. The therapeutic commitment, Bugental asserted, is to "my responsiveness to my patient's being as he struggles to emerge from non-being" (or nonawareness; p. 289). It is not, Bugental went on,

> to the patient's inherent worthiness or *to* his goodness. . . . Often such a focus seems so desirable and so humane that it is an easy temptation to yield to it. Usually when this happens, however, I find that what has happened is that I have suppressed annoyance or anger with the patient by not meeting him as he is in the contact but redirecting my attention to the imputed worth, goodness . . . or whatever. I am increasingly of the opinion that genuine committed being with my patient must deny any assumptions about the value of the patient now or in the future. (p. 289)

This chapter focuses on Rollo May's "awe-based" approach to therapy. By awe-based approach to therapy (which is my own term), I mean an approach that stresses the humility and wonder—or sense of adventure—toward living. I also mean an approach that derives from Rollo's existential–humanistic orientation to psychology. His orientation was existential because it pertained to people's many-faceted relationships to existence (e.g., physiologically, cognitively, affectively), and it was humanistic because it stressed a profoundly personal understanding of those relationships.

In the first part of the chapter, I show how radical openness to the radical mystery of existence was integral to Rollo's practice philosophy. I also show how this awe-based approach both dovetails with and diverges from Carl Rogers's person-centered therapeutic orientation. In particular, I show how Rollo's metapsychology highlights the self/world struggle, wonder, and mystery, whereas Rogers's metapsychology accentuates the self/world compatibility, integration, and unity.

In the second part of the chapter, I show how these respective metapsychologies have significant implications for the theorists' views of psychological growth and therapy. For example, whereas Rollo emphasizes activism and encounter in the therapeutic relationship, Rogers stresses understanding and warmth; and whereas both approaches can be seen as critical to an awe-based therapy, Rollo's, as illustrated by his "case of Phillip," appears to proceed with more depth. I conclude the chapter with a discussion of the role of awe-based psychology within the larger field of psychology. I contend that in great part due to Rollo's influence, awe-based psychology is on the rise again, and it is particularly notable in the area of existential–humanistic therapy.

THE DAIMONIC CORE

One way to understand Rollo's radical openness to radical mystery is to elucidate his position of the daimonic. The daimonic for Rollo is any natural human function that has the capacity to overtake the entire organism (May, 1969). One can view the daimonic in terms of the creative and destructive forces of the personality and, by implication, of nature:

> A special characteristic of the daimonic model is that it considers both creativity on one side, and anger and rage on the other side, as coming from the same source. That is, constructiveness and destructiveness have the same source in human personality. The source is simply *human potential*. (May as cited in Diamond, 1996, p. xxi)

Hence, if human potential can draw on cultural, genetic, circumstantial, and ultimately cosmic sources, it must be both abundantly potent and exceedingly volatile at the same time. This is precisely Rollo's point. We, like the universe, are unfinished products, motivated continuously by multiple levels of influence. The therapeutic task is to help each person to compose a life out of those levels of influence and not simply a makeshift prop.

What this means existentially is that choice—although tempered by the past—is a moment-to-moment pivot point. There are no automatic outcomes or pat behavioral tendencies—only a plentitude of decision points, unaccounted-for impulses, and unknown possibilities. In other words, it's messy "in there" as well as "out there"; well-being is gained through many hard-won steps against a background of continual ambiguity. This understanding is vividly illustrated by all the stories about people who appear to be raised in decent cultural circumstances (e.g., by "ordinary" families) only to find that they engage in appalling acts of cruelty (as was evident in a number of recent wars; e.g., see Lifton, 1986; Rossi Monti, 2010). It is also evident in people who appear to have derived from some of the most depraved circumstances imaginable yet somehow have managed to rise above them (e.g., Frankl, 1959; Simonton, 1994; Tedeschi & Calhoon, 1995). Although Rollo acknowledged a certain value to presuppositions about human personality (e.g., patterns of psychological and physical vitality), he would persistently question orthodoxies about these presuppositions, whether they derived from deterministic theories such as behaviorism and psychoanalysis or so-called liberal axioms such as those of his fellow humanists.

A CLASSIC DEBATE

Carl Rogers, a liberal theorist par excellence, held views about human nature that directly contradicted Rollo's experiences of clinical reality. Although Rollo respected Rogers, he questioned his worldview, particularly as it affected therapeutic practice. For example, Rogers's metapsychology (or philosophy of psychology) emphasized both a "formative tendency" and a drive toward unity—neither of which Rollo would countenance. Rogers (1978) wrote:

> There is a formative tendency in the universe, which can be traced and observed in stellar space, in crystals, in microorganisms, in organic life, in human beings. This is an evolutionary tendency toward greater order, greater interrelatedness, greater complexity. In humankind it extends from a single-cell origin . . . to a conscious awareness of the organism and the external world, to a transcendent awareness of the *unity* [emphasis added] of the cosmic system. (p. 26)

What Rogers implies here is that there is a natural telos or purpose in all things that aim toward existential unity. When these natural inclinations are harnessed, Rogers intimated, life and ultimately the universe are likely to become harmonious partners, ensconced in a mutually sustaining, systemically rewarding collaboration. "The basic nature of human beings when functioning freely," Rogers (1961) elaborated, "is constructive and trustworthy" (p. 194).

Hence, the question for Rogers was how to free the natural inclinations of human beings toward order and harmony. To respond to this question, however, he had to first identify the obstacles that stood in the way of people achieving such equanimity, and he found those in the therapeutic setting— among them guilt, anxiety, fear, and rage. On the other hand, what Rogers didn't seem to fully appreciate, and what Rollo later elaborated, is that each of these so-called conflicts are also springboards to a fuller and potentially richer life experience. Rollo viewed them not so much as states to be assuaged (or soothed over) but as states to be acknowledged, grappled with, and rechanneled into productive directions. Yet Rogers's research (and no doubt life biases) led him to believe that conflicts were ultimately encumbrances to human flourishing and that "facilitative" human relationships could transform them. These facilitative relationships featured three main elements: empathy (or acceptance), congruence (or personal integrity), and unconditional positive regard (or consistent prizing of the other as a person). The basic idea of these relationships was to provide a warm and supportive mirror to people so that they could feel the safety to understand and make constructive choices about their life conflicts. Techniques such as reflective listening (e.g., parroting, paraphrasing) would be used to convey acceptance of people's struggles and confirmation of the resources people possess to transform those struggles.

The problem is the following: To what extent can "unconditional" (or consistent) warmth be received by people who have learned to distrust such warmth or who are persistently angry, dependent, or repressed? To what extent are they reached by that warmth, or to what extent might it divert them from the opportunity to face "cold, hard" facts about their intra- and interpersonal suffering (Diamond, 1996)? Another problem is in regard to what is meant by empathic acceptance and mirroring. Is the acceptance embracing chronically self-destructive behavior patterns or protracted docility? Does the mirroring reflect a client's overt as distinct from "whole bodied" presentation? Is the mirroring chiefly passive and neglectful of the person (i.e., the therapist) who is doing the mirroring?

In an interview in 1987, Rollo stated the following about Rogers's overall approach:

> Rogers' main problem is that he leaves out evil [by "evil," Rollo essentially means intensively disturbing emotions]. You see . . . when you go into a patient's hell, [one] also has some hell of [one's] own and that can't be left out. Sometimes the therapist gets irritated and if he does, I think it's very important to ask the patient, "What could you have said, what's going on here that makes me suddenly irritated?"
>
> [For example,] . . . in the two films about psychotherapy [*Equus* and *Ordinary People*], . . . the therapist and patient have to get mad at each other before they could really trust each other. Especially in *Ordinary*

People that's clear. This boy [the patient] couldn't really trust this man [his therapist] until he could get angry with him and have . . . a real struggle between the two of them. Then he knew he could trust him.

Now Rogers leaves that out entirely; [though] I'm sure one would get real good out of a session with Rogers. . . . [Still,] the therapists Rogers trains . . . also make gross mistakes [because] they've never been taught to deal with their own daimonic. (May as cited in Schneider, Galvin, & Serlin, 2009, p. 432)

The capacity to "assert some freedom," Rollo elaborated in another venue

put[s] an added responsibility upon us to affirm realistically the anxiety involved, the precarious and limited nature of this freedom, and the fact that our belief in the human being can work for good only when the individual can face the world with all its inner and outer cruelty, its failure, and its tragedy. (May as cited in Greening, 1984, p. 21)

It was in this light, then, that in one of the most ambitious investigations of client-centered therapy ever undertaken—the so-called Wisconsin Schizophrenia Project (Rogers, Gendlin, Kiesler, & Truax, 1967)—Rollo criticized Rogers's trainees. While Rollo was certainly not pervasively critical in his overall evaluation of the project, and he resonated notably with much that Rogers and his group held valuable, the issue of passive therapeutic affirmation was a continual point of contention for him. In their follow-up report about the project, Rogers et al. (1967) noted that for Rollo,

the therapist's over-identification with [the] patient . . . seem[ed] to "take away the patient's opportunity to experience himself as a subject in his own right, to take a stand against the therapist, to experience being in an interpersonal world ("I sometimes got the feeling there were not two people in the room" [Rollo was quoted]). To summarize, much of the potential dynamic of the relationship with the therapist is absent. [Again the editors quote Rollo:] "I think the lack of this dynamic of interpersonal relationships is a consequence of a misuse of the 'reflecting' technique, so that we get only an amorphous kind of identity rather than two subjects interacting in a world in which both participate, and in which love and hate, trust and doubt, conflicts and dependency, come out and can be understood and assimilated." (p. 438)

Rollo elaborated this point in the context of the case of "Brown" and found that progress is attributable not so much to the Rogerian techniques but to the attitude the therapist brought to his encounter. This attitude, he went on,

is in my judgment more critical for the patient's progress than any technique as such. The harmful effects of the air of going along on the surface in some of the sessions, being two-dimensional, are avoided to a considerable extent by the fact that there is nothing whatever superficial about the therapist's concern for the patient. . . . This is what has the profoundly powerful effect upon the other person. My belief, nevertheless, is obviously that the therapy would go along better, effect change on a deeper and more lasting level, if the underlying feelings, including the negative aggressive ones, were brought out and experienced directly in the relationship between patient and therapist. (Rogers et al., 1967, p. 439)

What is vital for Rollo in these observations is not so much the specific technique the therapist applies but the intensity of his engagement with the client that effects the most positive change. To put it another way, the optimal points of contact exhibit a commitment to unveiling the client's deepest points of struggle, and these cannot often be tapped through simple or passive reflection. What can tap them, according to Rollo, is a commitment on the part of the therapist to radically open to the manifold layers of the client's battle (including that with the therapist) and to stand ready at any appropriate point to call attention to those layers, to hold them up to the client, and to explore their unfolding dimensions. Rollo's further point is that this exercise is not a passive process, but one that is both impassioned and involved. The therapist's own responses, in other words, are integral to what she or he mirrors back to the client, as well as the risks she or he is willing to take to call attention to experiences that might not be overtly displayed by the client. In these ways, the therapy can move in a direction of holistic (rather than truncated) encounter and enable the fuller ranges of affect and embodiment to be addressed. Rollo noted with another patient in the Wisconsin study, for example, just how the therapist "misused" the reflecting technique. He wrote that

> nowhere is *anger* reflected by the therapist. Other negative emotions like aggression, hostility, and genuine conflict (as distinguished from mere misunderstanding) are almost entirely absent in what the therapist reflects. It seemed clear to me that the patient was angry. . . . When . . . Jones is trying to pin the therapist down on whether he believes in rights for mental patients, isn't the patient trying to express a current of anger? The fact that this isn't brought out seems to me partially to account for the patient's consequent resignation and "I-can't-expect-anything" attitude. If this anger were brought out, assumedly, then the patient might have gone on to bring out what is behind his obsessional concern for "rights" . . . But what I missed was a living-out of what the patient was experiencing in the world right there. (Rogers et al., 1967, p. 469)

Now, to be fair, later Rogerian adherents, such as Brian Thorne (2003), disagreed with Rollo's assessment. Thorne contended that despite Rollo's reservations, the Wisconsin study actually highlighted the value of authentic client engagement and spurred person-centered theorists to feature it in their follow-up formulations. He also contended that Rogers himself became struck by the centrality of therapist authenticity (or as he put it, congruence) following the Wisconsin study and in later years made that the cornerstone of his facilitative triad. Recently, there have been other person-centered theorists who have extended the accent on therapist authenticity to what they call "relational depth." Deriving from existential principles Rollo largely etched out, relational depth is now an emerging edge in the person-centered repertoire (e.g., see Mearns & Cooper, 2005).

Despite these developments, however, there is little doubt that key differences between Rollo and Rogers persisted to the end of their lives—and these differences have significant implications for the future of psychotherapy. As late as 1981 (6 years before Rogers's death), Rogers wrote that

> my major difference with Rollo [is] around the question of the nature of the human individual. He sees the demonic as a basic element in the human makeup, and dwells upon this in his writing. For myself, though I am very well aware of the incredible amount of destructive, cruel, and malevolent behavior in today's world [but] . . . I do not find that this evil is inherent in human nature. In a psychological climate that is nurturant of growth and choice, I have *never* known an individual to choose the cruel or destructive path. Choice *always* seems to be in the direction of greater socialization, improved relationships with others. . . . So I see members of the human species, like members of other species, as essentially constructive in their fundamental nature, but damaged by their experience. (Rogers as cited in Greening, 1984, p. 12)

I am struck by two points in this comment by Rogers—his misquotation of Rollo's notion of the "daimonic" as "demonic," and his omission of the human being's fundamental relation to existence (above and beyond nurturing environments). As for his mischaracterization of Rollo's notion of the daimonic, as opposed to demonic, as a "basic element of the human makeup," there is an illuminating irony. Rollo would have oversimplified the human plight had he said that human beings are inherently demonic (i.e., blatantly destructive), but he did not say that; he said that human beings are inherently daimonic, which is an ambivalent disposition pertaining to people's capacity for either creative or destructive choices. The fact that Rogers mischaracterized Rollo says more about Rogers's oversimplification of the human situation than about Rollo's purported biases. As to Rogers's omission of humanity's relation to existence above and beyond nurturing environments, much could be elaborated. Suffice it to say that the arousal of fear, anxiety, power seeking, and the like do not seem confined to the dynamics of human interaction but extend to our relations with our mortality, our enigmatic universe, and our manifold impulses (Becker,

1973; Kagan, 2009; Pyszcynski, Solomon, & Greenberg, 2003). Some children appear to be born shy and timid, others brazen and aggressive (Kagan, 2009). Many adults have deep-seated fears of heights or of strange environments, and most of us are disquieted by our fragilities. These issues are human and cosmological, and no simple formula, including communitarian ones, will safely eradicate them.

That said, how do we optimally broach our paradoxical lives? What does Rollo have to say about attaining the vital or optimal experience? To uncover these perplexities, we now turn to the hopeful side of Rollo's multi-layered practice philosophy, a side that I term "awe-based," and an evolving direction for the existential–humanistic field.

TOWARD AN AWE-BASED PSYCHOLOGY

In the summer of 1992, Rollo wrote: "The blocking of one's capacity for wonder, and the loss of the capacity to appreciate mystery can have serious effects upon our . . . health, not to mention the health of our whole planet" (p. 5).

With this acute observation, Rollo set the stage for a radical new under-standing of psychological struggle as well as resiliency. I call this under-standing "awe-based" and apply it directly to therapy. What do I mean by awe-based? I mean a practice philosophy that stresses the humility and won-der, thrill and anxiety, or in short, the adventure of living (Schneider, 1993, 2004, 2009). I also mean a metapsychology that embraces life's mystery, as Rollo eloquently implied, in all its stark poignancy.

When therapy is done right, according to this purview, it helps cli-ents shift between crippling fear and brazen wonder, crushing fixation and enlivening possibility. How does such a therapy unfold? Just consider how Rollo worked with Phillip,[2] a middle-aged architect who experienced paralyz-ing jealousy toward his girlfriend, Nichole (May, 1981). Repeatedly, Rollo worked with Phillip to identify not just what he thought about Nichole but also how he felt with her. To amplify this experience, Rollo invited Phillip to envision a dialogue with Nichole following a cruel joke she made about making love to another man. What they discovered from this dialogue is that although Phillip "knew" that Nichole's joke was cruel, he didn't feel it and used many devices to rationalize the cruelty, such as her poor upbringing.

---

[2]It is fairly well established that Rollo's case of Phillip, like several of his published cases, also involved parts of Rollo's own life-experience. While this adds an intriguing dimension to the facts of Rollo's case with Phillip, it also, in my view, personalizes and thereby bolsters the credibility of Rollo's awe-based perspective.

But Rollo would have none of the rationalization. Here is what he mirrored back to Phillip:

> May: Phillip, I notice that you show Nichole how much she hurts you. You react like Pavlov's dogs—you make sure she sees how you bleed. But you don't tell her how you really feel. You never simply say to her, "Look, I love you and I don't want you running around the country having sex with other men."
>
> Phillip: I thought I had said that.
>
> May: I haven't heard it. I've only heard how much her sleeping with so and so hurts you, how all your lacerations are bleeding from her going away for that weekend.
>
> Phillip: I don't want to make demands on her.
>
> May: You think you're not making demands on her by showing her all this blood? . . . You always prefer to be hurt rather than to take care of yourself even if it hurts someone else. (May, 1981, p. 44)

As Rollo pressed Phillip to delve deeper into his dialogue with Nichole, and by implication the coercive women in his childhood, he contacted his anger toward them, along with his capacity to defy and adapt without them. Or as Rollo put it: "Anger, was for Phillip, a path to freedom. The times when he had become angry . . . were times when he had gained valuable insights, which he then expressed constructively" (May, 1981, p. 47). Rollo then elaborated the larger context of this dynamic, Phillip's anger "against destiny":

> The concept of destiny makes the experience of anger necessary. The kind of person who "never gets angry" is, we may be sure, the person who also never encounters destiny. . . . Experiencing the emotional state of anger and conceiving of destiny means that you are freed from regarding yourself as too "precious"; you are able to throw yourself into the game, whatever it may be, without worrying about picayune details. (May, 1981, p. 47)

The capacity to become angry, to defy, connects directly with the capacity to discover new resources, not merely in the context of one's girlfriend or mother but in the context of life as a whole, mortality as a whole. After many revisitations to the scene of Phillip's docile relationships with life, Rollo helped Phillip move from "precious" victim to active agent and from reticent bystander to emboldened risk taker.

Yet along with his newfound autonomy, Phillip also experienced despair, which is not an infrequent occurrence in awe-based existential treatment (May, 1981; Schneider, 2008). The price of authenticity is often anxiety, and one of the chief anxieties is despair. This was particularly evident in the last session with Rollo when Phillip felt "sad, lost, and especially lonely" (May, 1981, p. 48). But there were also hints of "rebirth" in his loneliness, and Rollo was acutely sensitive to them (p. 48). While he did not want to downplay the real fears Phillip experienced in separating from key figures (including Rollo himself) to whom he was previously, albeit toxically at times, attached, Rollo also did not want to take away from Phillip's potential to transform those fears. "In that hour," Rollo wrote, "I wanted to support [Phillip's] confidence without taking away the force of his despair, since despair may well lead to the deepest insight and the most valuable change" (p. 51). Rollo informed us that Phillip indeed contacted the potential for constructive change in that final session. In a spontaneous yet relevant reverie, Phillip recalled a time when he had just graduated from college and decided to teach English at a Turkish school for boys. He described the loneliness he felt there and the isolation he experienced as a foreigner with a small and lackluster group of students. After a protracted period of struggle with these painful affects, he eventually "broke down" in a manner of speaking and resigned to bed rest for a couple of weeks (p. 49).

But this was not the end of Phillip's reverie. As he delved deeper into the memory, he fervently recalled the lifestyle change that emanated from his period of "collapse." In this recollection, he described wandering around and "drawing poppies in the fields and old mosques of Istanbul. He gave up his habit of rigidly planning his life and began to take the flow of energy as it came" (May, 1981, p. 49). That spring, he told Rollo with rising intensity, "had been the prelude to the best summer I ever had" (p. 50). He went on to describe how he traveled to the Caspian Sea that summer and "by accident" met up with a group of artists and started sketching villages all along the sea (p. 50). That was the summer, he continued with enthusiasm, that inspired him not only to become an architect but also to lose his virginity!

This radiant recollection, then, this hint of emancipated possibilities, imbued the closing moments of therapy, but they also imbued Phillip's transformative path. For just as despair both dampened and rekindled his energies in Istanbul, it dampened and rekindled his possibilities with Rollo, and that led to an encouraging termination. Another way to state all this is that Rollo helped Phillip contact the "more" of his experience; although feeling lost, sad, and lonely were the triggers for his despair, the more he was able to stay present to those dimensions, the more he opened to memories and possibilities that superseded them. This doesn't inevitably happen in psychotherapy, but it does happen frequently, and it provides the impetus for major life transition. Summing up, Rollo wrote:

> We know in psychotherapy that times of despair are essential to the client's discovery of hidden capacities and basic assets. Those therapists are

misguided who feel it incumbent upon themselves to reassure the patient at every point of despair. For if the client never feels despair, it is doubtful whether he ever will feel anything below the surface. There is surely value in the client's experience that he has nothing more to lose anyway, so he may as well take whatever leap is necessary. That seems to me to be the meaning of the sentence from folklore "Despair and confidence both banish fear." (May, 1981, p. 51)

SUMMATION AND DISCUSSION

One could say that by helping Phillip to shift from fear to wonder, wonder to fear, and then fear to wonder once again, the ground was prepared for an awe-based transformation. By supporting Phillip to be present to his experience, Rollo helped Phillip discover the "more" of his experience and this in turn encompassed both Phillip's crushing despair (humility) and emboldening possibility (wonder). In this light, then, Rollo held up a series of mirrors to Phillip, some more active than others, to help him mobilize choice. The first mirrors reflected Phillip's acquiescence to Nichole, his mother, and his sister. The second set of mirrors reflected Phillip's growing outrage at this acquiescence and his desire to break free. The next set of mirrors reflected Phillip's resistance to his outrage and his impulses to revert back to his safe but miserable ties. The fourth set alerted him to his unwillingness to settle for these stifling ties and his vociferousness in opposing them. The fifth set of mirrors sparked him to actually separate from his disabling ties and to seek alternative directions. The sixth set alerted him to the anxieties of this separation—sadness, loneliness, and disorientation. And the final set of mirrors helped him to realize the richness, even in his anguish, of an evolving life.

Rollo's route to an awe-based transformation is neither simple nor cosmetic. It is not molded in the "rose-colored" tradition of American liberalism. But it is not fashioned in the hangdog expression of European conservatism either. It is a richer, rounder synthesis of both, and it aims to reconstitute both. In short, Rollo's awe-based therapy points to a new, though scandalously old, yearning of humanity—to find joy beyond and even above the seductive clamors for happiness. In his own words:

Happiness depends generally on one's outer state; joy is an overflowing of inner energies and leads to awe and wonderment. . . . Happiness is the absence of discord; joy is the welcoming of discord as the basis of higher harmonies. Happiness is finding a system of rules which solves our problems; joy is taking the risk that is necessary to break new frontiers. (May, 1981, p. 242)

CODA

I have called depth existential therapy—particularly in its final stages—a "rediscovery of meaning and awe" (Schneider, 2008, p. 80). What I mean by this is that clients in such therapy address not only symptoms, such as Phillip's lack of assertiveness with Nichole, but also profound struggles, dormant desires, and budding expansions of their approach to life. Hence, through the presence he cocreated with Rollo, Phillip was able to contact deep yearnings to break free—sexually, intellectually, and spiritually. Through the rediscovery of his past, he developed a new appreciation for sensuality; for the beauty of the environment; for aesthetic design; and for travel, adventure, and discovery. Hence, Phillip rediscovered meanings in his life well beyond his capacity for assertiveness with women; he discovered a sense of the humility and wonder, or in short, the awe of living.

Now, Rollo was well aware of these "additional benefits" to Phillip's therapy. He was well aware of the additional benefits that existential therapy offers to people generally and that cross into dream life, philosophical and literary inquiry, myth, and spirituality. However, what is perhaps most important at present is that the world of psychotherapy, and leading researchers in particular, are (re)discovering these benefits as well (e.g., Elkins, 2010; Mendelowitz & Schneider, 2008; Schneider & Langle, in press).

In a landmark review, leading psychotherapy researcher Bruce Wampold (2008) wrote that there is an "alternative common factor" in existential therapy that makes it "intriguing" as a foundational approach (p. 4). He went on to identify this factor as the facilitation of "meaning" in clients' lives—above and beyond simply a "nurturing therapeutic environment" (p. 4). He also suggested that "the focus on reflective and meaning-making aspects" of existential therapy—"as illustrated by the incorporation of meditation and Eastern principles"—is "very important" for mainstream therapies as a whole (p. 3). Summing up, Wampold concluded: "It could be that an understanding of the principles of existential therapy is needed by all therapists, as it adds a perspective that might . . . form the basis for all effective treatments" (p. 6).

REFERENCES

Becker, E. (1973). *The denial of death*. New York, NY: Free Press.

Bugental, J. F. T. (Fall, 1967). Commitment and the psychotherapist. *Existential Psychiatry, 6*, 285–292.

Diamond, S. (1996). *Anger, madness, and the daimonic*. Albany, NY: SUNY Press.

Elkins, D. N. (2010, August). *What the dodo bird overlooked: Additional benefits of various psychotherapies*. Paper presented at the 118th Annual Convention of the American Psychological Association, San Diego, CA.

Frankl, V. (1959). *Man's search for meaning*. Boston, MA: Beacon Press.

Greening, T. (Ed.). (1984). *American politics and humanistic psychology*. Dallas, TX: Saybrook.

Kagan, J. (2009). *The long shadow of temperament*. Boston, MA: Belknap Press.

Lifton, R. J. (1986). *The Nazi doctors: Medical killing and the psychology of genocide*. New York, NY: Basic Books.

May, R. (1958). The origins and significance of the existential movement in psychology. In R. May, L. Binswanger, & E. Angel (Eds.), *Existence: A new dimension in psychiatry and psychology* (pp. 3–36). New York, NY: Basic Books.

May, R. (1969). *Love and will*. New York, NY: Norton.

May, R. (1981). *Freedom and destiny*. New York, NY: Norton.

May, R. (1991). *The cry for myth*. New York, NY: Norton.

Mearns, D., & Cooper, M. (2005). *Working at relational depth in counseling and psychotherapy*. London, England: Sage.

Mendelowitz, E., & Schneider, K. J. (2008). Existential therapy. In R. Corsini & D. Wedding (Eds.), *Current psychotherapies* (8th ed., pp. 295–327). Belmont, CA: Thompson Brooks/Cole.

Pyszcynski, T. A., Solomon, S., & Greenberg, J. (2003). *In the wake of 9/11: The psychology of terror*. Washington, DC: American Psychological Association.

Rogers, C. R. (1961). *On becoming a person*. New York, NY: Houghton Mifflin.

Rogers, C. R. (1978). The formative tendency. *Journal of Humanistic Psychology, 18*(1), 23–26. doi:10.1177/002216787801800103

Rogers, C. R., Gendlin, E. T., Kiesler, D., & Truax, C. (Eds.). (1967). *The therapeutic relationship and its impact*. Madison: University of Wisconsin Press.

Rossi Monti, M. (2010). You will be like god: Fascination of force and social conformism in two war episodes. *Journal of Humanistic Psychology, 50*(1), 6–37. doi:10.1177/0022167809338069

Schneider, K. J. (1993). *Horror and the holy: Wisdom-teachings of the monster tale*. Chicago, IL: Open Court.

Schneider, K. J. (2004). *Rediscovery of awe: Splendor, mystery, and the fluid center of life*. St. Paul, MN: Paragon House.

Schneider, K. J. (2008). *Existential–integrative psychotherapy*. New York, NY: Routledge.

Schneider, K. J. (2009). *Awakening to awe: Personal stories of profound transformation*. Lanham, MD: Aronson.

Schneider, K. J. Galvin, J., & Serlin, I. A. (2009). Rollo May on existential psychology. *Journal of Humanistic Psychology, 49*, 419–434.

Schneider, K. J. (in press). The renewal of humanism in psychotherapy: Summary and conclusion. *Psychotherapy*.

Simonton, D. K. (1994). *Greatness: Who makes history and why*. New York, NY: Guilford Press.

Tedeschi, R., & Calhoon, L. (1995). *Trauma and transformation: Growing in the aftermath of suffering*. Thousand Oaks, CA: Sage.

Thorne, B. (2003). *Carl Rogers*. Thousand Oaks, CA: Sage.

Tillich, P. (Speaker). (1963). *Romanticism* (Part 1). [CD recording T577 116, Paul Tillich Compact Disc Collection]. Richmond, VA: Union PSCE.

Wampold, B. (2008, February 6). Existential–integrative psychotherapy: Coming of age. [Review of the book *Existential–integrative psychotherapy: Guideposts to the core of practice* by K. J. Schneider]. *PsycCRITIQUES, 53*(6). doi:10.1037/a0011070

2

WHENCE THE EVIL? A PERSONALISTIC AND DIALOGIC PERSPECTIVE

PETER F. SCHMID

Humanistic psychology often has been confronted with the reproach that the phenomenon of evil is not taken seriously or considered sufficiently. However, among the main characteristics of humanistic psychology in general, the person- or client-centered approach in particular holds a belief in the human's freedom of choice and responsibility. This understanding of the human as person implies the challenge of an authentic confrontation with and the necessity of taking a stance toward the phenomenological fact of what we call "evil" and the "dark or negative side" of human experience and behavior. Asking ourselves who we really are and how we can best relate to each other—or the other way around!—has been triggering the challenging question about the nature of evil from the very beginning of our reflection upon ourselves.

Facing the threat of a nuclear war, two great humanistic authors, Rollo May (1909–1994) and Carl Rogers (1902–1987), dealt with the problem,

DOI: 10.1037/13941-002
Humanity's Dark Side: Evil, Destructive Experience, and Psychotherapy, A. C. Bohart, B. S. Held, E. Mendelowitz, and K. J. Schneider (Editors)
Copyright © 2013 by the American Psychological Association. All rights reserved.

discussed it, and arrived at rather divergent positions that they expressed in their famous exchanges (May, 1982/1989; Rogers, 1981/1989b, 1982/1989c). On the basis of their views, I discuss some aspects of the question of evil in this chapter.

I follow some of its traces in ontology, anthropology, theology, ethics, politics, and individual and social psychology. I also discuss implications and consequences for the place of negativity in the therapeutic process on the basis of an existential view of an encounter and a dialogue-oriented psychotherapy that truly deserves the name *person-centered*. First, I consider two fundamental philosophical and anthropological positions in the occidental history of humankind in regard to the issue of evil and then look closer at May's and Rogers's stances. I argue that May's critique ignored Rogers's emphasis on choice and responsibility. Rogers believed that a facilitative relationship helps clients grow in a constructive or prosocial direction. The key difference is that the Rogerian therapist does not believe that the kind of confrontation used by May is needed.

Next, I compare and assess the implications of a *being-centered* or *person-centered* philosophy in the views of Rogers and May on the one hand, and in contemporary philosophy on the other hand. And finally I sketch how a genuinely personalistic and dialogical anthropology might comprehend what we call *evil*. I argue that evil arises from the refusal of personalization. As a result, an in-depth person-to-person encounter in therapy is needed, based on the conviction that the focus of attention has to move from the general question "What is the nature of the human being" to "Who are you?" (see also Schmid, 2010a, 2010b).

UNDE MALUM?

Where Does Evil Come From?

Why have we been dealing with this question from time immemorial? It preoccupies us because of our experience, since the "dark" or "negative" side of nature, the human being included, puzzles us, makes us suffer, fascinates us. It is one of the questions that seems unanswerable. It continuously challenges us to take a stance. We cannot get it out of our minds, no matter whether we try to come to grips with nature through research or cope with human behavior by trying to understand and to empathize. We cannot get it out of our doings, even if we try to do our best. We cannot get it out of our experiences, even if we try to ignore it, to fight it, or to keep cool. Even after the outrageous cruelties and tyrannies of the 20th century—Auschwitz, Hiroshima, the Gulag Archipelago—after 9/11, in the face of the threat of a nuclear war or of worldwide terrorist attacks.

And why is dealing with this question important to psychotherapists and counselors? There are two reasons. First, it is necessary in order to understand human nature—even to determine whether there is such thing as a human nature. Second, it is necessary in order to adequately practice psychotherapy and counseling.

What Does *Evil* Mean?

Beginning with Plato, philosophers have distinguished between physical evil (*malum physicum*, including illness, pain, ugliness, accidents, natural disasters; megalomania and delusion; structural evil), metaphysical evil (*malum metaphysicum*, Leibnitz's term for the imperfect world, including finiteness, limits, and death), and moral or ethical evil (*malum morale*, including evil intentions and actions) deriving from freedom. Only the last type of evil is of interest in this chapter.

Etymologically, *evil* (like the German *Übel*) stands for "exceeding due limits" (Hoad, 1986). Similarly, the German *böse* comes from *baus*, which originally means "blown up, swollen." On the contrary, the Latin word *malus* means "small, minor, inferior."

Both Rollo May and Carl Rogers used the term in a broad sense. May (1982) spoke about "angry, hostile, negative—that is, evil—feelings of the clients" (p. 245), "violent rage or collective paranoia in time of war or compulsive sex or oppressive behavior" (p. 240), and "destructive possession" (1969, p. 131). Rogers used the term to designate "destructive, cruel, malevolent behavior" (1981, p. 237); religiously motivated terrorism, "murderous impulses, desires to hurt, feelings of anger and rage, desires to impose our will on others" (1982, p. 254), "the dark and often sordid side of life" (1958, p. 17).

I do not see anger or aggression as evil per se, although they may be evil depending on the context, the givens, and the motives. The aim of this chapter is not to find a conclusive definition of evil. As a working definition, I use "hostile, destructive, malevolent intentions, and actions that cause suffering; in short, anything that is 'against the good life.'"

The question discussed in humanistic psychology and in this chapter is, Whence the evil? Where does evil come from if all people aim at what they consider to be *good*? The question is not, What is evil? Although these questions are of course interrelated, we ask why? whence? how come? and how to overcome? And the corresponding ethical question has to be, How do you deal with evil? Which action do you take in the face of the phenomenon of evil? How do you respond to those persons that you experience as evil-minded or evil-doing? How do you handle the experience of evil, if you find out that you yourself have evil thoughts or impulses or act evilly? I do not want to speculate; I am dealing with a phenomenological issue of original experience.

TWO FUNDAMENTAL POSITIONS

For Pythagoras, the *one* was the fullness and the good as such. Division or split was the beginning of all evil because it meant loss of this unity.

Among others—for example, the pessimistic stance of Schopenhauer (that everything is evil) or the optimism of Leibnitz (that this is the best of all possible worlds)—there are two classical answers to the question of the origin of moral evil: Either evil is there from the beginning as a fundamental force in the universe as the opposite to the good, or it is a deficiency of the good and has no being in itself. These two positions characterize the essential difference between dualistic religions and world views on the one hand and monotheistic religions and such philosophies that believe in one sole source of all being on the other hand.

Dualism: Good Versus Evil

Is evil there from the beginning? Is there an evil principle opposite to a good one? a good god and an evil god? a good law and an evil one that rule the world? The classical dualistic world view can be found, for example, in Parsism, Manichaeism, Priscillianism, and gnosticism. In Zoroastrianism, the classical Persian religion of Zarathustra, two fundamental principles compete: Ahura Mazda or Ormuz, the good god of creation and order; and Angra Manju or Ariman, the bad one, the god of lying, destruction, and death. The human's free will decides between them and thus decides the fate of the cosmos. In Manichaeism and Neoplatonism, to simplify it, the soul is the good and the body the evil.

Two principles that rule the world are in Heraclitus's philosophy of the interplay of opposites; they can be found in gnosticism (light vs. darkness; "soma sema" ["το μεν σωμα εστιν ημιν σημα"]—the body as grave for the soul), and they form Schelling's idea of history as fight between light and darkness, good and evil.

A dualistic antagonism is, of course, the basis of Freud's (1920/1998) metapsychology, developed after World War I: All human behavior, and in fact all that exists, is the result of the ongoing fight of libido and aggression, Eros and Thanatos, the drives of connection and union—of enhancement and love, on the one hand, and destruction and death—today we might speak of entropy—on the other hand. The interior of the human being is the venue of this battle. In the development of the infant, evil is everything that has to do with deprivation of love; later, *evil* becomes a generic term for any disturbance of living together by the human drive of aggression, including self-destruction. For Freud, this reality is not only psychological but also metapsychological. The goal of life is death; everything will end as inorganic matter, as it once was, before there was life; fossilization is the perspective of redemption (Safranski, 1999, p. 248).

Rollo May

May (1982) also holds a dualistic position in postulating that the human's potentialities are "the source *both* of our constructive and our destructive impulses" (p. 240). This does not come as a surprise, if you take May's professional background in psychoanalysis into account. May, analysand of Erich Fromm, had attended seminars with the second founder of psychoanalysis, Alfred Adler, in Vienna in the early 1930s, had worked as a psychoanalyst in private practice, and had his primary professional association with the William Alanson White Institute of Psychiatry, Psychoanalysis and Psychology in New York from 1948 until 1975, the year of his move to California (Kirschenbaum & Land Henderson, 1989, pp. 229–230).

Despite his big leap from conventional analysis and its mode of therapy to existentialism and humanistic stances, May's basic convictions were obviously influenced by psychoanalytical thinking. For example, when he writes about "potentialities, driven by the daimonic urge" (May, 1982, p. 240), we clearly see that his view is rooted in Freudian ideas. This daimonic urge needs to be integrated into the personality, which in May's view is the purpose of psychotherapy—again undoubtedly an analytical position. As for Freud, for May evil is an ontological, not just a moral, problem. The gnostic thesis of the failed creation returns (Safranski, 1999, p. 249).

May, in his efforts at reconciling Freud and the existentialists, turned his attention to motivation. His basic motivational construct is the daimonic as the entire system of motives, different for each individual. It is thought to be composed of a collection of specific motives called *daimons* and has obvious parallels with Freud's id (see also Cooper, 2003, p. 84).

The term *daimonic*, from the Greek δαιμονιον [daimonion], that is, "the divine, the divine power or little god," was earlier used by Xenophon, Socrates, and Nietzsche (and influenced Schopenhauer's "will to live" concept) to describe the warning inner voice of the deity, an ethical intuition (not to be confused with demonic from demon, which means an evil spirit).

May was convinced that the daimonic urge (again, not to be confused with demonic) is a central motive for each individual to face life and the principal source of our potential to develop constructively as well as destructively. Unlike Rogers's actualizing tendency (see below), May's daimonic "urge for self-affirmation is not in any a priori sense directionally set. It could be expressed either constructively or destructively"—that is (and here there is no difference with Rogers), "humans are inherently capable of both good and evil" (Patterson, 2008, p. 29).

According to May, it is important to "integrate" the daimonic forces; otherwise, if one daimon becomes so important that it takes over, the result is destructive activities, or "daimonic possession." Therefore, May (1982) concluded that confronting these issues is crucial (p. 240). He emphasized that "the issue of not confronting evil is the most important error in the humanistic movement" (p. 249). Because—and here May (1969) seems to be inconsistent—"not to recognize the daimonic itself turns out to be daimonic, it makes us accomplices on the side of the destructive possession" (p. 131). Why does May call destructive possession *daimonic*, if the daimonic is neither good nor evil in itself?

One Sole Source: Evil as the Minor Good

According to the classical doctrine of both Greek and Judeo–Christian philosophy, evil, the κακον [kakon], is not a principle of its own; it has no being. *Esse qua esse bonum est*—All being as being is good (Augustine). Therefore, evil is a deficiency in being; it lacks full being: *Malum privatio essendi et boni* (Thomas Aquinas). As already said, the Latin word malus means "minor, inferior."

Strictly speaking, the imperfect *is* not. What *is*, as far as it *is*, is good and perfect. Evil is an absence of being that ought to *be* there, but *is* not. Thus it is στερησις [steresis], *privatio* (Latin *privare* means "deprive, rob of"; deprivation means losing a quality, a withdrawal; see Wucherer-Huldenfeld, 2007). Evil is deprived of (full) being; it misses something, namely, that which it should be. It is deprivation, imperfection, a defect of being; ultimately something that has no substance, no being, that does not exist. Το ουκ ον [To uk on] (Origenes), *privatio entis* or *privatio essendi et boni*: Evil is the absence of what should be, of the being and the good. It is similar to darkness, which is the absence of light and not something in its own right. Or like blindness: The organ is good, blindness is a lack of its functioning. Or a hole: A hole is not; the less there is, the bigger it becomes. Aristotle's famous example is the deformed infant: It can only survive if it does not fall short of a minimum of being.

The deprivation of the good is experienced as not only a harmless missing but a reversal of the good that is missed. It is not there as it should be (cf. the loss of a front door key; Wucherer-Huldenfeld, 2009, p. 136).

This is the thinking of many philosophers from Pythagoras, Plato, Epictetus, Augustine, Boethius, Dionysius Pseudo-Areopagita, Thomas Aquinas, and Christian metaphysics to Leibnitz, Spinoza, Hegel, Goethe (see Goethe,1808/1832/1966, with Mephistopheles as the "devil" who always aims at evil and yet causes good, vv. 1336–1337), Heidegger, Buber, and many others.

The Bible holds a similar conviction. After the creation, "God saw everything which he had made and it was very good" (Gen. 1:31). The primeval narrative of the Fall of the Human Being (Gen. 3) states that

- Evil does not originate in God,
- nor is its origin in a counter-divine power—the devil is a fallen angel, a creature, and not another god (Schmid, 2000; 2001)—and
- it is also not part of the created order: humanity is made in God's image (Schmid, 1998c). In the paradise there was no evil.

The root cause of all evil is the human's voluntarily turning away from *the* good, from God. This estrangement leads to the inability to become perfect, to become what we could be. Only God, and that means love, can overcome evil. Ultimately, in a Judeo–Christian view evil is the negation of the good (and thus of God).

Martin Buber (1952/1986, p. 192) wrote that evil cannot be done wholeheartedly; only the good can be done wholeheartedly. Humans lie to their being when they deny their true self. He coined the term *Vergegnung* instead of *Begegnung*, *miscounter* instead of *encounter*, the denial of encounter, going astray, missing each other instead of meeting.

Carl Rogers

The philosophy of Rogers is deeply rooted in this strand of tradition, as his basic assumptions and his theories prove. The following names some of them:

- the belief that something *could* be there, but *is* not or not yet (e.g., further personality development);
- the basically constructive nature of the formative and the actualizing tendencies;
- the need of "the Other" (in the sense of encounter philosophy, e.g., a person providing facilitative conditions) for the actualizing tendency to work;
- a fundamentally constructive, trustworthy, and forward-moving human nature, as opposed to a beast to be tamed (Rogers directly attacked Freud and Nietzsche for the latter view, and Nietzsche furthermore believed that evil was a construct of the weak, who resented being defeated in the struggle for life; this construct of evil served to hinder the strong from acting);
- the proactive direction of humans' movement under facilitative conditions;

- voluntary choice;
- the fully functioning person who has all of the qualities of a person in fullness (as in the Bible's paradise lost)—and the actual person's lack of some of these in different graduations: being alienated, estranged from their true nature—from what could and should be, but is not; and
- *unconditional positive regard*, the psychological technical term for love in the meaning of *agape* (Rogers, 1951, pp. 154–155; Schmid, 1989, pp. 255–257; 1996, pp. 253–259, 533–540), transcending negative assessment and self-assessment.

One of the most important roots of Rogers's, as well as May's, thinking is in the Christian tradition. He had been brought up in a Christian tradition and had been a student of theology. "I am influenced by the Judeo–Christian stream of thought," Rogers (1965, p. 10) confessed. Following Goldstein, he held the idea that there is only one motivational force, the force of actualization. (See Rogers, 1951, 1963; Patterson, 2008, p. 31.)

But, contrary to widespread misinterpretation, Rogers did not postulate that humans are basically good. "In my experience every person has the capacity for evil behavior. I, and others, have had murderous and cruel impulses, desires to impose our will on others" (Rogers, 1982/1989c, p. 254).

Actualization does not necessarily go in a prosocial direction. But Rogers saw it as an empirical observation that human beings have the potential to be constructive in an *individual and social* way and the actualizing tendency makes people *naturally and spontaneously* grow in this direction (see Bohart, 2007) *if* the individual finds himself or herself in a facilitative relationship: "If the elements making for growth are present, the actualizing tendency develops in positive ways. In the human these elements for growth are . . . a climate of psychological attitudes" (Rogers, 1982/1989c, pp. 253–254).

So, whatever evil might be, according to Rogers it is a matter not only of the individual or of society but also of relationship.

Rogers was heavily criticized by many: "Your viewpoint is devilishly innocent" (Warren Bennis to Rogers; Rogers & Bennis, 1976). Despite accusations that Rogers underrated the forces of evil (see Thorne, 2003, p. 79), Rogers was not naïve. It is ridiculous and against the facts to think that Rogers did not recognize the dark side or held too rosy a view of human nature. But unlike others, he did find "members of the human species *essentially* constructive in their fundamental nature, but damaged by their experience" (Rogers, 1981/1989b, p. 238). The following are some examples.

> It disturbs me to be thought of as an optimist. My whole professional experience has been with the dark and often sordid side of life, and I know, better than most, the incredibly destructive behavior of which

man is capable. Yet that same professional experience has forced upon me the realization that man, when you know him deeply, in his worst and most troubled states, is not evil or demonic. (Rogers, 1958, p. 17)

The presence of terrorism, hostility, and aggression are urgent in our days. I am very well aware of the incredible amount of destructive, cruel, malevolent behavior in today's world—from the threats of war to the senseless violence in the streets. It is cultural influences which are the major factor in our evil behaviors. (Rogers, 1981/1989b, pp. 237–238)

I am quite aware that out of defensiveness and inner fear individuals can and do behave in ways which are incredibly cruel, horribly destructive, immature, regressive, anti-social, hurtful. Yet one of the most refreshing and invigorating parts of my experience is to work with such individuals and to discover the strongly positive directional tendencies which exist in them, as in all of us, at the deepest levels. (Rogers, 1961, p. 27)

In a statement Rogers (1957/1989a) summarized his conviction:

I do not discover man to be well characterized, in his basic nature, by such terms as *fundamentally hostile, antisocial, destructive, evil.*

I do not discover man to be, in his basic nature, completely without a nature, a tabula rasa on which *anything* may be written, nor malleable putty which can be shaped in *any* form.

I do not discover man to be essentially a perfect being, sadly warped and corrupted by society.

In my experience I have discovered man to have characteristics which seem inherent in his species, and the terms which have at different times seemed to me descriptive of these characteristics are such terms as *positive, forward-moving, constructive, realistic, trustworthy.* (p. 403)

He expressed his conviction similarly in exchanges with Paul Tillich, May's teacher at the Union Theological Seminary in New York.

People sometimes say to me, "What if you create a climate of freedom? A man might use that freedom to become completely evil or antisocial." I don't find that to be true, and that is one of the things that makes me feel that . . . in a relationship of real freedom the individual tends to move not only toward deeper self-understanding, but toward more social behavior. (Rogers & Tillich, 1966/1989, p. 68)

And in his review of a book by the theologian Reinhold Niebuhr, he wrote,

It is in his [Niebuhr's] conception of the basic deficiency of the individual self that I find my experience utterly at variance. He is quite clear that the "original sin" is self love . . . I could not differ more deeply from the notion that self love is the fundamental and pervasive "sin." (Rogers, 1956, p. 14)

About the psychoanalyst Karl Menninger, Rogers (1957/1989a) said,

> When a Freudian such as Karl Menninger tells me (as he has, in a discussion of this issue) that he perceives man as . . . "innately destructive," I can only shake my head in wonderment. (p. 405)

To sum it up, here is his creed in the formulation (from his 1957 "note on the nature of man"):

- The human being is not fundamentally evil,
- not without a nature, and
- not essentially perfect.
- Constructiveness is inherent in the human species.

In short: "I find in my experience no such *innate* tendency toward evil" (Rogers, 1982/1989c, p. 253, italics added).

Evil—The Price of Freedom

If the human being's nature is essentially constructive, this again raises the question: *Unde malum?* Whence the evil?

The traditional answer to the question of why we have the problem of moral evil is the freedom of the human being. If humans are free, they have the freedom of choice, free will. Its misuse is, according to Kant, what is evil.

Rogers's answer to the *unde malum* problem not only reflects the traditional Western position, his view "is the essence of a phenomenological position, when carried to its logical conclusion," as Brian Thorne (2003, p. 86) remarked.

Rogers stated that whether evil impulses and desires become evil behavior depends on two factors, namely, (a) *social conditioning* and (b) *voluntary choice*. With this statement Rogers acknowledged the power of imposed conditions of worth, of forces outside our awareness, *and* free will. By stressing the human being's capacity for free choice, he rejected the absolute behaviorist position and the analytic position of the overall rule of the unconscious (see Thorne, 2003, pp. 86–87). However, like the psychodynamic theoreticians, Rogers acknowledged the role of social conditioning in early childhood—see his remarks on Hitler (Rogers, 1982/1989c, p. 254) and Alice Miller's investigations of Hitler's upbringing, as quoted by Tony Merry (1995, pp. 31–33) in his chapter titled "If People Are So Constructive, Why Do They Do Such Destructive Things?" (pp. 29–34).

It is worth noticing that May (1982/1989), in his rebuttal to Rogers (1982/1989c), referred only to one of the elements mentioned by Rogers, namely, culture; he blamed Rogers for not seeing the individual's responsibility, thus clearly ignoring Rogers's stance on free will. Rogers, then, is definitely in the tradition of those who see evil as the "price of freedom" (Safranski, 1999), as part of the "drama of freedom."

CONSEQUENCES FOR PSYCHOTHERAPEUTIC PRACTICE

Rogers (1982) correctly wrote that the question of "origin makes a great deal of difference philosophically" (p. 253), but of course the different images of the human being have consequences for the practice of psychotherapy, too. What are they?

May's (1982) answer was that "aspects of evil need to be brought out in therapy" (p. 17). So, it follows for May that "the daimonic needs to be directed and channeled" (1969, p. 126) and integrated (1969, 1982).

To take care "to integrate something" means to have a goal for the client. Not unlike Fritz Perls, the cofounder of gestalt therapy, with his background in Freudian analysis, Rollo May could not think of a therapy in which the therapist does not have to guide the client in some way and to confront him or her with matters the therapist thinks are crucial for the client. Despite their move toward existential, humanistic, phenomenological convictions, neither Perls nor May made the radical shift to a fully *client*-centered psychotherapy. Yet, even so, the question remains, why is it considered necessary in therapy to stress the confrontation with evil and not the confrontation with good?

Rogers's answer to this question is that evil is a subject in therapy, as is every other subject. The avoidance of aggressive, hostile, negative, destructive, evil issues by therapists—as critically annotated, for example, by reviewers at the Wisconsin Schizophrenia Project (Rogers et al., 1967), as well as at other occasions—is clearly a professional error on the part of the therapist—quite often probably because therapists have not confronted their own dark side. But to avoid paying attention to the dark side is definitely not at all something that is inherent to the image of the human being in the person-centered approach.

Some person-centered therapists tend to avoid confronting their own and their clients' feelings of aggression and dealing with so-called negative feelings or thoughts. They obviously feel attracted to a seemingly harmless therapeutic approach that in fact is a watered-down version of what appeared to be too radical a challenge to professional experts. Rogers and others needed time to dare to encounter these sides of their clients in the required depth. As an *encounter*—a term that originally was used for hostile meetings only (note that there is *counter* in the word)—psychotherapy always involves the risks of being surprised by the Other and of meeting the challenge of the unexpected (see Schmid, 1996; Schmid & Mearns, 2006).

BEING-CENTERED OR PERSON-CENTERED?

Two Divergent Positions?

May and Rogers were similar in many ways. Both moved from theology to psychology (in a way Rogers is "the Catholic" as his view on society shows parallels to the idea of an "original sin"; May is "the Protestant" in this debate). Both were influenced by Otto Rank and his theory of will. Both were dedicated to the idea of a genuinely humanistic, existence-based psychology, and both were concerned with political implications.

May believed that humans have both constructive and destructive *inherent* impulses; Rogers was convinced of the constructive and prosocial nature of the inherent actualizing tendency and stressed that what is generally thought of and referred to as evil is, more accurately, an outward expression of a person's internal estrangement, his or her incongruence between the actualizing tendency and the self-actualizing tendency, his or her striving to self-actualization.

Although May and Rogers have two quite different anthropological positions originating in different philosophical backgrounds with different practical consequences, they are more alike than they appear at first sight, because both are grounded in conventional ontological thinking, concerned with being and essence.

Mearns's Objection

A comment by Mearns on the issue sheds light on the fact that contemporary men and women no longer find that traditional ontological categories provide sufficient solutions to their experiences. His answer to the *unde malum* problem is anxiety. Mearns's—as he says "disparaging"—definition of evil is "a hypothetical construct used to describe someone whom we fear and whom we do not understand" (Mearns & Thorne, 2000, p. 59).

This admittedly crude position indicates that a *discussion* of the question, whence the evil?—a question that comes from experience, not from a philosophy that has lost touch with the real world—derives from abstract ontological categories that might well be outdated, because we no longer think about our experiencing and our existing in those conceptual categories. On the contrary, we need existential answers to existential questions.

Ontological or Dialogic?

Both May and Rogers discussed the problem of evil in the traditional ontological categories of being and essence. Both believed that there is a human nature (Bohart, 2009) and discussed human nature in a one-sided, substantialistic way (i.e., mainly concerned with the substance of this nature). Both of them were occupied with the following questions: What is *in* the individual? What substance does the individual possess?

May was close to Kant in his belief that evil is inherent to the human being. Rogers took a nontraditional stance in his epistemology; that is, he questioned whether we need "a" reality, a "real" nature of reality (Rogers, 1978), thus proving to be one of the first constructivists. Rogers thought in ontological categories (despite the fact that he responded to May's repeatedly uttered demand for ontology, "Rollo, if you want an ontology you write one. I don't feel the need for it" [Kirschenbaum, 2007, p. 236]). Paradoxically, when Rogers refused the idea that the human being has "to fulfill an evil nature" (Rogers, 1982, p. 253), he seems to have been even more concerned with ontology than was May.

With the debate about an existing or nonexisting evil *in* the individual comes the idea that evil is a substance that exists or does not exist. Thus, Rogers and May show that they were captives of traditional ontological categories. But this is inappropriate for a truly personalistic understanding of the human being. Comprehending a human holistically as a person is the underlying idea of the person-centered approach. Thus, both May and Rogers had inconsistent beliefs. Whereas Schneider (2009) blamed Rogers for not being sufficiently being-centered, I find that in this respect *both* took a "being-centered" view, thus failing to grasp the full notion of "being and becoming a person" because of their focus on the substance.

A PERSONAL–DIALOGIC POSITION

Now, almost 30 years after the May–Rogers debate, we must advance a philosophy that is based on anthropological foundations in theory and practice.

Personal Anthropology

Within philosophy, the paradigm has shifted from general philosophy to anthropology, the philosophy about the human being. Philosophy has transitioned from being-centered to person-centered—that is, from metaphysics or ontology to existentialism, phenomenology, personalism, and dialogical philosophy. The question for today's philosophers is not about *being as such* but about *personal being* (*Personales Sein*, Wucherer-Huldenfeld, 1994/1997). This is an ongoing process and a perspective to be continuously developed.

The pertinent question for anthropology and therefore for a genuinely humane psychology—reflecting the paradigmatic shift from natural science to human science—is no longer Kant's "What is the human being?" but rather, "Who is this (specific) human being?" Moreover, in the light of dialogical philosophy, "Who are you?" This question deals with the person-to-person relationship and the encounter, interrelatedness, and dialogue (see Schmid, 1991, pp. 19–21, 1994, 1996, 1998a, 1998b, 1998c, 2006, 2007a). (The *quid* [what?] addresses the essence, the nature, the *quis* [who?] addresses the person both in their substantiality and interrelatedness.)

So the pertinent question is not, "Was Rogers being-centered enough?" (Schneider, 2009), but instead, "Was Rogers person-centered enough?" In other words, in which direction do we need to further develop humanistic psychology?

The Meaning of *Person*

To think in a person-centered way, we need to understand the notion of *person*—that is, we need to clarify what is meant when talking about the person. The issue at stake is the process of being and becoming a person, in other words, personalization.

Philosophically, the person-centered approach is founded on the conviction that human beings should be regarded as persons. To be a person means that the human being is intrinsically and dialectically both substantial and relational: The human being is from oneself and thus autonomous, and from relationship and thus interdependent. This dialectic view overcomes a one-sided substantialistic position. Human beings have an innate capacity, need, and tendency to develop on their own and in relationships. Both autonomy and interrelatedness constitute the one human nature. Thus, the two essential dimensions of person-centered anthropology are independence and interconnectedness. This image of the human being is the essential conclusion of an ongoing process of reflection about ourselves in the European tradition during more than two millennia from the Jews and Greeks via the Muslims until today. Therefore, the human is now understood as a *substantial–relational* being, autonomous *and* interdependent, characterized by self-responsibility *and* solidarity.

The development of the personality theory and theory of interpersonal relationships of the person-centered approach has led to an improved realization of the relational dimension of personhood. This relational dimension can be termed *encounter* (Schmid, 1994, 1998a), *meeting at relational depth* (Mearns & Cooper, 2005), *relationship-oriented approach,* or *dialogical* (Schmid, 1996, 2007a, 2009b). Such an image of the human being—with its profoundness and radicalism and the dialectical balance of substantiality and relationality—can only be found in a genuine person-centered approach. (See the detailed description in Schmid, 1991, 1994, 1998c, 2007a, 2009b.)

The challenge of the person-centered approach is to understand the client as the sole expert on the path of therapy in terms of both its content and its method. Clients are the agents that make therapy work (Bohart & Tallman, 1999); the therapist's task is to facilitate, that is, to offer a fostering relationship to the client based on the conviction of a fundamental We, open for personal encounter. Personalization, the actualizing tendency toward personality development, is supported and facilitated by a personal responsiveness to the client's existential needs. The challenge of such responsiveness is to realize and unconditionally value the otherness of the Other (e.g., by renouncing predetermined diagnostic categorization) and to enter into a dialogue that is considered to be already there at the very beginning of therapy (Schmid, 1989; 2002; 2009a, 2009b).

The Person and Evil

Such a consequently personal anthropology overcomes thinking in conventional ontological categories. From a phenomenological point of view this includes the issue of what we call evil and the dark or negative side of human experience, imagination, and behavior. Understanding a human being as a person requires an authentic confrontation with, and taking a stance toward, these phenomenological facts. If we experience those phenomena—by our fellow humans' behavior, by our own ideas, wishes, and actions—then it is a matter of authenticity, integrity, and credibility to deal with them philosophically, theoretically, and in the therapeutic practice. This means that we must take seriously that evil is foremost an elementary *experience* to a human being and not so much a matter of terminology or metaphysical discussion.

Thus, everything is evil that is against the person. From a personalistic perspective, *evil is to avoid personalization*, to not actualize the potential of fully being and becoming a person in terms of the substantial as well as the relational dimension ("miscounter") of personhood. Evil is alienation from oneself, acting contrary to the best of one's knowledge and belief, that is, against one's conscience *and* ignoring the call of the Other by refusing to respond and therefore to be responsible (see Schmid, 2002, 2009b). Evil is to refuse the demand for authenticity and solidarity, to avoid becoming who you are, to avoid encountering other human beings, to avoid autonomy and responsibility, to avoid sovereignty and engagement, to ignore one's possibilities, and to ignore dialogue and the fundamental human We—in short, evil is to escape from genuinely being and becoming a person.

The perspective that as human beings we are not only *in* relationships but we *are* relationship (Schmid, 2006) overcomes what Emmanuel Levinas

(1957/1983, p. 189) called *egology*, that is, being concerned with the I. The relevance particularly for a genuinely humanistic, client- or person-centered therapy is obvious: As long as psychotherapists are concerned with questions like "What do I have to do as a therapist?" therapy is more therapist-centered than client-centered. Only a therapy that is genuinely oriented toward the person is rooted in and grasps toward a consciousness and self-understanding of being-with and being-for.

Ratio mali, the cause ("reason") of evil, is not to be found in objective substantial realities but in personal and interpersonal qualities and attitudes (see Rotter, 1993, pp. 104–105). It is a *no* to all perspectives of personalization held at once—toward oneself and toward others, a refusal to embrace both authentic self-realization and self-fulfillment *and* authentic relationship as being-for-each-other by being-with and as being-counter to each other (Mearns & Schmid, 2006; Schmid & Mearns, 2006). The cause of evil is inauthentic responding or the denial of responding to the dialogical situation we find ourselves in within this world. It is particularly the unwillingness to deal with the unknown, the strange (Schmid, 2009b).

Conditional Positive Regard: Evil as Deprivation of Love

Evil is everything that opposes personal being. If the meaning of being consists of being-for-each-other, then evil is opposition to love. Therefore— and with all due cautiousness and carefulness because of the multiple meanings of the word *love*—evil is the failure to love oneself and the other. To love is used here in the meaning of αγαπη (agape) as Rogers (1951, 1962) used the term, a personal posture that he carefully and in detail described as "unconditional positive regard." In a personal–dialogical perspective love is the fulfillment of dialogue (Rombold, 1984, II, p. 86).

"To love means to open ourselves to the negative as well as the positive—to grief, sorrow, and disappointment as well as to joy, fulfillment, and an intensity of consciousness we did not know was possible before" (May, 1969, p. 100).

Unde malum? From a personalistic and a person-centered philosophy, the answer is *privatio amoris*, deprivation of love. It is evil to deprive oneself and others of respect, regard, and acknowledgment as a person. It is evil to withhold love toward oneself and others.

The result is definitely not an overly positive view of human nature. We all owe each other and ourselves love. To not acknowledge this interpersonal condition in the therapeutic encounter and dialogue is, theologically speaking, a sin. From the point of view of psychotherapy science, it is a professional blunder. According to a person-centered view, the so-called negative in the therapeutic process is the *conditionality of positive regard*, or the deprivation of love (an idea that can be found in both Freud and Rogers; see above).

This is true not only for the cocooned client–therapist relationship (which would mean that the problem of evil is reduced to an individual phenomenon) but also for groups and for society as a whole (when we consider the societal dimension *structural* evil can be reflected). Because psychotherapy must be seen as a question of social ethics (Schmid, 2007b), the question of evil is also and today predominantly a question of social dimensions and therefore of social ethics, social psychology, sociology, and politics. After all, "psychotherapy is political or it is not psychotherapy" (Schmid, 2007b).

REFERENCES

Bohart, A. C. (2007). The actualizing person. In M. Cooper, M. O'Hara, P. F. Schmid, & G. Wyatt (Eds.), *The handbook of person-centred psychotherapy and counselling* (pp. 47–63). Houndmills, England: Palgrave Macmillan.

Bohart, A. C. (2009, August). *Carl Rogers, Rollo May, and humanity's dark side*. Symposium conducted at the 117th Annual Convention of the American Psychological Association, Toronto, Ontario, Canada.

Bohart, A. C., & Tallman, K. (1999). *How clients make therapy work: The process of active self-healing*. Washington, DC: American Psychological Association. doi:10.1037/10323-000

Buber, M. (1986). *Bilder von Gut und Böse* [Images of good and evil] (4th ed.). Heidelberg, Germany: Lambert Schneider. (Original work published 1952)

Cooper, M. (2003). *Existential therapies*. London, England: Sage.

Freud, S. (1998). Jenseits des Lustprinzips [Beyond the pleasure principle]. In S. Freud, *Gesammelte Werke* [Collected Works], (Vol. 13, pp. 1–69). London, England: Imago. (Original work published 1920)

Goethe, J. W. v. (1966). *Faust: Der Tragödie erster und zweiter Teil* [Faust: The first and second part of the tragedy]. Stuttgart, Germany: Reclam. (Originally published: Part I 1808; Part II 1832)

Hoad, T. F. (Ed.). (1986). *The concise Oxford dictionary of English etymology*. Oxford, England: Clarendon Press.

Kirschenbaum, H. (2007). *Carl Rogers: Life and work*. Ross-on-Wye, England: PCCS Books.

Kirschenbaum, H., & Land Henderson, V. (Eds.). (1989). *Carl Rogers: Dialogues*. Boston, MA: Houghton Mifflin.

Levinas, E. (1983). *Die Spur des Anderen: Untersuchung zur Phänomenologie und Sozialphilosophie* [The trace of the Other: Investigation on phenomenology and social psychology]. Freiburg, Germany: Alber. (Original work published in 1957)

May, R. (1969). *Love and will.* New York, NY: Dell.

May, R. (1989). The problem of evil: An open letter to Carl Rogers. In H. Kirschenbaum & V. Land Henderson (Eds.), *Carl Rogers: Dialogues* (pp. 237–239). Boston, MA: Houghton Mifflin. (Original work published 1982)

Mearns, D., & Cooper, M. (2005). *Working at relational depth in counselling and psychotherapy.* London, England: Sage.

Mearns, D., & Schmid, P. F. (2006). Being-with and being-counter: Relational depth—The challenge of fully meeting the client. *Person-Centered & Experiential Psychotherapies, 5,* 255–265. doi:10.1080/14779757.2006.9688417

Mearns, D., & Thorne, B. (2000). *Person-centred therapy today: New frontiers in theory and practice.* London, England: Sage.

Merry, T. (1995). *Invitation to person-centred psychology.* London, England: Whurr.

Patterson, C. H. (2008). *Understanding psychotherapy: Fifty years of client-centred theory and practice.* Ross-on-Wye, England: PCCS Books.

Rogers, C. R. (1951). *Client-centered therapy: Its current practice, implications, and theory.* Boston, MA: Houghton Mifflin.

Rogers, C. R. (1956). Review of Reinhold Niebuhr's "The self and the dramas of history." *Chicago Theological Seminary Register XLVI, 1,* 13–14.

Rogers, C. R. (1958). A discussion of Reinhold Niebuhr's the self and the dramas of history [concluding comment by B. M. Loomer, W. M. Horton & H. Hofmann]. *Pastoral Psychology, 9*(5), 15–17. doi:10.1007/BF01758621

Rogers, C. R. (1961). The process equation of psychotherapy. *American Journal of Psychotherapy, 15,* 27–45.

Rogers, C. R. (1962). The interpersonal relationship: The core of guidance. In C. R. Rogers & B. Stevens, *Person to person: The problem of being human* (pp. 89–104). Moab: Real People.

Rogers, C. R. (1963). The actualizing tendency in relation to "motives" and to consciousness. In M. R. Jones (Ed.), *Nebraska symposium on motivation* (Vol. 11, pp. 1–24). Lincoln, NE: University of Nebraska Press.

Rogers, C. R. (1965). A humanistic conception of man. In R. Farson (Ed.), *Science and human affairs* (pp. 18–31). Palo Alto, CA: Science and Behavior Books.

Rogers, C. R. (1978). Do we need "a" reality? *Dawnpoint, 1*(2), 6–9.

Rogers, C. R. (1989a). A note on the "nature of man." In H. Kirschenbaum & V. Land Henderson (Eds.), *The Carl Rogers reader* (pp. 219–235). Boston, MA: Houghton Mifflin. (Original work published 1957)

Rogers, C. R. (1989b). Notes on Rollo May. In H. Kirschenbaum & V. Land Henderson (Eds.), *Carl Rogers: Dialogues* (pp. 237–239). Boston, MA: Houghton Mifflin. (Original work published 1981)

Rogers, C. R. (1989c). Reply to Rollo May's letter to Carl Rogers. In H. Kirschenbaum & V. Land Henderson (Eds.), *Carl Rogers: Dialogues* (pp. 251–255). Boston, MA: Houghton Mifflin. (Original work published 1982)

Rogers, C. R., & Bennis, W. (1976). *Reflections, with Carl Rogers and Warren Bennis.* American Personnel and Guidance Association. Psychological Films.

Rogers, C. R., Gendlin, E. T., Kiesler, D. J., & Truax, C. B. (1967). *The therapeutic relationship and its impact: A study of psychotherapy with schizophrenics.* Madison, WI: University of Wisconsin Press.

Rogers, C. R., & Tillich, P. (1989). Paul Tillich and Carl Rogers—A dialogue. In H. Kirschenbaum &. V. Land Henderson (Eds.), *Carl Rogers: Dialogues* (pp. 64–78). Boston, MA: Houghton Mifflin. (Original work published 1966)

Rombold, G. (1984). *Anthropologie I+II.* Unpublished manuscript.

Rotter, H. (1993). *Person und Ethik: Zur Grundlegung der Moraltheologie* [Person and ethics: The foundation of moral theology]. Innsbruck, Austria: Tyrolia.

Safranski, R. (1999). *Das Böse oder Das Drama der Freiheit* [Evil or the drama of freedom]. Frankfurt, Germany: Fischer.

Schmid, P. F. (1989). *Personale Begegnung: Der personzentrierte Ansatz in Psychotherapie, Beratung, Gruppenarbeit und Seelsorge* [Personal encounter: The person-centered approach to psychotherapy, counseling, group work and pastoral care]. Würzburg, Germany: Echter.

Schmid, P. F. (1991). Souveränität und Engagement: Zu einem personzentrierten Verständnis von "Person" [Sovereignty and engagement: Towards a person-centered understanding of "person"]. In C. R. Rogers and P. F. Schmid, *Personzentriert: Grundlagen von Theorie und Praxis* [Person-centered: Foundations of theory and practice] (pp. 15–164). Main, Germany: Grünewald.

Schmid, P. F. (1994). *Personzentrierte Gruppenpsychotherapie: Ein Handbuch: Vol. I: Solidarität und Autonomie* [Person-centered group psychotherapy: A handbook. Vol. I: Solidarity and autonomy]. Cologne, Germany: EHP.

Schmid, P. F. (1996). *Personzentrierte Gruppenpsychotherapie in der Praxis: Ein Handbuch. Vol. II: Die kunst der begegnung* [Person-centered group psychotherapy in practice: A handbook. Vol. II: The art of encounter]. Paderborn, Germany: Junfermann.

Schmid, P. F. (1998a). "Face to face": The art of encounter. In B. Thorne & E. Lambers (Eds.), *Person-centred therapy: A European perspective* (pp. 74–90). London, England: Sage.

Schmid, P. F. (1998b). *Im Anfang ist Gemeinschaft: Vol. III. Personzentrierte Gruppenarbeit in Seelsorge und Praktischer Theologie* [In the beginning there is community: Vol. III. Person-centered group work in pastoral care and practical theology]. Stuttgart, Germany: Kohlhammer.

Schmid, P. F. (1998c). "On becoming a person-centered approach": A person-centred understanding of the person. In B. Thorne & E. Lambers (Eds.), *Person-centred therapy: A European perspective* (pp. 38–52). London, England: Sage.

Schmid, P. F. (2000, May). Personalisation oder Mephisto wird Supervisor [Personalization or Mephisto becomes a supervisor]. In P. F. Schmid (Chair), *Wie führe ich ein ehrenwertes Leben?* [How to lead an honorable life]. Symposium conducted at the meeting of PCA, Vienna, Austria.

Schmid, P. F. (2001). "Puzzling you is the nature of my game." Von der Faszination und dem Verdrängen des Bösen [On the fascination and repression of evil]. *Diakonia, 32,* 77–83.

Schmid, P. F. (2002). Anspruch und Antwort: Personzentrierte Psychotherapie als Begegnung von Person zu Person [Demand and response: Person-centered psychotherapy as encounter person to person]. In W. Keil & G. Stumm (Eds.), *Die vielen Gesichter der Personzentrierten Psychotherapie* [The many faces of person-centered psychotherapy] (pp. 75–105). Vienna, Austria: Springer.

Schmid, P. F. (2006). *"In the beginning there is community": Implications and challenges of the belief in a triune God and a person-centred approach.* Norwich, England: Norwich Centre Occasional Publication Series.

Schmid, P. F. (2007a). The anthropological and ethical foundations of person-centred therapy. In M. Cooper, M. O'Hara, P. F. Schmid, & G. Wyatt (Eds.), *The handbook of person-centred psychotherapy and counseling* (pp. 30–46). Houndsmill, England: Palgrave Macmillan.

Schmid, P. F. (2007b). *Psychotherapy is political or it is not psychotherapy: The actualizing tendency as personalizing tendency.* Keynote lecture at the 3rd national conference of the British Association for the Person-Centred Approach: Past, Present and Future, Cirencester, England.

Schmid, P. F. (2009a, June). *Beyond question and answer: The challenge to facilitate freedom.* Paper presented at the International Conference on PC Counseling & Psychotherapy Today: Evolution & Challenges, Athens, Greece.

Schmid, P. F. (2009). *Freedom to respond. Dialogue—Foundation and challenge of humanity.* Carl Rogers Award Address: Paper presented at the 117th Annual Convention of the American Psychological Association, Toronto, Canada.

Schmid, P. F. (2010a). Die person und das böse. Zum Problem des Bösen in der Humanistischen Psychologie [The person and evil. On the problem of evil in humanistic psychology]. In M. E. Aigner, R. Bucher, I. Hable, & H.-W. Ruckenbauer (Eds.), *Räume des Aufatmens* [Rooms to breathe] (pp. 440–459). Berlin, Germany: Lit Verlag.

Schmid, P. F. (2010b). The person and evil. In J. Leonardi (Ed.), *The human being fully alive.* Ross-on-Wye, England: PCCS Books.

Schmid, P. F., & Mearns, D. (2006). Being-with and being-counter: Person-centered psychotherapy as an in-depth co-creative process of personalization. *Person-Centered & Experiential Psychotherapies, 5,* 174–190. doi:10.1080/14779757.2006.9688408

Schneider, K. (2009, August). Ontology and depth: Rollo May's inseparable duo [abstract]. In A. C. Bohart (Chair), *Carl Rogers, Rollo May, and humanity's dark side.* Symposium conducted at the 117th Annual Convention of the American Psychological Association, Toronto, Ontario, Canada.

Thorne, B. (2003). *Carl Rogers* (2nd ed.). London, England: Sage.

Wucherer-Huldenfeld, A. K. (1994/1997). *Ursprüngliche Erfahrung und personales Sein* [Original experience and personal being]. Vol. I: 1994 / Vol. II: 1997. Vienna, Austria: Böhlau.

Wucherer-Huldenfeld, A. K. (2007). Was besagt Privation? Zur Sprache der Abwesenheit. [What does privation mean? About the speech of absence]. *Jahrbuch für phänomenologische Anthropologie und Psychotherapie, 23*, 22–39.

Wucherer-Huldenfeld, A. K. (2009). *Wie sollen wir mit dem Übel umgehen? Skizze einer praktischen "Theodizee."* [How shall we deal with evil? Outline of a practical "theodicy"]. Unpublished manuscript.

3

DARTH VADER, CARL ROGERS, AND SELF-ORGANIZING WISDOM

ARTHUR C. BOHART

Darth Vader, the villain who is the central figure in the *Star Wars* movies, is an interesting figure to consider from a person-centered point of view. He first appears in *Star Wars Episode I: The Phantom Menace* as a 9-year-old boy under the name Anakin Skywalker. He and his mother are slaves. He is described as generous toward others. He is also recognized as having unusual powers, such as having the ability to see future events. He is discovered by one of the Jedi Knights, a special group of individuals with unusual powers that are based on their ability to mobilize and use "the Force" in the service of good. They undertake to train Anakin as a Jedi.

The first three movies in the series (the prequel trilogy, Episodes I–III) trace Anakin's gradual transformation from a Jedi into someone who gets seduced by the "dark" side of the Force. The person who seduces Anakin is Palpatine, a senator who is secretly planning to take over the government of the Republic and to create a Galactic Empire. He promises Anakin unlimited

DOI: 10.1037/13941-003
Humanity's Dark Side: Evil, Destructive Experience, and Psychotherapy, A. C. Bohart, B. S. Held, E. Mendelowitz, and K. J. Schneider (Editors)

power. In particular, Palpatine tells him that the dark side of the Force can be used to bring the dead back to life. This power appeals to Anakin because he has had a vision in which the princess whom he loves, named Padme Amidayla, dies in childbirth.

Toward the end of the first three movies, Anakin has opted for the dark side of the Force and has taken on the name Darth Vader. He fights his old Jedi mentor and is nearly destroyed. He is rebuilt by Palpatine as a creature who is half-man, half-machine. While this is going on, unbeknownst to him, his wife, Padme, has given birth to twins and has died in childbirth. The twins are hidden from Darth Vader and grow up to become freedom fighters for the Republic. One of them, Luke Skywalker, becomes the hero of the next three films.

These following films chronicle the adventures of Luke and his companions as they fight against Darth Vader, Palpatine, and the empire. Both the Emperor and Darth Vader have tried to seduce Luke to the dark side. When Luke is brought before his father, he says to him, "I know there is good in you." When efforts to seduce Luke prove ineffective, Luke must fight his father as the Emperor looks on. The Emperor continually baits Luke to give into his anger and to kill his father, but at the fateful moment when he might easily do so, he refuses. The Emperor then starts to use his own power to destroy Luke. Finally Darth Vader rises up and slays the Emperor, thereby saving his son and ending the Galactic Empire. In so doing, he is mortally wounded. However, before dying, he tells his son that Luke has saved him.

What is interesting about Darth Vader from a person-centered point of view is Luke's statement near the end: "Father, I know there is good in you." In 1982 Rollo May accused Carl Rogers of believing that people are basically good and of being naive about the nature of evil in human affairs. In another publication, Rogers, Gendlin, Kiesler, and Truax (1967) asked several therapists to listen to and comment on tapes of psychotherapy. May was one of the commentators. May argued that person-centered therapy did not provide an environment within which clients were given permission to experience and confront anger, something that May believed was important for growth in therapy.

On the basis of the Darth Vader example, did Rollo May accurately characterize Carl Rogers and the person-centered point of view? From that point of view, what does it mean to say that there is "some good" in someone? Must clients confront their anger in order to change? In this chapter, I explore these questions. I start by discussing the notion of the actualizing tendency. I then move to a consideration of how person-centered therapy works, with a focus on the process of self-organizing wisdom. I then consider how person-centered therapy might conceptualize and help someone like

Darth Vader to grow toward more wise and socially positive behavior. Finally, I discuss what processes in therapy seem to be the most facilitative of self-organizing wisdom.

CARL ROGERS, THE ACTUALIZING TENDENCY, AND SELF-ORGANIZING WISDOM

The person-centered perspective sees people as *having the potential to be good*. This is different from seeing them as basically good. Rogers did hold that a therapeutic relationship characterized by unconditional positive regard, empathic understanding, and therapist congruence would help people develop in ways that were socially sensitive and responsible. These conditions would facilitate the movement of what he called the *actualizing tendency* in a positive direction.

The Actualizing Tendency

According to Rogers, one overarching motive—the actualizing tendency—underlies all of human behavior (Bohart, 2008a; Rogers, 1959). The actualizing tendency is the tendency of the organism to maintain and enhance itself. Rogers's view of this tendency does not posit that actualization will necessarily go in a positive direction. As I (Bohart, 2008a) have said:

> It is important to note that for Rogers, the existence of this tendency is biological. It is not fundamentally moral. Nor does it necessarily go in a morally positive direction. At the human level one could learn and become better and better at being a sadistic monster. All it postulates is a tendency to proactively grow and adapt. (p. 49)

It is accurate to see the person from Rogers's point of view as having a potential for developing in a positive, prosocial fashion. Almost like a gene, however, whose potential can be expressed in different ways depending on environmental circumstances, the individual's potential for developing prosocially will depend on the proper circumstances. The wrong circumstances can lead the person to develop in a negative direction.

Darth Vader is a good illustration. As a child he is described as having been generous. Yet as an adult he is capable of great evil. What has happened in between? Various forces have conspired so that his attempt to maintain and enhance his life has led him in a negative direction. As a child he lived in slavery, and the enslavement of his mother and himself may have left a mark on him. As a young adult he is prone to being headstrong and becomes angry when people do not treat him with the respect he thinks he deserves, particularly the Jedi who are training him. This energy, bound up in his tendencies toward being headstrong and angry at perceived injustice, could be a positive force if integrated into the personality effectively, but the Jedi do not help him master this. Instead, they treat him in a relatively dictatorial and judgmental fashion, imposing what Rogers would call *conditions of worth*. Then he discovers that his mother has been kidnapped and brutally mistreated by a tribe of creatures. She dies. In his rage, he kills every member of the tribe. He appears to be shocked at his own behavior, but once again no one empathically listens in a way that would help him process what he has done. Finally, Emperor Palpatine plays on him, feeding his anger at the way he has been treated by the Jedi, promising unlimited power, and hinting that if Anakin turns to the dark side, he will have the power to restore the dead to life. This is particularly important to Anakin because he has had a vision of his wife dying in childbirth.

The harsh circumstances in which Anakin Skywalker has grown up have conspired so that the actualizing tendency has gone in a negative direction rather than a positive one. However, it would be a mistake to say that he is fundamentally "good" or "bad." Rather, he is a person, like each of us, having the potential for both. In fact, it could be said that Darth Vader's turn toward evil is actually fueled in part by his potential for good. If we consider love to be "good," then it is his capacity to love his mother that causes him to engage in the evil act of mass slaughter in the name of revenge. His desire for untoward power comes from his love for his wife and his fear about her dying.

Actualization and Personality Change in Psychotherapy

So how would a Rogerian therapist treat Darth Vader to facilitate his turning to the good side of the Force? Is it true that Rogers's presumably overly optimistic view of human nature, or at least the Rogerian method, which relied on unconditional positive regard, empathic understanding, and congruence, would cramp people's capacity to tune into their own dark sides and confront them in order to grow? *Must* Darth Vader be led by the therapist to confront his anger? May asserted as much when asked to evaluate tapes of client-centered therapy from the Wisconsin Schizophrenia Project (Rogers et al., 1967) and argued that the Rogerian method cramped the expression of client anger.

The core idea of the Rogerian vision of personality change is a *radical* belief in the intrinsic capacity of the individual to grow in the direction he or she needs, given the proper circumstances. What I mean by this is that individuals, at an intrinsic or implicit level, "know" the direction in which they need to go. They also know how they will move forward toward resolution or "healing" of personal problems if they can be given the proper conditions for that implicit knowing to operate.

As Rogers (1961) said,

> It is the client who knows what hurts, what directions to go, what problems are crucial, what experiences have been deeply buried. It began to occur to me that unless I had a need to demonstrate my own cleverness and learning, I would do better to rely upon the client for the direction of movement. (p. 12)

And

> The central hypothesis of this approach can be briefly stated. It is that the individual has within himself or herself vast resources for self-understanding, for altering his or her self-concept, attitudes, and self-directed behavior—and that these resources can be tapped if only a definable climate of facilitative psychological attitudes can be provided. (Rogers, 1986/1990, p. 135)

The organism is built with the potential to move toward more organized, integrated, and effective ways of coping with the world. Under the proper conditions, the organism will take steps toward what Karen Tallman and I have called *self-healing* (Bohart & Tallman, 1999, 2010). This means that the human organism will (a) in its own good time deal with whatever it needs to grow; (b) as it moves forward, generate its own creative insights and new ideas; (c) move outward to engage in the behavioral experiments requisite for growth; and (d) move toward confronting whatever thoughts, feelings, emotions, or memories that may need confronting if that is part of the self-healing process for that particular individual.

This organismic capacity, or wisdom, will operate in the proper psychological climate. I shall have more to say about this later. For now I note simply that the therapist does not need to guide the client to get in touch with feelings, challenge dysfunctional cognitions, expose him or her to traumatic experience, take behavioral risks, gain insight, differentiate or individuate, get over splitting, nudge the client to confront avoided material from childhood, or do any of the other things other types of therapists think are necessary. Clients in their own good time, as part of their own intrinsic natural healing processes, will deal with whatever is needed for them to grow. Given that each client self-organizes in her or his own way, confronting trauma may or may not be necessary for growth, for instance. Forgiving abusive parents may or may not be needed in order to grow. Confronting anger may or may not be needed.

This capacity for *self-organizing wisdom* (Wood, 2008) is therefore the organism's capacity to generate productive change. This capacity is not primarily conscious, although conscious activities in therapy, such as self-reflection, can contribute. To quote Gendlin (1984),

> Roger's method brought it home that the decisions a person must make are inherently that person's own. No book knowledge enables another person to decide for anyone. That goes for life decisions and life-style as well as, moment by moment, what to talk about, feel into, struggle with. Another person might make a guess, but ultimately personal growth is from the inside outward. A process of change begins and moves in ways even the person's own mind cannot direct, let alone another person's mind [italics added]. (p. 297)

Rogers's view is different from other views that hold that therapy involves unearthing that which is unconscious or avoided in order to make it conscious. Rogerians do not believe that insight is necessary for change (Eckert & Biermann-Ratjen, 1990). The closest to this in the person-centered camp is the view of Gendlin (1996), who identified a process that he called *focusing*. This process involves tuning into the implicit lived complexity of one's experiencing of the world and articulating it (e.g., Gendlin, 1968). In contrast to the idea of insight, it is not what is learned through this process that is corrective. Rather, the process itself leads to organismic reorganization.

Therefore Rogers's view differs from those of Freud, Rollo May, and others who believed that individuals must consciously confront their dark sides in order to grow. This is not because Rogers naively believed people were basically good but, rather, because he believed—naively or not—that people had the basic potential to change (Shlien & Levant, 1984) in productive directions given the proper supportive interpersonal conditions. Given those conditions, clients might evolve in such a way that they find themselves confronting their anger or their dark sides. On the other hand, individuals do not necessarily need to confront their anger. It is an individual matter. Nothing in Rogerian therapy, at least theoretically, precludes confronting anger. In fact, according to Maureen O'Hara (2009), a colleague of Rogers, there were many times when people working with Rogers were able to get angry.

Because of this radical faith in the individual's organismic capacity for self-healing, the primary thing the therapist has to do is to *be present* in a way that facilitates the client's capacity for self-organizing wisdom to become operative. The Rogerian method is designed to provide both maximum support and freedom for this process to go in its own intrinsically wise direction. It is for this reason that Rogerians reject diagnosis of clients, having agendas for clients, believing that therapists must guide clients in various ways, and so on.

Self-Organizing Wisdom

The term *self-organizing wisdom* comes from John Wood (2008). Theoretically, self-organizing wisdom is part of the actualizing tendency. It is the organismic capacity to adapt to life problems creatively and productively in a manner that takes into account the wishes and needs of others. It is called self-organizing *wisdom* because it goes in a positive direction. It is not mere creativity. Creativity could lead to a person becoming more effectively evil. It is also not the equivalent of wisdom per se (see Staudinger, 1996, and Sternberg, 2004, 2007, for views on the nature of wisdom). A person may not start out being wise in therapy, but the self-organizing wisdom process may move her or him toward more wise ways of being and behaving.

The concept of self-organizing wisdom needs to be contrasted with a related idea, the belief that "wisdom" can be found in even the most dysfunctional behavior. The idea of implicit wisdom behind dysfunctional behavior is widely shared. Gendlin (1967) argued that there is a "positive thrust" underlying dysfunctional behavior. Boukydis (1984) said

> Everybody is right or rational in what he is doing at some level. If a person gets listened to long enough on why he is the way he is, something will be heard that suddenly makes sense out of the way he is being. (p. 309)

Linehan (1997), from a dialectical behavior therapy point of view, expressed a similar idea with her concept of level five validation: the idea that what the client is doing has some wisdom in it in the moment. She distinguished this from level four validation, which is the idea that what the client is doing was once wise in the past but not now. Linehan was not claiming that the client's dysfunctional behavior was not dysfunctional. What she was claiming is that, as she often said, there is a "nugget of gold in the bucket of sand."

The idea that there is some wisdom at the root of dysfunctional behavior, however, is not the same as self-organizing wisdom. Self-organizing wisdom is a process that moves the person toward wiser ways of being in the world. Theoretically it should lead to clients generating wiser choices, wise experiments to further growth, wise creative ideas, wise insights into their problems, and wise new steps toward solving their problems. However, helping clients identify the wisdom underlying their dysfunctional behavior can be a step in fostering the self-organizing wisdom process.

Is there any evidence for the existence of self-organizing wisdom? No specific research studies have been conducted on this. However, there is both informal and formal evidence compatible with it. First, in terms of informal evidence, a number of therapeutic methods rely on it. The fact that Rogerian therapists do not specifically guide clients toward solutions yet clients grow in person-centered therapy (Elliott & Friere, 2010) suggests that relying on the process of self-organizing wisdom works. Gendlin's (1996) focusing technique involves having clients follow instructions on how to turn their attention inward and listen to themselves. They are not given clues about what they are to think or what they might discover. However, through following the instructions, a self-propelled process happens in which clients find themselves generating new words and symbols to capture experience. Transcripts of focusing sessions in which clients verbalize their internal experience illustrate the self-propelled, emergent nature of the process. Similarly, in eye movement desensitization and reprocessing (e.g., Shapiro, 2002), there are case examples and transcripts that illustrate clients going through a creative, productive, forward-moving process generated from within, with the therapist doing little more than waving her fingers. Finally, the inner guide exercise (e.g., Zilbergeld & Lazarus, 1987) is another example. Clients are taken in their imaginations to a quiet safe, relaxing place. They await the arrival of their "inner guide." They can then ask this inner guide questions about their problems. Zilbergeld and Lazarus (1987), two behavior therapists, reported a case in which a client, June, said, "I ran into someone—the strongest, wisest person I ever met" (p. 147). Zilbergeld and Lazarus noted, "With the help of her advisor, June was able to resolve quickly several important issues in her life" (p. 147).

In terms of formal research evidence, a study by Staudinger and Baltes (1996) asked participants to do something similar to consulting an inner guide. Participants were given a problem to solve—for example, a friend threatening suicide—and then asked to think out loud about what they would do. Staudinger and Baltes found that individuals came up with wiser solutions when they imagined a dialogue with a friend than did those who merely thought about the problem. Evidence also supports the idea that unconscious thought can be creative and sophisticated (e.g., Bargh & Morsella, 2008; Dijksterhuis & Nordgren, 2006).

Research on psychotherapy has shown that clients can be generative contributors (Bohart & Tallman, 2010). They do not merely learn what therapists provide but often creatively refashion what they get from therapists to meet their needs. For instance, Greaves (2006) found the following in a qualitative study of 13 clients:

> The clients exhibited initiative and engaged in meaning-making processes to make sense of their difficulties, redefine and remoralize themselves, and try out new ways of being. Not only did they act in planning and management capacities, they also played the role of truth-seeker, motivator, advocator, and negotiator to further the pursuit and attainment of their goals. They blended their own wisdom with their therapist's expertise in idiosyncratic ways, after having prepared their therapist to potentially offer the most appropriate assistance. (p. xii)

Finally, I and two graduate students found, in a study of one client working with an existential-psychodynamic therapist, evidence that the client showed gains in wisdom on Mickler and Staudinger's (2005) scale for measuring self-related wisdom over a 12-session course of therapy (Bohart, Wickes, & Berry, 2010). We also found evidence that person-centered therapy does indeed promote "wisdom-making" behavior on the part of clients.

This evidence lends support to the idea of self-organizing wisdom. Further research is needed.

Implications of Self-Organizing Wisdom for Therapy Practice: What If Someone Like Darth Vader Went to Therapy?

So, what if someone like Darth Vader had gone to therapy? It is hard to imagine such a person doing so. Why would he? He has immense power, although he has suffered several defeats at the hand of his son. It is hard to imagine him acknowledging that, for instance, he experienced any conflict or pain that he could not handle. However, he might go to talk to someone who could help him better use his evil powers.

So, suppose we visit a galaxy long ago and far away. There, Darth Vader goes to see Darth Therapist, the resident therapist on his battle cruiser. Darth Therapist's job is not to help people grow in positive directions, but rather to help them become more effectively evil. In fact, Palpatine the Evil Emperor was Darth Vader's original Darth Therapist. When Darth Vader was still Anakin Skywalker, a young member of the Jedi Knights, it was Palpatine who gently led him along the slippery slope to evil. How did he do that? He played on Anakin Skywalker's fears and his anger at his Jedi Knight teachers by implying that they were withholding power from him. He promised him powers that he could use to right the wrongs he observed in the world.

But what if, somehow, the rebel coalition had managed to sneak a real Rogerian therapist aboard and substitute him for Darth Therapist? Darth Vader comes in to talk to someone who he thinks is Darth Therapist. But instead of having the therapist play on his fears, Darth Vader suddenly finds himself being empathically listened to.

"My son, Luke Skywalker, who fights for the rebels, escaped again."

"Eluded you again, eh?"

"Yes. It is most frustrating to almost have him and then through some bit of misfortune have him get away."

"*Somehow* he manages to escape no matter what you do and you don't understand it."

"Yes. Luck seems to be on his side. I thought the dark side of the Force was more powerful than the light side. Yet it seems as if some fate is protecting him."

"You're wondering to yourself: 'Is the dark side really stronger?' It's making you doubt. And you wonder if you're up against some kind of force helping him that you don't know about."

"Yes. I have never been defeated so often" (beginning to sound angry). "It makes no sense."

"Absolutely not. I have been very successful in the past. I am quite angry."

"It's as if you're saying, 'I don't get what is going on and it makes me very angry.'"

"Yes, it most certainly does! But it is not just anger. I have not doubted myself for a very long time, since before I became Darth Vader. Yet I am finding doubt creeping in and I know that that can be dangerous."

"Doubt."

"Yes. Doubt. I do not remember having such doubts since way back when I was first struggling with joining the dark side and abandoning the Jedi Knights."

"Doubt about yourself. 'What am I doing wrong?'"

"Yes, doubt, but not just about what I am doing wrong. More like the path I'm taking. I wonder if I am getting in my own way . . . if I am defeating myself on purpose. After all, he is my son."

"Are you deliberately sabotaging yourself to save your son?"

"Yes. After all he is my son . . . all I have left of my wife, Padme" (said in a sad voice).

"And I must admit, now that I open myself up to it, it bothers me that I am pursuing my own son. I have not thought about that at all. I have just assumed that the Emperor's idea of turning him to the dark side was a good idea. But he is my son. Do I want to do that? Would that be what Padme would have wanted?" His voice has gotten soft and begins to crack.

"I wonder what it would be like to listen to my son. I have not felt like a human being for a very long time. It is difficult to, when one is half machine. But I still have emotions, and it seems I do still care. I lost my wife, the only person I cared about after my mother." (He stops.)

"It is hard for me to admit but I almost feel as if tears are coming to my eyes. Yet I must not cry. I am now half electronic circuitry. If I cried I could cause a short in the machinery and die. I must control my emotions. And yet . . . ."

And the dialogue might go on. We could imagine Darth Vader beginning to open up to implicit and long-forsaken aspects of his personality, to begin to see the broader picture, to begin to incorporate new aspects of his experience into his ideas. He might begin to question his constructs, such as those imposed by the Emperor, he might begin to balance his desires for power and revenge with a more deeply human side. He might actually begin to move toward discovering the "good" in him. He might even join the rebel forces!

Of course, this is fictitious and a simplified version of what might take many sessions in real life. However, it is meant to demonstrate how the client's self-organizing wisdom might begin to operate. As Darth Vader talks, he begins to turn inward and to reflect. This is one of the key ways that clients think productively in therapy (Bohart, 2001). He begins to become more receptively open (Bohart, 2008b). As he does so, new aspects emerge in his internal "arena." He finds doubts beginning to surface. He finds himself revisiting old experiences. He finds himself beginning to stand back and to notice pros and cons of the path he has chosen. He begins to get in touch with deeply personal aspects of himself on which he has not focused in a long time. As he does so, he moves out of a simplistic either/or stance and toward reclaiming his personhood.

In so doing, he makes a brief stop on anger along the way, but the process is not so much that of his confronting his anger as that of its emerging as a natural part of the self-healing process. The therapist does not have to direct the client's attention to it, but simply listen to it as another part of the client's meaning-making process. The client soon moves on to deeper aspects that are more personally relevant to the process.

Theoretical Examination

Let us examine this process theoretically. What I have tried to show is that the Rogerian position does not assume that people are basically good. What it does assume is that within all persons there is the potential for goodness. All persons have the potential for fellow feeling, that is, a potential capacity to care for others. While Rogers never said where this came from, we can imagine that it is part of the genetic heritage of being a human being. It might also have been, in Darth Vader's case, reinforced by experiences in childhood of having been cared for.

In therapy, the person-centered therapist treats the client as someone (a) fundamentally worthy of being respected as a person no matter how dysfunctional or evil their behavior has been and (b) someone capable of potentially wise and adaptive behavior no matter how harmful or ineffective their behavior has been in the past. If, in therapy, a proper empathic atmosphere is provided, persons will move out of entrenched stances. They will begin to access different perspectives, they will search their experience and bring in discrepant aspects, they will begin to balance priorities. They will begin to balance what is good for them with what is good for others. With this in mind, I move to two thorny theoretical questions relevant to the debate between Rollo May and Carl Rogers. If people have this capacity for self-organizing wisdom, why don't they act wisely more often? Indeed, why is it that they may act evilly? In addition, why, theoretically, do the conditions of Rogerian therapy make the process go in a positive direction?

Self-Organizing Wisdom and Evil

It is cliché to say that people often do not act wisely. We eat foods that are bad for us, do not exercise enough, make poor decisions in our personal lives, do not deal effectively with our emotions, and so on. Furthermore, we can often act evilly. Zimbardo (2007) showed how easily ordinary people can turn to evil.

There are two questions: Why, in everyday life, do we not use our capacities for self-organizing wisdom more often? and, Why, in psychotherapy, does a process characterized by deep respect for the personhood of the client and by empathic listening seem to facilitate this process?

The two questions are interrelated, but I will take the second question first. Why might the person-centered therapy process lead individuals not only to be more creative in dealing with their personal lives but also to have that creativity move in wise and prosocial directions at the same time?

First, as I have previously noted, creativity is not the same as self-organizing wisdom. Why could not individuals in Rogerian therapy develop in ways in which they use their creativity for antisocial ends? Why, for instance, when empathically listened to, might Darth Vader not move toward using his creativity to figure out better ways to destroy the Republic and to find ways of converting his son to the dark side?

From the Rogerian point of view, the theoretical reason is that when therapists relate to clients with unconditional positive regard, empathic understanding, and congruence, they are not merely creating conditions facilitative of openness and creativity, they are creating conditions facilitative of clients developing their *personhood*. In a sense the goal of person-centered therapy is, to paraphrase Rogers (1961), to "become a person."

What does it mean to become a person? Aren't we already persons? In one sense, yes, and Rogerian therapy depends on the idea of the therapist relating to the client as a person right from the start. However, although we are already persons, we can develop our personhood further. Many individuals have had their sense of themselves as persons lost or fragmented. The process of therapy is to help them reclaim that, or, as feminist therapists have said, to help clients find "their own voices," which again brings us back to the question, what does it mean to become a person?

What is a person? Peter Schmid (2004; see also Chapter 2, this volume) noted that Rogers always assumed that persons were "incurably social" (Rogers, 1965, p. 20). Schmid agreed that the nature of the person is fundamentally social and said that persons are not merely *in* relationships but *are* relationships. There are two aspects to being a person: individuality and interrelatedness. Individuality is the side that has been most focused on by Western culture and by much of Western psychology. The emphasis is on the individual as an autonomous agent, capable of making his or her own choices, having the right or freedom (within reasonable limits) to decide what is the best life path for him or her, and to hold his or her own values. The second aspect, according to Schmid, is interrelatedness. That is, persons are persons only in relationships to other persons. We discover our personhood in human relations, and our autonomy makes sense only as it exists and is balanced within relationships with others. Persons are therefore both autonomous and interconnected. The process of establishing authenticity as a person is that of balancing individuality and interrelatedness.

It follows that persons can lose their sense of themselves as persons through two routes: first, through losing touch with their own inner experience, choices, and values; second, through losing touch with connections with others.

Schmid (2004) argued that person-centered therapy is a *personalizing* process. As clients are supported as they seek their own voices, as they seek to find and own their own unique experience, cutting through the welter of shoulds, "ways to be," and criticisms that have been imposed upon them from outside, they begin to reclaim themselves as "authentic sources of experience" (Bohart & Greenberg, 1997).

At the same time, this process is taking place in the context of a deeply personal relationship with an Other who relates to them as persons and recognizes them as persons. *They discover their sense of personhood in relationship to another person who is more than just a therapist playing a professional role*. Therefore, automatically, as part of the same process, their sense of relationship and connection with others is being deepened. It is as you, the therapist, who is a person, with your own values, preferences, choices, and locus of control, relates to me, the client, as a person with my own values, preferences, and locus of control, and models for me the value of listening and being present in positive and facilitative ways, that I discover the relational aspect of my personhood as well.

In saying this I need to emphasize that, for the Rogerian, it is the therapist as person that is healing. It is not professional expertise or the trappings of professionalism. The therapist is a person who empathically witnesses (Kleinman, 1989) other people's experience. By treating clients with respect, by witnessing their struggles as they try to make sense out of their experience, by having faith that they can and do make sense and then helping them sort out that sense, therapists treat clients in ways that help them take themselves seriously, hear their own voices, and create more constructive ways of being in the world. At one point, Rogers said that the therapy encounter is a "meeting of persons" and therapeutic change is a by-product of that (Cissna & Anderson, 1994).

It is important to recognize that the Rogerian therapist does not look for the good in people per se. Rather, he or she looks for the "person" in people.

As a result, the Rogerian therapist is open to whatever comes up from the client: bad or good, anger or sadness, fear or happiness. It is that openness, that willingness to greet whatever comes up and to listen to clients and how they relate to whatever comes up, that provides the context wherein clients' self-organizing wisdom becomes operative.

This makes listening the sine qua non of Rogerian therapy. Empathic listening is not compassion. Empathic listening is careful and sensitive receptivity to what the client is saying, doing, and experiencing in the moment. It is an attuned "staying with" the organism's process as it engages in ongoing self-disclosure and exploration. It is the recognition of the client as an individual who, at some level, fundamentally makes sense, no matter how crazy or disturbed he or she may seem. It is helping the client get in touch with his or her own "sense-making process" that is therapy.

But is this not a truism? Don't all therapists listen? Don't all therapists treat persons as persons? From a Rogerian perspective the answer is "not necessarily." There are many therapists from any persuasion who do. For instance, Westra, Aviram, Barnes, and Angus (2010) recently found that cognitive–behavior therapists who operate in a person-centered way are more effective than cognitive–behavior therapists who stick to manuals (see also Chapter 8, this volume).

However, there are many therapists who primarily listen to clients to gather information: to find out what diagnosis to give them, to find out what is wrong with them from the therapist's theoretical point of view, to figure out what intervention strategies to use. They do not necessarily place an emphasis on listening and relating to clients as whole persons with hopes and fears, triumphs and defeats, life stories that tell who they are, and so forth. Leitner (2009), writing from his experiential-constructivist point of view, gave the following example:

> I first saw Tom on intake at a Veteran's Hospital. He was clearly agitated and confused and was, at times, incoherent. His family filled us in on his increasingly bizarre behavior over the last week (including hiding in his closet petrified about what hallucinatory voices said). When the admitting physicians excused themselves to make arrangements for his hospitalization, I said to him, "You seem really confused about things." Tom's eyes welled with tears and he said, "I am so confused I cannot even think." His desperation and despair were palpable. I told him that it broke my heart to see him in such pain. He looked at me and replied, "As long as I don't think about Vietnam, I don't get confused." I then suggested that, perhaps while he was in the hospital, we could talk about whatever happened in Vietnam.
>
> I was met with incredulity when I argued that perhaps clients like Tom were saying things that were personally meaningful and important. For example, when I suggested that Tom's confusion and erratic

behavior might be related to something that happened to him in Vietnam, I received a lecture on the nature of schizophrenic thought disorganization. Tom was attributing his confusion to Vietnam due to a desperate search for a cause when the reality was that a schizophrenic process was the cause. . . . Sadly, I saw Tom again a few days later on the inpatient unit. He was on heavy doses of neuroleptics and speaking even a few words required great effort. To this day, I still wonder what might have happened in Vietnam. (pp. 364–365)

Unfortunately stories like this are not uncommon (see also Honos-Webb & Leitner, 2001). For instance, Sabat (2001) in *The Experience of Alzheimer's* noted how often professionals "listen" to Alzheimer's patients and "hear" their disease rather than hearing persons struggling to communicate through their disease. These professionals probably would not agree that they are not treating their patients as persons. In fact, they would believe themselves to be compassionate and caring, and they probably are. However, although they have compassion for their patients and are trying to help them, by assuming that what patients say is "crazy talk" or "due to the Alzheimer's," they are not relating to their patients as if there are persons inside trying to get out, so to speak. This frequently happens with schizophrenics, and yet there is evidence, too, that when schizophrenics are treated as persons many can recover without the use of drugs (Mosher, Hendrix, & Fort, 2004).

Theoretically, from a person-centered point of view, it is listening to persons as persons, in a personalizing way, that creates the conditions whereby the self-organizing wisdom process goes in a positive, or prosocial, direction. This makes sense if we look at wisdom from the perspective of Sternberg (2004, 2007). Wise people deal with problems by trying to find balance: balance between their use of different kinds of intelligence (practical, analytic, creativity; Sternberg, 2007) and balance between what is good for themselves and good for others (Sternberg, 2004). From a person-centered point of view, to develop as a person is to work to balance concern for self with concern for others, as a result of the process of being responded to as a person by that other person, the therapist.

It follows from this discussion that individuals act unwisely or even evilly in everyday life either because they are not in touch with themselves as persons in the moments when they make unwise decisions or because they do not have context or room enough to engage in the balancing, self-organizing wisdom-making process. In other words, they may feel harried or harassed or under pressure by others to make a decision. They may have no one who will listen to them in such a way as to give them adequate space whereby they can look at things in context and find balance.

If this is so, then it may be that self-organizing wisdom is most likely to happen only under certain conditions, and those would be conditions wherein people are deeply reminded of themselves as persons. This may happen through empathically feeling the pain of another or being reminded of deeply important personal experiences. One bit of anecdotal evidence to support this is the story of when President Sadat of Egypt and Prime Minister Begin of Israel met at Camp David during the presidency of Jimmy Carter to try to hammer out a Middle East peace accord. After 12 fruitless days nothing had been accomplished, with Begin refusing to sign the accords. The night before the conference was to adjourn, Begin and Carter were talking. They began to reminisce and talk about their grandchildren. The next day Begin approached Sadat and they reached an accord (Rogers & Ryback, 1984).

Other evidence is in accord with the Rogerian hypothesis developed here. First, the work of Staudinger and Baltes (Staudinger, 1996; Staudinger & Baltes, 1996) on wisdom is compatible with the person-centered perspective in that they emphasize, and have research to support, that what they called *interactive minds* facilitate the development of wisdom. Second, Zimbardo's (2007) *The Lucifer Effect: Understanding How Good People Turn Evil* summarizes a considerable amount of evidence that is compatible.

Briefly, Zimbardo documented how easy it is for good people to engage in evil acts. Two famous experiments are his Stanford Prison Experiment (Haney, Banks, & Zimbardo, 1973) and the Milgram (1974) studies. In the Stanford experiment, students played the roles of prisoners and guards in a mock prison. Within one day guards began to lose their humanity and treat prisoners brutally. Some prisoners began to have mental breakdowns. A number of parameters were involved, but the important one involved conditions that led prisoners, guards, and Zimbardo himself to lose their sense of personal identity. Zimbardo called this process *de-individuation*. He has been vocal in pointing out the similarities between his study and what happened at Abu Ghraib during the Iraq war.

Zimbardo also documented many other studies that show that evil often happens in situations where people lose a sense of self and personal responsibility. In some cases, such as that of Rwanda, where people went on killing rampages against people they had formerly thought of as neighbors, it was because of a mass ideology to which individuals conformed, thereby losing touch with their own inner moral voices. In the Milgram (1974) studies, people were willing to inflict severe shock on others simply because they conformed to the authority of someone who passed himself off as an expert. From a Rogerian point of view, it could be argued that the experimenter imposed a "condition of worth" on the experimental participants, in essence implying that "I won't respect you if you don't obey." In such a situation, persons lost at least partial touch with their own inner locus of control. In addition, under pressure from the experimenter to respond, persons did not have the freedom, support, or space to reflect, from which their capacity for self-organizing wisdom might have led to wiser solutions.

CONCLUSION

What I have outlined here is a theory of why people, from a person-centered point of view, are expected to grow in ways that are personally beneficial, becoming more socially responsible and sensitive at the same time. I have tried to show why I do not believe Rollo May (1982) was accurate in his criticisms of Rogers, either in his assumption that the person-centered theory of being is based on the idea that people are basically good or by arguing that person-centered therapy is unable to handle anger and other potentially "dark side" aspects of the human being. I have taken Wood's (2008) concept of self-organizing wisdom and have shown how it is the core of effective Rogerian therapy. I have tried to explain how treating people as persons is at the base of why self-organizing wisdom is expected to go in a positive direction in therapy. Finally, I have briefly discussed factors that get in the way of self-organizing wisdom operating in everyday life. I have cited evidence that is in accord with these Rogerian positions.

I conclude by making two points. First, the Rogerian hypothesis is that treating persons as persons, by relating to them with unconditional positive regard, empathic understanding, and congruence, is both necessary and sufficient for therapeutic personality change (Rogers, 1957). Empirically, it remains to be seen whether it is true that relating to persons as persons is both necessary and sufficient to help individuals get over all the various psychological disorders with which they struggle; certainly therapists from other orientations would disagree. Exactly how potent a factor this is in therapeutic change in general remains to be seen. Second, the Rogerian hypothesis is that any therapist who treats persons as persons will likely be successful, no matter what their orientation. What this means is that what I have said for the person-centered point of view is not limited to it. As with Westra et al. (2010), who found that "person-centered" cognitive behavior therapists were more effective than non–person-centered ones, there is nothing to preclude therapists from other points of view from treating persons as persons in a way that facilitates their self-organizing wisdom, while also using techniques and procedures of the other orientations.

REFERENCES

Bargh, J. A., & Morsella, E. (2008). The unconscious mind. *Perspectives on Psychological Science, 3*, 73–79. doi:10.1111/j.1745-6916.2008.00064.x

Bohart, A. C. (2001). How can expression in psychotherapy be constructive? In A. C. Bohart & D. J. Stipek (Eds.), *Constructive and destructive behavior: Implications for family, school, & society* (pp. 337–364). Washington, DC: American Psychological Association. doi:10.1037/10433-016

Bohart, A. C. (2008a). The actualizing person. In M. Cooper, M. O'Hara, P. F. Schmid, & G. Wyatt (Eds.), *The handbook of person-centered psychotherapy and counseling* (pp. 47–63). New York, NY: Palgrave Macmillan.

Bohart, A. C. (2008b). How clients self-heal in psychotherapy. In B. E. Levitt (Ed.), *Reflections on human potential: Bridging the person-centered approach and positive psychology* (pp. 175–186). Ross-on-Wye, Wales: PCCS Books.

Bohart, A. C., & Greenberg, L. S. (1997). Empathy: Where are we and where do we go from here? In A. C. Bohart & L. S. Greenberg (Eds.), *Empathy reconsidered: New directions in psychotherapy* (pp. 419–449). Washington, DC: American Psychological Association. doi:10.1037/10226-031

Bohart, A. C., & Tallman, K. (1999). *How clients make therapy work: The process of active self-healing.* Washington, DC: American Psychological Association. doi:10.1037/10323-000

Bohart, A. C., & Tallman, K. (2010). Clients as active self-healers: Implications for the person-centered approach. In M. Cooper, J. C. Watson, D. Hölldampf (Eds.), *Person-centered and experiential therapies work* (pp. 91–131). Ross-on-Wye, Wales: PCCS books.

Bohart, A. C., Wickes, C., & Berry, M. (2010, August). Self-organizing wisdom in person-centered therapy: Theoretical and empirical analyses. In H. Levitt (Chair), *Studying clinical wisdom: Research on therapists and clients' wisdom-related processes.* Symposium conducted at the 118th Annual Convention of the American Psychological Association Convention, San Diego, CA.

Boukydis, K. M. (1984). Changes: Peer-counseling supportive communities as a model for community mental health. In D. Larson (Ed.), *Teaching psychological skills: Models for giving psychology away* (pp. 306–317). Florence, KY: Cengage Brooks/Cole.

Cissna, K. N., & Anderson, R. (1994). The 1957 Martin Buber—Carl Rogers dialogue, as dialogue. *Journal of Humanistic Psychology, 34*(1), 11–45. doi:10.1177/00221678940341003

Dijksterhuis, A., & Nordgren, L. F. (2006). A theory of unconscious thought. *Perspectives on Psychological Science, 1,* 95–109. doi:10.1111/j.1745-6916.2006.00007.x

Eckert, J., & Biermann-Ratjen, E.-M. (1990). Client-centered therapy versus psychoanalytic psychotherapy: Reflections following a comparative study. In G. Lietaer, J. Rombauts, & R. Van Balen (Eds.), *Client-centered and experiential psychotherapy in the nineties* (pp. 457–468). Leuven, Belgium: Leuven University Press.

Elliott, R., & Friere, E. (2010). The effectiveness of person-centered and experiential therapies: A review of the meta-analyses. In M. Cooper, J. C. Watson, & D. Hölldampf (Eds.), *Person-centered and experiential therapies work* (pp. 1–15). Ross-on-Wye, Wales: PCCS books.

Gendlin, E. T. (1967). Therapeutic procedures in dealing with schizophrenics. In C. R. Rogers, E. T. Gendlin, D. J. Kiesler, & C. B. Truax (Eds.), *The therapeutic relationship and its impact* (pp. 369–400). Madison, WI: University of Wisconsin Press.

Gendlin, E. T. (1968). The experiential response. In E. Hammer (Ed.), *Use of interpretation in treatment* (pp. 208–227). New York, NY: Grune & Stratton.

Gendlin, E. T. (1984). The politics of giving therapy away: Listening and focusing. In D. Larson (Ed.), *Teaching psychological skills: Models for giving psychology away* (pp. 287–305). Monterey, CA: Brooks/Cole.

Gendlin, E. T. (1996). *Focusing-oriented psychotherapy.* New York, NY: Guilford Press.

Greaves, A. L. (2006). *The active client: A qualitative analysis of thirteen clients' contributions to the psychotherapeutic process.* Unpublished doctoral dissertation, University of Southern California, Los Angeles.

Haney, C., Banks, C., & Zimbardo, P. (1973). Interpersonal dynamics in a simulated prison. *International Journal of Criminology and Penology, 1,* 69–97.

Honos-Webb, L., & Leitner, L. M. (2001). How using the DSM causes damage: A client's report. *Journal of Humanistic Psychology, 41,* 36–56. doi:10.1177/0022167801414003

Kleinman, A. (1989). *The illness narratives: Suffering, healing, and the human condition.* New York, NY: Basic Books.

Leitner, L. M. (2009). Theory, therapy, and life: Experiential personal construct psychology and the "desert places" of a therapist. In R. J. Butler (Ed.), *Reflections in personal construct theory* (pp. 361–374). Chichester, England: Wiley-Blackwell.

Linehan, M. M. (1997). Validation and psychotherapy. In A. C. Bohart & L. S. Greenberg (Eds.), *Empathy reconsidered: New directions in psychotherapy* (pp. 353–392). Washington, DC: American Psychological Association. doi:10.1037/10226-016

May, R. (1982). The problem of evil: An open letter to Carl Rogers. *Journal of Humanistic Psychology, 22*(3), 10–21. doi:10.1177/0022167882223003

Mickler, C., & Staudinger, U. (2005). *Manual for the assessment of self-related wisdom.* Bremen, Germany: Jacobs Center, International University Bremen.

Milgram, S. (1974). *Obedience to authority.* New York, NY: Harper & Row.

Mosher, L. R., Hendrix, V., & Fort, D. C. (2004). *Soteria: Through madness to deliverance.* Philadelphia, PA: Xlibris.

O'Hara, M. (2009, August). Human visionaries reconsidered in the face of 21st century challenges. In A. C. Bohart (Chair), *Carl Rogers, Rollo May, and humanity's dark side.* Symposium conducted at the meeting of the American Psychological Association, Toronto, Canada.

Rogers, C. R. (1957). The necessary and sufficient conditions of therapeutic personality change. *Journal of Consulting Psychology, 21*(2), 95–103. doi:10.1037/h0045357

Rogers, C. R. (1959). A theory of therapy, personality, and interpersonal relationships, as developed in the client-centered framework. In S. Koch (Ed.), *Psychology: A study of a science* (Vol. III, pp. 184–256). New York, NY: McGraw-Hill.

Rogers, C. R. (1961). *On becoming a person.* Boston, MA: Houghton-Mifflin.

Rogers, C. R. (1965). A humanistic conception of man. In R. Farson (Ed.), *Science and human affairs* (pp. 18–31). Palo Alto, CA: Science and Behavior Books.

Rogers, C. R. (1990). A client-centred/person-centred approach to therapy. In H. Kirschenbaum & V. L. Henderson (Eds.), *The Carl Rogers reader* (pp. 135–152). London, England: Constable. (Original work published 1986)

Rogers, C. R., Gendlin, E. T., Kiesler, D. J., & Truax, C. B. (Eds.). (1967). *The therapeutic relationship and its impact*. Madison, WI: University of Wisconsin Press.

Rogers, C. R., & Ryback, D. (1984). One alternative to nuclear planetary suicide. In R. F. Levant & J. M. Shlien (Eds.), *Client-centered therapy and the person-centered approach: New directions in theory, research, and practice* (pp. 400–422). New York, NY: Praeger.

Sabat, S. R. (2001). *The experience of Alzheimer's disease*. Oxford, England: Blackwell.

Schmid, P. F. (2004). Back to the client: A phenomenological approach to the process of understanding and diagnosis. *Person-Centered & Experiential Psychotherapies, 3*(1), 36–51. doi:10.1080/14779757.2004.9688328

Shapiro, F. (Ed.). (2002). *EMDR as an integrative psychotherapy approach*. Washington, DC: American Psychological Association.

Shlien, J. M., & Levant, R. F. (1984). Introduction. In R. F. Levant & J. M. Shlien (Eds.), *Client-centered therapy and the person-centered approach: New directions in theory, research, and practice* (pp. 1–16). New York, NY: Praeger.

Staudinger, U. M. (1996). Wisdom and the social-interactive foundation of the mind. In P. B. Baltes & U. M. Staudinger (Eds.), *Interactive minds: Life-span perspectives on the social foundation of cognition* (pp. 276–315). New York, NY: Cambridge University Press.

Staudinger, U. M., & Baltes, P. B. (1996). Interactive minds: A facilitative setting for wisdom-related performance? *Journal of Personality and Social Psychology, 71*, 746–762. doi:10.1037/0022-3514.71.4.746

Sternberg, R. J. (2004). Why smart people can be so foolish. *European Psychologist, 9*(3), 145–150. doi:10.1027/1016-9040.9.3.145

Sternberg, R. J. (2007). *Wisdom, intelligence, and creativity synthesized*. New York, NY: Cambridge University Press.

Westra, H. A., Aviram, A., Barnes, M., & Angus, L. (2010). Therapy was not what I expected: A preliminary qualitative analysis of concordance between client expectations and experience of cognitive–behavioural therapy. *Psychotherapy Research, 20*(4), 436–446. doi:10.1080/10503301003657395

Wood, J. K. (2008). *Carl Rogers' person-centered approach: Toward an understanding of its implications*. Ross-on-Wye, Wales: PCCS Books.

Zilbergeld, B., & Lazarus, A. A. (1987). *Mind power: Getting what you want through mental training*. New York, NY: Ivy.

Zimbardo, P. (2007). *The Lucifer effect: Understanding how good people turn evil*. New York, NY: Random House.

II

CLINICAL ENCOUNTERS
WITH THE DARK SIDE

INTRODUCTION: CLINICAL ENCOUNTERS WITH THE DARK SIDE

In this section, authors from different theoretical traditions discuss how they approach the problem of the dark side in human beings, with implications for both therapy and larger organizations.

James Hollis (Chapter 4) writes from a Jungian perspective. He argues that as therapists we have to face a basic dilemma: Should we avoid such terms as *evil* and simply be pragmatic? He wonders, while we should not impose our moral categories on clients, do we collude with evil and enable its perpetuation if we use contemporary euphemisms to describe it, such as "disorder"? He focuses on the concept of the *shadow*, or those parts of ourselves that we disown. These are not necessarily "bad" parts. However, by disowning them we create the possibility for engaging in destructive behavior toward others directly, or indirectly through projection of our fears and anxieties onto them. We also may behave destructively toward ourselves as a result. Hollis, like Schmid, traces some of our difficulties back to different theological notions, either ones that encourage us to accept the notion that there is evil in life so that we can more effectively cope with it, or ones that may create the illusion that we can strive for conscious ego control in such a way that we may end up disowning or denying it. For Hollis, life is messy, contradictory, and something that we have to continually face up to, accept, and realize we do not have control over. For effective therapy, it is important for clients to confront their shadow sides. To do that, therapists, too, must confront their shadow sides.

Edward Mendelowitz (Chapter 5) challenges the reader to engage in a process of his or her own self-examination. His chapter is not written in the typical academic expository style. Rather, through quotations drawn from psychology, philosophy, literature, and film, he presents a chorus of perspectives. A central theme is that opening to life's complexities is essential for becoming more fully human: We cannot rely on comforting myths and must confront "the radical ambiguity of things." Mendelowitz points beyond either–or encapsulations of good versus evil to an "engendering of self-examination" and the "integration of elements." Mendelowitz's chapter is, in the end, a contemplation of Nietzsche's "pathos of nobility and distance": an inquiry into—and exhortation concerning—who we are and what we might be.

Larry M. Leitner (Chapter 6) presents an innovative experiential personal-construct point of view that integrates ideas from Kelly's personal-construct theory and the humanistic psychology focus on experiencing and on relationship. Personal construct theory (Kelly, 1963) has been seen as one of the first "cognitive" approaches to psychology, although Kelly's approach was more than purely cognitive. It also was different from those of the most influential modern cognitive theorists: Aaron Beck and Albert Ellis. Beck and Ellis, who have often been called "rational" cognitive theorists, focus on the "correctness" or "incorrectness" of beliefs, as if it could be said that certain beliefs were rational or irrational. In contrast, constructivists assume that many different personal constructions of reality may work. The question is not which are right or wrong, but how a person's constructs help him or her navigate reality. Leitner combines this constructivist view with an emphasis on the felt experiential aspects of personal functioning. In particular, he emphasizes the importance of relationship in affirming a deep sense of self. Evil arises when humans treat one another in ways that are deeply disconfirming or invalidating of core meaning constructs. Experiences that lead people to freeze their ability to relate in open new meaning-making ways with one another engender destructive behavior. The goal of therapy is to restore the capacity to relate in an open intimate way and thereby to make new meaning. Consonant with other authors in the book, such as Miller and Hollis, Leitner questions how psychology itself may be complicit in supporting disconfirming relationships that may block people's capacity to create new meaning in relationship to others.

John Briere (Chapter 7) is one of the leading experts on trauma psychology (e.g., Briere & Lanktree, 2011). He writes from the perspective of someone who has worked with both perpetrators and victims of abuse and acts such as torture. In considering how to think about working with someone who either has been abused or has abused, Briere discusses two dimensions that are typically used in deciding whether what someone has done is evil. The first is *intention*. To what degree does the role of the intention of the perpetrator make a difference in how his or her act is viewed, and in the impact of how his or her act is experienced? Along with this, Briere discusses the role of free will. From these considerations, Briere discusses the Buddhist notion of dependent origination—that all things arise from concrete conditions and sustaining causes—as a treatment remedy. If we understand the context from which evil behavior arises, we are less likely to make attributions of independent behavior to the perpetrators. Briere discusses the role of forgiveness in treatment in this context. Consonant with other authors, Briere argues that intervention should be at the social and at the individual levels.

In a lively and unorthodox chapter, Arnold A. Lazarus (Chapter 8) writes from his integrative "multimodal" (Lazarus, 2006) approach to psychotherapy. This was originally grounded in the cognitive–behavioral tradition and in our view provides a good representation of how cognitive–behaviorists might view issues of evil in psychotherapy. Lazarus acknowledges that he has not worked extensively with perpetrators of evil. However, he has worked with people who have been hurt by perpetrators. He has worked with lesser forms of human destructiveness. He first grapples with the nature of evil by way of discussing how he, as a clinician, decides how to deal with it in his work. He discusses the ideas of Albert Ellis, who believed there were no evil persons, just evil acts. Lazarus holds that Ellis's methods of separating the deed from the person is most useful for working with those who suffer from neurotic disorders but perhaps not for antisocial personalities. Lazarus concludes by demonstrating his approach with the case of a woman who was acting destructively toward herself. She did this by describing herself as evil on the basis of violations of her conservative religious strictures. She had previously seen a therapist who had challenged what she had perceived as her "dysfunctional beliefs," such as her belief in God, to no avail. Lazarus not only helps her with skills training but also finds an empathic way of challenging her dysfunctional beliefs that helps her cope with them.

Maureen O'Hara and Aftab Omer (Chapter 9) broaden the discussion and examine everyday dark behavior that emerges in organizations involved in efforts to bring good to the world. The chapter is based on case material gathered over two decades of inquiry into organizations dedicated to social services, social change, and education that engage in cruel and unjust treatment against their members and sometimes their clients. A "virtuous" organization may cohere around a myth of its own innocence. When this myth is falsely maintained by the denial of actions, attitudes, and values counter to the organization's stated view of itself, the consequences are harmful and sometimes devastating. Situated within an American culture that historically has mobilized powerful defenses against an awareness of its own propensity for and perpetration of evil, well-meaning organizations often fall into similar patterns of false innocence and perpetrate cruelty while proclaiming virtue. O'Hara and Omer suggest some principles and practices that can enable organizations to foster a reflexive awareness both to prevent and to remedy these harmful dynamics and to assist psychotherapists working with victimization.

REFERENCES

Briere, J. N., & Lanktree, C. B. (2011). *Treating complex trauma in adolescents and young adults*. Thousand Oaks, CA: Sage.

Kelly, G. (1963). *A theory of personality: The psychology of personal constructs*. New York, NY: Norton.

Lazarus, A. A. (2006). *Brief but comprehensive psychotherapy: The multimodal way*. New York, NY: Springer.

4

THEOGONIES AND THERAPIES: A JUNGIAN PERSPECTIVE ON HUMANITY'S DARK SIDE

JAMES HOLLIS

A few hours ago I met with a 61-year-old woman who is the daughter of a military couple whose substance abuse and contentious, violent marital relationship caused her and her five siblings to live in hell. One of her mother's many visiting lovers raped her when she was 11. She told no one of this trauma until after reaching 40 years of age because she knew that she would be doubly violated as their scorn and blame would be visited upon her rather than her assailant. Throughout her childhood until she left for college, she rose at 5:00 a.m. every morning to rouse, feed, and dress her younger siblings. Driven by a steady hum of anxiety, shame, and self-loathing, she promptly found a man to take her away from all that but who would predictably abuse and betray her. Her self-treatment plan also included residing for decades in the underworld of alcoholism, and, had she not had children for whom she felt responsible, she would many times have preferred to take her life to end her pain. Today, sober and productive, she remains in terror of relationships, is

DOI: 10.1037/13941-004
Humanity's Dark Side: Evil, Destructive Experience, and Psychotherapy, A. C. Bohart, B. S. Held, E. Mendelowitz, and K. J. Schneider (Editors)

afraid of risking feeling anything, and is dying of loneliness. That she has been lost in a very dark wood, to borrow Dante's metaphor, for a very long time is obvious and profoundly grievous. Only now, as she faces the last decades of her life, has she sought therapy to possibly fashion a life not defined by darkness.

However horrible the circumstances of her life, the history of abuse, the chronicles of shame and self-degradation, the relentless angst in which she lives her journey, can we say that she has suffered *evil?* If we use that term as therapists, what do we mean? Whence does such ontological conviction emanate? And how are we to work in its presence? Are we to avoid moral categories and simply manage pragmatic costs with pragmatic treatment plans? When Menninger (1988) asked "Whatever became of sin?" was he right to redeem this concept for our profession, which so often has treated the darkest of human behavior as derivative of defective genes, hormonal imbalances, interfering complexes, or cultural relativisms? We are rightly cautioned not to impose our own moral categories, prejudices, and complexes onto our patients, but are we then sometimes led to collude, however unwittingly, with evil and its perpetuation? In his fine book, *Explaining Hitler: The Search for the Origins of His Evil,* Rosenbaum (1999) offered a range of perspectives on modernism's favorite whipping boy. Having done so, he then raised a disturbing challenge to his own project: Were it possible to understand Hitler, would it make him less culpable?

As therapists, we have to face a basic dilemma: Should we avoid such terms as *evil* and simply be pragmatic? Do we collude with evil and enable its perpetuation if we use contemporary euphemisms, such as *disorder,* to describe it? In this chapter, I employ Jung's concept of the *shadow* to provide another, perhaps more helpful perspective on the problem. The shadow represents all that the person wishes to disown within his or her psychic life that embodies such autonomous energy that it continues to break through into daily life, even in the face of suppression, repression, or projection. Engaging the personal or collective shadow is both humbling and burdensome, but only through such willingness to be accountable can its energies ever be integrated into the personality. If we do not do this work, we project the shadow onto others, which can lead to hysteria, scapegoating, and violence to others or ourselves. Furthermore, when we ignore our shadow (energies), we diminish ourselves and live unconscious, timorous lives.

COMPARATIVE VIEWS OF EVIL

When we begin to examine the problem of evil and the encounter with both "natural" evil (e.g., earthquakes, hurricanes, cancer) and "moral" evil (i.e., the suffering that we bring to ourselves or others as a result of our choices), we immediately encounter the shadow issue of the Western theological traditions. The Eastern traditions often embraced a polytheistic view, as in Hinduism, in which there are multiple divinities, operating in multiple, diverse ways without contradiction, wherein human hope is vested in the possibility of conducting this phase of a cosmic history in such fashion as to relieve the burden for the next incarnation. In Buddhism, the problem is centered in the grasping, imperialistic activities of the insecure but inflated ego that wishes control, sovereignty, and an exemption from suffering. For the Buddhist, the key may be found in the transformation of ego consciousness from this delusional effort to control to the relief of "letting be," of going with the flow of energies in constant transformation, and in relinquishing an inflated identification with the ego state as the core of our being.[1]

The Western theologies, however, placed all their chips on the theistic square, the one where there is a single deity, omnipotent, omniscient, omnipresent, and possessing moral character (this last quality not infrequently looking rather like ours, by the way). Given these attributes, such a supreme being cannot be claimed to be looking elsewhere, preoccupied, impotent, or indifferent when suffering or injustice occurs. From this troubling nexus rises the shadow aspect of the Western theologies, a discipline called *theodicy*, whose task it is to reconcile this core contradiction. No matter how much sophistry or strained logic may be required to make it work out, the unitary nature of divinity is to be preserved at all costs. Although many of the arguments of theodicy appeal to the intellect, few satisfy the heart. Moreover, this theodicy project haunts Western therapies, given our frequently unexamined presuppositions that there is a collective expectation for societal behavior, a putative definition of sanity, and a horror of the amoral as evidenced in our slow evolution from "moral insanity" to "character" disorders to "personality" disorders and perhaps in the contemporary use of the euphemism *disorder* rather than *evil*.

JUNG'S CONCEPT OF THE SHADOW

It does not require a great deal of psychological awareness to perceive that generally these theologies, these *imago Deis*, arise from projections and often tell us more about the psychic state of the theologian than the mysterious Other. Jung (1973) even wrote a book on this subject, *Answer to Job*, recommending psychotherapy for such split tribal or collective imagoes as

---

[1]This idea finds its Western expression in the "Serenity Prayer" of twelve-step groups, or in the German word for "serenity," *Gelassenheit*, which could literally be translated as "the condition of having let be."

they shunt the dark side of the cosmos off onto a scapegoat figure, a devil or a Satan, rather than an imago that embraces the totality of being. Such splits Jung named *the shadow*, which may be experienced on both the personal and the collective levels. More recently, an extensive series of letters with Father Victor White, an English Dominican, on the subject of evil has been published (Lammers & Cunningham, 2007). In this exchange, Jung contended with the Roman Church's position that God is the *Summum Bonum* and resides untouched by evil, evil being merely the *privatio boni*, the absence of the good. Jung argued for the ontological status of evil and asserts that any theogony that does not include the dark side of the cosmos is simply incomplete.

Most commonly, the shadow manifests in our personal lives through the *unconscious* as it spills into one's self-defeating choices, one's narcissistic agenda, or even one's unlived life transmitted to one's children who carry it into subsequent generations. The greatest burden the child must bear, Jung asserted, is the unlived life of the parent. Thus, wherever we are blocked, oppressed, lacking permission, so our children will be similarly blocked, will struggle in an overcompensated way to break free from our heritage, or will unconsciously evolve a "treatment plan," ranging from anaesthetizing the conflict to distracting oneself from it or trying to solve it in ourselves or others. The way in which many of us in the healing professions carry this vast, impossible assignment of "fixing" what is wrong in others is replicated through what Jung called the archetype of "the wounded healer." It is disgraceful that so many of our training procedures neglect this intrapsychic pathologizing feature that lies deep within the soul of most therapists and drives many to steady states of anxiety, stress, substance abuse, and burnout. This unaddressed configuration alone, this engine of vocational identification, represents one of the prime shadows of our profession.

The shadow is not synonymous with evil per se. It is a metaphor to embody whatever ego consciousness, personal or collective, prefers to disown. That within me that makes me uncomfortable about me, that I prefer to repress, deny, discard, is my shadow. Accordingly, the shadow may also embody some of my best qualities, such as creativity, desire, spontaneity—all movements of affect, which at some point in our development proved costly or contradictory to the norms of our family or cultural context.

The shadow is *projected onto others*. What I wish to disown in myself I will see in you and condemn. (The mote in my neighbor's eye is so much more evident than the log in my own.) Often, what we dislike most about others is how they embody aspects of our own shadow. On the collective level, shadow projection is the origin of bigotry, prejudice, sexism, ageism, and every categorical animosity. The more stressed the cultural climate, the more unconscious and fearful the populace, the more we will seek someone to blame, some scapegoat who may carry the weight of our own psychological laziness. Having visited Buchenwald, Mauthausen, Dachau, Bergen-Belson, and Auschwitz and having read this morning's newspaper, I know that the rail tracks of such projections lead to concentration camps, to pogroms, and to killing fields scattered around the planet. And, as I live in an angst-ridden, divided country, I see such shadow projection manifesting as hysteria, scape-goating, and incitements to violence.

One may *be subsumed by the shadow* and revel in it: *Laissez les bons temps rouler* ("let the good times roll") . . . get stoned . . . enjoy the pure righteous-ness of anger . . . lose your mind . . . bask in the sweet seduction of *Schaden-freude*. As the shadow contains enormous energy, we often draw upon it and are exhilarated. As Nietzsche once observed, it is amazing how good bad reasons and bad music sound when one is marching off to meet the enemy.

One may *make the shadow conscious* and be summoned to humility before its leveling of ego presumptions, fantasies, inflations. Usually we come to this accounting the hard way because of the damage we have done to ourselves or others or because we are called to consciousness by the accumulative debris of consequences that trails behind our separate histories. Even more, the great-est of our shadow accounts arises from the narrow, diminished, timid lives we lead. We, and many of our clients, live timorous lives, and our own psyche expresses its contrary point of view through the symptomatology of depres-sion, desuetude, drugs of all kinds—including fundamentalisms, distractions, diverse disorders of desire, and the sundry forms of *mauvais foi* ("bad faith") of which Sartre accused us. As Jung variously said, we all walk in shoes too small for us. Most of all, we suffer from the general aimlessness of our lives. The summons to shadow accountability always asks us to grow up, to stop blaming our parents or our partners, and to risk wholeness rather than good-ness. While the presenting symptoms our clients bring will vary, most of them are suffering less from the evils of this world than from the unlived life that smolders untended within them.

One might argue that these considerations of the shadow are more phil-osophical than psychological. To that I would reply yes, these are philosophi-cal matters, and some of the greatest minds of antiquity wrestled with these same matters. I wish that more therapist training programs paid attention to philosophy because we are, finally, the sum of our "philosophies," whether conscious or not. Every *complex* is an embodied philosophy, rooted in the subject's past, a splinter personality, a somatic manifestation, a miniscript or scenario, and a tendency toward repetition. Many of our traumata have phenomenologically generated philosophies of self and world, and all of us have a tendency to commit "the fallacy of overgeneralization"; namely, what appeared to be true back then gets extrapolated to subsequent futures and cre-ates those noisome patterns that confound our deepest fantasies of freedom of choice. Would that more therapists were trained in the various argumentative fallacies that philosophers have smoked out through the millennia because our clients and their culture are awash in them. Similarly, however irrational the world is, and however quirky and idiosyncratic our sensibilities, we all could use that old tool, reason, to chart a path through the dark woods of our lives from time to time. And finally, developing a mature philosophy of life, one that asks accountability of us, one that acknowledges the reality of attachment and loss, one that summons us to the highest, will serve anyone well on whatever stormy seas our fate provides us.

One of the peripheral virtues of working with dreams is that the client's ego is summoned to a dialogue with a different, deeper source within. The dreams are, after all, one's own, but from whence does such ingenuity, such creativity and perspicacity, arise, and what is its intent? When the client engages the fact that there is a profound wisdom astir, what Jung called the "2-million-year-old person within," then he or she acquires greater access to a personal path and may recover personal authority theretofore traded away in the thousand adaptations that dependency once obliged. From both the extrapsychic dialogue of therapy and the intrapsychic dialogue of introspection, a larger life may unfold, and the shadow world may grow more luminous and inform a larger range of conscious choices.

THE INHERENT TRAUMA OF HUMAN EXISTENCE

Tiresias, the venerated blind prophet of ancient Greece, once observed that we sometimes see things not meant to be seen. So the therapist sometimes encounters the darkest of humanity's possibility, not only in the experience of evil's visitation but also in its deliberate practice.

While doing an internship in a psychiatric hospital decades ago, I encountered a woman who expressed the wish—and would often act out until she achieved her desire—to be "restrained," namely, bound in bedsheets to her bed and completely immobilized. Her presenting issue was a generalized anxiety disorder of such magnitude that making choices during the day filled her with so much terror that, restrained, she felt relief in having no choices to make at all.

What we do is always "logical," if we understand the psycho-logical premise our behavior serves or treats. Jungians learned a great deal from the work of the anthropologists Lévi-Bruhl and Levi-Strauss, who pointed out that the "savage mind," the mind to which each of us repairs when under primal stress, embodies a unique albeit a symbolic, associational, dereistic logic rather than the linear, discursive logic of ego consciousness. Most of us would find our anxiety mounting if we were rendered helpless by being bound to our beds. This sad woman felt freed of the burden of entering life with all its attendant vexatious choices.

When I spoke with her about her behaviors she explained that, among other things, her mother used to place splinters of wood under her fingernails every morning when she was a child. At first, I thought this and other lurid accounts were the products of a psychosis, but buried in her huge file were field reports from long ago written by the family services operative who managed to take her away from that house because the mother did in fact perpetrate those monstrous morning ministries and more, until tipped off by schoolteachers. To see this grown woman in such terror is to experience the magnitude of ontological evil. She haunts me to this day, as do the instruments on view at the *Straffenblock*, or punishment wing, at Buchenwald, just outside the lovely city of Weimar, which once housed the likes of Goethe, Schiller, Nietzsche, Wagner, and other luminaries of the human spirit.

So, too, am I haunted by the morbidly obese woman who was passed around by her parents as a sexual partner to their visiting friends. So, too, does the woman who was laughed at by her social worker for talking about the "three hearts housed in her body": one pumped blood, one was broken forever because of the death of her son, and one grieved for the rest of the world. I believe she had greater felt humanity than that social worker, and numerous others on staff who protected their unexamined lives and fragile hold on things by ridicule, distancing, and gallows humor. To keep even our one heart open in that place was to invite the minions of hell to enter.

All of us suffer from posttraumatic stress disorder (PTSD), for life is traumatic, existentially overwhelming, flooding us with a magnitude of experience too large to wholly assimilate. No wonder we have to repair to sleep to allow the psyche to keep processing that material and metabolizing its toxins. When people are deprived of sleep, and dreaming especially, in laboratory settings over time, they tend to hallucinate, so urgent is it for that material to be processed. Although this engagement with trauma is difficult enough on an individual basis, it may be accumulatively iatrogenic for therapists and professional health care providers as we take in these referred toxins over time. One colleague compared it to invisible silica drifting down from the ceiling, slowly filling our bodies and souls until the *pneuma*, the spirit, is laden, saturated, and finally quenched. I recall one of the senior analysts in Zurich who once confessed that when her week was over, she wept for her most troubled patient. And if they were all doing all right, she wept for herself.

As we know, an elemental treatment for PTSD is to tell one's story over and over, in the company of a trusted other, until that material has been metabolized. Without diminishing the encounter with evil that some of our clients have suffered, the therapist has to continuously support the idea that what happens *to* us is not *about* us, as such, though it occupies a regnant portion of our experience. Beneath the level of ego consciousness, we all exercise the mechanism of magical thinking, with paranoid tendencies toward embroidering. "I am what happens to me," we conclude as we internalize our world as a statement *to us about us*, and continue serving that charged "message." (As novelist Faulkner put it, "the past isn't dead; it's not even past.") Reinforcing the idea that the traumata arose from the exigencies of life, from the pathology of another person, from the occasional collusion of time and agency, is critical in developing another region of the psyche, which not only can challenge the messages implicate in the trauma but can learn to govern from a larger psychic space. As Jung said of our core complexes and wounds, we may not solve them, but we can outgrow them.

If we look at humanity's dark side, we are obliged in the name of philosophical honesty to consider whether the idea of *dark*, the idea of *evil* itself, is not primarily an "ego" problem, the problem of splitting when the universe itself is not split—it simply is. As a John Steinbeck character put it, "there ain't no good and there ain't no evil; there's just stuff folks do." In other words, whatever we personify when we speak of nature naturing (*natura naturans*) or nature natured (*natura naturata*), such a force does not consider or care about the problem of evil or that of light and dark. What agencies people have personified as "the gods" apparently do not either, although there are, of course, religions such as Christianity in which a compassionate deity is professed to have entered the world in human form to share and possibly redeem suffering. The polytheisms have an easier time of all this because the divine powers are not obliged to be consistent or compassionate, or anything but "the god." Classical Buddhism is accordingly more an existential psychology that addresses our core condition: *angst*. The ego, then, is not tasked with that impossible agenda of sovereignty, which serves as the core, silent assumption of so many modern psychologies and therapeutic methods. Most of our psychological theories and treatment plans invest heavily in the fantasy of ego sovereignty and control through cognitive restructuring and behavioral modification. These fantasies will, to the classical Buddhist, only deepen delusion and set the ego up for further angst, as these stratagems ultimately fail. Similarly, most popular theologies set up the believer, either by infantilizing him or her through guilt and anxiety or by seducing him or her with intimations of happiness, material prosperity, and longevity. When any of these psychological or theological assumptions falters under the burden of reality, the individual is typically left to account for the discrepancy by indicting the gods, or themselves, for their shortcomings. Gautama noticed this tendency two-and-a-half millennia ago when he said that the ego attitude itself was the problem. Is it not interesting that we are still stubbing our toes on this recalcitrant tendency of ego inflation these many centuries later? And that the implicit healing fantasy of most of our methods may compound this dilemma?

It is the nature of *psyche*, an energy system geared toward its own development and preservation, to differentiate into components that may support or impede those agenda. The phenomenology of being itself splits and creates such epiphenomena as ego consciousness and the splintered fragments of diverse drives, complexes, and reticulated personal and cultural scenarios. These differentiations of psyche, not unlike the leaf, blossom, stalk, and seed of the plant, conduct their agenda through multiple structures and functions. Yet this same utilitarian variegation also begets splits, conflicts, suffering, neurosis. In the Edenic myth, for instance, one may eat of *the Tree of Life*, but *the Tree of Knowledge* is forbidden. Living unconsciously in service to instinct is psychic wholeness; serving the divergent agenda of consciousness, however, leads to fragmentation, inner division, and ultimately spills out into violent contention within one's own species. Various fantasies of "homecoming," of "heaven," of "wholeness," of "happiness," of "returning to nature," of "the simple life" serve this nostalgia for the lost unity of instinctual being. But there is no going back. The saddest lines in the English language are perhaps those of Milton describing how our mythopoeic ancestors wound their solitary way out of Eden, forever.

So, in response we devise the epiphenomenal armamentaria of theology, psychology, treatment plans to perpetuate the fantasy of return, forgetting Freud's reminder that our much more modest, perhaps achievable, task is to move from the neurotic miseries of life to the normal miseries of life. While we may or may not agree that the problem of evil, of humanity's "dark side," is the unavoidable casualty of splitting ego consciousness, we will nonetheless have to contend always with the heart, and with the irreducible sum of human suffering. As Pascal noted in the 17th century, the heart has reasons that reason knows not. And as Yeats agreed, whatever our theoretic preferences, in the end we are left only "with our blind stupefied hearts."

BRINGING THE SHADOW INTO CONSCIOUSNESS

The problem with the unconscious is that it is *unconscious*. We cannot with any certainty say that it exists, yet we have as much right to speak of it as an entity as astrophysicists have to speak of black holes, whose existence they posit because of their effect on surrounding bodies. That so much of our histories seem to spill into the world from places unknown to consciousness appears to legitimize the existence of such a premise. From the limited purview of consciousness, however, the whole presumption is revolutionary and unsettling. It is unsettling to think that the ego may be only a thin wafer on a large, tenebrous sea when we have invested so much in its seaworthy character, ride its tossing structure, and cling to it as a fixity. From the standpoint of the immature or threatened ego, even the rest of our psychic reality may be considered a "dark side." The partner of one of my analysands has resisted personal therapy on the grounds that "I know what I think," which is the equivalent of saying, "I think I think what I think." Similarly, the secret imperialism of Freud's "where Id was, there Ego shall be" also suggests something of the Ego's attitude to this terra incognita. So, in exploring the shadow, we are asked to be accountable not only for the unknown but for the little pieces we can know, but prefer not to.

In speaking to groups on the theme of the shadow, I have developed daylong workshops in which, after a general introduction to the concept of the shadow and examples on the societal and historical front, we explore the theme on a very personal basis. While the privacy of each participant is protected, each is asked to journal on the spot in response to some provocative questions. These workshops have led to some engaging conversations, and I believe no little increase in personal awareness. Although the questions themselves are simple enough, they do stir the pot and bring much otherwise neglected material to the surface. Rather than focus on the issue of evil per se, and in the spirit of broadening the topic of humanity's dark side, let me share some of the questions and brief amplifications here.

1. (a) Of your many, many virtues, a list too large to encompass in this brief few hours, can you identify perhaps three of them which you believe show up in your life with reasonable consistency?
   (b) What are the opposites of those virtues, those manifestations of a darker side to a personality, which of course are most remote from your intentions?
   (c) Can you identify specific occasions where the practice of the virtues you listed in 1. (a) above brought harm to you or someone else?
   (d) Can you identify specific occasions where the opposite of your virtues as listed in 1. (b) above turned up in your life?

This very simple four-part question begins to shift the ground beneath the ego and its pretensions. All of us wish to think of ourselves as generally righteous people, citizens of goodwill, who, hopefully, will make beneficent contributions. However, a sober assessment of history, ours and that of the world, suggests that even the very best of intentions may lead to unforeseen harm to self and others. And, however vigilant we wish to be, the whole range of human possibility sooner or later leaks into the world through us. The general effect of even this first question is disquietude and an aroused sensitivity that other forces may be afoot. If anyone ever doubted it, the first question alone begins to underline the role of the unconscious in the governance of daily life, and the reminder that we do not in fact know what we think, nor are we arrogantly able to chart a course of moral certainty.

2. Examine the key relationships of your life, domestic and business. Where does the shadow manifest in patterns of avoidance of conflict or compliance with the pressure of the moment, leading to consequences which are not in your interest or perhaps that of others?

Again, this question demonstrates the ubiquity of subterranean agendas, old patterns of adaptation, Quisling-like evasions of accountability that allow us to slip-slide away from the encounter with the anfractuosities of life.

3. Examine the patterns of your intimate relationships, either current or past. What annoys you most about that partner? Where have you encountered such annoyance before?

This question begins to get at the question of how we project our shadow onto our partners, and indeed may select them in order to do so. We chose them for good reasons, and only a very few of those reasons were conscious. In the face of highly charged messages, especially the unconscious ones, we have a tendency to serve the instructions through repetition, or may be caught in overcompensation by trying to get away from a dynamic pattern (and thereby being still defined by it) or by having worked out a treatment plan such as a numbing addiction, a life of distraction, or gasp, by being a therapist and trying to fix them in everyone else.

4. Where do you repeatedly undermine your interests, shoot yourself in the foot, cause yourself familiar griefs? Where do you avoid risking what you intuit to be your larger self?

Again, the shadow manifests most tellingly in our collusion with it. Even when we know what is needed, we often repeat patterns compulsively. As Paul said in the Letter to the Romans, though we know the good, we do not do it. Why? He tended to mark it up to "sin," the impossibility of perfection, and an imperfect will. All of that may be true, but he did not know much about the vastness of the unconscious and the fact that the contrary tendencies are also part of who we are. In fact, the most astute psychological comment ever to come from the ancient world is from the Roman playwright Terence, who two millennia ago said, "Nothing human is alien to me." This self-evident truth is the essence of shadow recognition, our common humanity, and yet each of us will have some place in our life where denial, evasion, suppression, repression, projection, or dissociation is reflexively employed to distance us and preserve the ego's fragile frame. None of us will wish to access our inner sociopath, embrace the murderer within—though we murder on a daily basis—confess our rampant narcissism, and none of us will want to confess how much we want to love and be loved.

5. Where are you "stuck" in your life, blocked in your development? What fears stand as sentinels to keep you from where you want to go, and from whence do they derive?

I have asked this question now on four continents, and no one has ever asked me, "What do you mean 'stuck'?" They ask for examples of every other question, but for this one they all start writing in a matter of seconds. It is of considerable psychological import that we can so readily identify where we are stuck, and yet we stay stuck. Often the pushback from those stuck places is reinforced by repeated failed attempts to get unstuck, and the person is further afflicted with shame, guilt, and diminished self-esteem. In addressing this question, I acquaint them with the chief premise of depth psychology, namely, that it is not about what it is about. Whatever the "stuck" place is, it is not about that issue, for that issue or task is on its own easily addressed. Rather, a metaphoric filament reaches down from the stuck place to a primal, archaic zone of the psyche where the earliest lessons about the twin threats to our survival—being overwhelmed and abandonment—were first met and suffered. In these superficial stuck places, we activate primal, archaic anxieties, and it is the admixture, the fuel from this archaic realm that overpowers the repeated efforts of ordinary ego consciousness to move forward. When one has grasped that "it is not about what it is about," then one can begin to realize that the archaic parts of the blocking mechanism can be confronted by the powers and resiliency the person has acquired over the intervening years. Many persons, whether it presents as writer's block, the need to lose weight, the need to address an addiction, or whatever, expressed a relief and a new resolve when they realized that the blockage arose not from their dilatory will but from matters long ago and far away, matters that an enlarged consciousness can now address.

6. Where do mother and father still govern your life, either through repetition, overcompensation, or your special "treatment plan"?

The unlived life of the parent, wherever they were stuck, becomes for all of us a compelling model, script, set of marching orders, or we spend enormous energy trying not to repeat our mother's life, or be like our father, or we evolve sophistic strategies to massage this issue and ignore its continuing role in our lives.

7. Where do you refuse to grow up, wait for clarity of vision before risking, hope for external solutions, expect rescue from someone, or wait for someone else to tell you what your life is about?

This question, like the one on "stuckness," is one to which the participants quickly respond. They, we, all know where we are avoiding showing up in our lives. All of us are aware where we would like someone else to take care of this nettlesome journey for us. All of us want to figure it all out, have the ambiguities resolved before we step into the abyss. This deferred accountability, this disowned personal authority, this evasion of responsibility is common to each of us in some area of our lives and is one of the chief manifestations of humanity's dark side. For those of us committed to democratic values, this flight from personal accountability not only sabotages the depth and integrity of our personal journey but also undermines the maturation necessary for a responsible, participatory democracy. No wonder our public sensibilities are characterized by their susceptibility to demagogues and to gurus, seduction by fads and fashions. They exhibit a short attention span, manifest a ready tendency to scapegoat, prefer simplistic solutions to complex matters, and relinquish personal authority so easily in times of distress. As one of Bertolt Brecht's characters said in response to how a tyranny is created, one does not have to organize the criminals, one has only to organize the people. As a result, the darkest side of our collective social structures has its origin in what we have avoided in our personal development.

MEANING ARISES FROM SUFFERING

In standing on this spinning planet and in doing this kind of work on a daily basis, we cannot help but be thrown back on existential perplexities: Why is there so much suffering, so much injustice? To what degree does one adopt a neutral, uninvolved approach? When is intervention possible, and necessary? How does our own philosophical *Weltanschauung* help or hinder our work? Is there a legitimate connection between theogony and therapy, and if so, what?

A long time ago, the problems of evil, injustice, and the ubiquity of suffering sent me to study philosophy and theology at the graduate level. As rich and provocative as those texts proved to be, I came to appreciate Whitehead's critique of "the bloodless dance of categories" and was left with little more than my own blind and stupefied heart. I recall listening to an interview over my car radio on November 23, 1963, as Kenny O'Donnell reflected on the assassination of his friend the day before. He said, "What's the good of being Irish if you don't know that sooner or later the world is going to break your heart." One does not have to be Irish to find our personal appointment with the darkest wood. Since that time, I have come to the conclusion that most of us no doubt reach, or we burn out, or we have to close up our spiritual shop and become automatons, namely: The ubiquity of suffering and injustice is pretty much a steady state. Just because we have been distracted for the moment does not remove the fact that horrible things are happening to people in any given moment. All we can bring to the table, then, is compassion, a steadiness that can sometimes assist healing, and the interpretive skills to help people find their position relative to their suffering. In his marvelous updating of the Job story, Archibald MacLeish (1961) moves his central character, a businessman named J. B., to observe that God does not love; God simply is. "But we do," his wife Sarah reminds him.

Sometimes we can help reframe the patient's suffering without evading it in any way. In my book *Swamplands of the Soul*, I make the point that in every swampland visitation—depression, loss, betrayal, guilt, and so on—there is always a psychological task, and addressing this task may move a person from victimhood and diminishment to proactive engagement and psychospiritual enlargement (Hollis, 1996). Mysteriously, healing often arises out of the therapeutic alliance itself, this most intimate of relationships. Well over a century ago, Pierre Janet observed what he called "the talking cure," the peculiar phenomenon that people somehow felt better having simply shared their suffering with him. What we can discern in this phenomenon is the importance of human relationship, of one person bearing witness to the suffering of another, and of being held in one's fallen state without judgment.

Surely one of the most delusory of ideologies in our cultural context is the fantasy of *happiness*. Happiness is a most transient state, and always contextual. (Remember the banquet of Damocles and his sword swinging over the head of the engorged diner?) When we are doing what is right for our soul, that is, *psyche*, we will be flooded from time to time by happiness, but the steady pursuit of it will lead to addictive behaviors, trivialization, and increased suffering. On the other hand, if the goal is *meaning*, that is, finding our purpose in our particular corner of the dark wood, then we will feel the richness of our journey. Part of our therapeutic task, so often necessary, is to undertake Freud's idea of *Nacherziehung*, namely, the reeducation of our values. Helping a person find his or her task amid suffering, loss, or disappointment moves him or her toward greater autonomy. Analytic psychology, as articulated by Jung, is ultimately a therapy of meaning. Although we begin our work in such swamplands as psychopathology, we are more importantly directed toward the task of finding meaning in those dismal places. What, in the face of these circumstances, is one called to *do*? What new attitudes are required, what persistence of will, and what changing agenda of values does this moment ask of one's life? When these questions are addressed directly, the person stays less stuck on the wounding and more engaged in the task that can lead him or her to enlargement. In the end, the attainment of happiness can be a trivial definition of life, but a more concerted dialectic among heart, brain, and soul may lead to a life well lived, a life in which one finds dignity, autonomy, and worth.

Jung repeatedly observed that we cannot take clients further than we have gone ourselves. Where we are stuck, the therapy will get stuck. We therefore have to bring to the table our own ongoing reflectivity, our own awareness of blind spots, and our own willingness to acknowledge what we do not know. We will not finally understand humanity's dark side, but we are here to bear witness, to bring the gift of compassion and shared journey to the client. All of us are in the same dark woods, albeit with different paths opening for us. Over 8 centuries ago, the writer of the Grail legend noted that when each knight took off in search of the Grail, each one went to a place in the forest where there was no path, for it would be a shameful thing to take the path someone has trod before. Before we can accompany anyone on the journey through the dark wood, we have to have undertaken our own. Wherever our own courage and resolve to see it through flags or fails, we will fail our patient, for what we have most to share with him or her is not our learning or our techniques, but rather who we have become, and what darkness we have faced in the world and in ourselves.

REFERENCES

Hollis, J. (1996). *Swamplands of the soul: New life in dismal places*. Toronto, Canada: Inner City Books.

Jung, C. (1973). *Answer to Job, collected works* (Vol. 11). Princeton, NJ: Princeton University Press.

Lammers, A. C., & Cunningham, A. (Eds.). (2007). *The Jung–White letters*. London, England: Routledge.

MacLeish, A. (1961). *J. B.: A play in verse*. New York, NY: Houghton-Mifflin.

Menninger, K. A. (1988). *Whatever became of sin?* New York, NY: Bantam.

Rosenbaum, R. (1999). *Explaining Hitler: The search for the origin of his evil*. New York, NY: Harper.

5

DECALOGUE, OR HOW TO LIVE A LIFE: ENGENDERING SELF-EXAMINATION

EDWARD MENDELOWITZ

Our whole life is startlingly moral. There is never an instant's truce between virtue and vice.

—Henry David Thoreau, *Walden*

The road from appearance to reality is often very hard and long, and many people make only very poor travelers. We must forgive them when they stagger against us as if against a brick wall.

—Franz Kafka, *Conversations With Kafka*

For we are like olives: Only when we are crushed do we yield what is best in us.

—The Talmud (in Hrabal)

This brief meditation on character and self-creation has its inception in the epistolary exchange on humanity's dark side that transpired between Rollo May and Carl Rogers toward the end of their respective lives. Rogers's largesse and early influence on my thought and work notwithstanding, May's richer literary approach is our point of departure. Like Nietzsche and Rank, May approached human nature with an artist's eye, seeing it as something of an unfinished canvas at which one ought to work throughout life. The chapter's nonlinear, collage-like approach is meant to frustrate the inflated left brain so as to effect a loosening of the traditional subject–object split and, thereby, an engendering of self-examination. Shards of poetry, literature, prose, and clinical narrative evoke a sense of the relativity of things: associations between real and fictional narratives, interrelations between madness and sagacity, the egregious acts of our most loathsome criminals and

Portions of this chapter have been adapted from Ed Mendelowitz's *Ethics and Lao-Tzu*, copyright 2008, with permission from University of the Rockies Press.

DOI: 10.1037/13941-005
Humanity's Dark Side: Evil, Destructive Experience, and Psychotherapy. A. C. Bohart, B. S. Held, E. Mendelowitz, and K. J. Schneider (Editors)

crimes and misdemeanors much closer to home. Mindful readers will note throughout an attentiveness to encounter and the breakdowns in communication underlying all thoroughgoing meditations upon ethics: the "pathos of distance" between who we are and what we might be. Message and form, as a consequence, are intricately merged.

A SORT OF INTRODUCTION

It has been more than 25 years since a serene summer evening in the Tiburon hills when Rollo May shared some thoughts with a small group of students on the age-old theme of humanity's dark side with some cautiously expressed hopes for one day a better world. He saw any number of things about which to feel sanguine and yet offered only a 50% chance of safe passage. I sat next to him and listened intently. It was a free-ranging discussion toward the end of a series of seminars ("Socratic discussions" is the phrase Rollo liked to employ) during which we had read through May's major works, discussing them then in his graceful yet far from ostentatious home.

May opined at some length about signs of life he discerned among the young, dissatisfied as they were with business as usual and eager for meaningful change. He mentioned the landing on the moon by the astronauts of Apollo 11 (and the vision from there of a blue water planet called Earth floating tentatively in space and unfettered by political divides) as a kind of metaphor for a more harmonious future politic and world. I listened with increasing perplexity, finally exclaiming that I did not share his vision or see quite so much reason for hope.

May misconstrued my comments at first, assuming that his remarks would seem too circumspect and reserved for us fledgling psychologists and that we would proffer, understandably, more upbeat assessments of the morrow. He related, touchingly, that my belief in advance reminded him of a conversation he had had many years ago with *his* mentor, the German philosopher and theologian Paul Tillich, noting that he, too, had once partaken of a perhaps necessary naïveté of youth. I was moved by his superimposition of the then-present moment (a present moment now almost 30 years past!) on that earlier imprint of his own student/teacher connection with Tillich. I corrected him, however, after which he exclaimed, "So you are more pessimistic than I!" "Yes," I said. "Well, that's because you are a Jew," he rejoined; "You know what I mean, don't you?" Intuitively, I think, I did. Rollo paused just long enough, however, to more concretely make his point: "It's because the Jews have taken it on the chin so many times."

May felt, it seems, that—with their bible of woe and tales of growth through suffering and without ultimate good news at the end of the line—the Jewish people had garnered through the generations a certain collective insight into the darkened aspects of human nature. The uses of adversity had always been one of May's bedrock ontological themes. A Hebraic reverie upon good and evil? I claim, really, no such thing. Rather, a collage-like meditation on character that is uniquely my own and for which no race, profession, or creed need take responsibility beyond normative influences. Moving beyond the neatness of philosophical/psychological/theological abstraction, we confront our very selves. Is there a better way to inquire into the essence of inmost and human things?

TIKKUN OLAM

Frieda Fromm-Reichmann was, along with their mutual mentor H. S. Sullivan, one of the two finest therapists Rollo May ever knew, though he recalled her as diminutive, awkward, and unprepossessing. Raised in an Orthodox German Jewish home, she was inspired in her life and work by the Judaic conception of *tikkun olam*, "repair" of a fallen world. According to legend, God at a certain moment in the evolution of the universe "retracted" upon Himself, thus causing a disturbance of the original unity and the shattering of its sacred vessels into shards. This primordial cosmic cataclysm, known as the "Breaking of the Vessels" (Afterman, 1992, p. 6), coincided, in effect, with the creation of the visible world. The Breaking of the Vessels finds, in turn, its earthly reverberation in a fragmented human consciousness, unable in its inchoate state to perceive revelation, the greater coherence of it all. Ever since this original retraction, the task of each human being has been to "repair the world," breaking through the husks of fallen shards to disclose the divine light hidden within. To redeem one person—to save a single life—according to Talmudic instruction, is to redeem the world. Such was the lofty touchstone for Rollo May's beloved teacher.

In Hannah Green's (1964, p. 24) autobiographical novel, *I Never Promised You a Rose Garden*, a psychotic adolescent girl recounts the course of her work with this tiny doctor "known and loved by madmen the world over." It is the strength of Fromm-Reichmann's character—and her patient's as well—amid a sea of normative deception and callousness that allows Deborah to emerge gradually from her inner world of Yr (a sanctuary once offering succor yet now threatening to consume), the relationship itself an exemplar of unselfconsciousness and engagement, humor and care.

When we first meet the miniscule psychiatrist in Green's novel, we find her lost in reverie about the Old Country, about madness and asylum and former patients in a villainous terrain she, as a Jewess, had been most fortunate to flee:

> Sometimes, she thought ruefully, the world is so much sicker than the inmates of its institutions. She remembered Tilda, in the hospital in Germany, at a time when Hitler was on the other side of its walls and not even she could say which side was sane. Tilda's murderous hate, bound down on beds, tube-fed, and drugged into submission, could still fade long enough to let the light in now and then. She remembered Tilda looking up at her, smiling in a travesty of genteel politeness from the canvas-bound bed, and saying, "Oh, do come in, dear Doctor. You are just in time for the patient's soothing tea and the end of the world." (Green, 1964, p. 18)

Deborah has that eerie precocity found oftentimes in childhood and early madness. And there is, too, a penchant for metaphor and yearning for justice in what is taken through embittered experience to be an untrustworthy, even sinister, world. She is angry at the cruelty of the fallen realms outside the facility that had brutalized both her and the others, driving them at first inward and, in the end, literally mad:

> Although those in the hospital wondered how springtime could come in spite of their particular pain, it came and was triumphant. It made the patients on D ward angry that the world which had murdered them did not suffer for its sins, but on the contrary seemed to be thriving. (Green, 1964, p. 174)

Deborah's inner world of Yr may be understood as a retreat from a traumatizing external reality into an interior place/space of her own choosing and creation—a kind of self-protective migration to safe haven within the mind. We are hardly surprised to learn that morality is both ambiguous and problematic even within the confines of asylum.

During one particular psychotherapy session, Deborah tells her doctor (affectionately christened "Furii" in a gesture that touchingly personalizes a relationship that will become, for a while, her very lifeline and hope) about an incident on the unit involving violent staff impropriety and about which she has complained without administrative acknowledgment or meaningful response:

> At last Furii agreed to mention it in the staff meeting, but Deborah was not convinced. "Maybe you doubt that I saw it at all."
>
> "That is the one thing that I do not doubt," the doctor said. "But you see, I have no part in what is to be done on the wards; I am not an administrative doctor."
>
> Deborah saw the match lighting dry fuel. "What good is your reality, when justice fails and dishonesty is glossed over and the ones who keep faith suffer?"

"Look here," Furii said. "I never promised you a rose garden. I never promised you perfect justice . . . " (She remembered Tilda suddenly, breaking out of the hospital in Nuremberg, disappearing into the swastika-city and coming back laughing that hard, rasping parody of laughter. "*Shalom aleichem*, Doctor, they are crazier than I am!") . . . "and I never promised you peace or happiness. The only reality I offer is challenge, and being well is being free to accept it or not at whatever level you are capable. I never promise lies, and the rose-garden world of perfection is a lie . . . and a bore, too!" (Green, 1964, pp. 121–122)

With such forthrightness and lack of pretense does a genuine relationship ensue, and Deborah's Yr voice with its incessant refrain ("You are not of them") gradually recedes as she learns that it may yet be possible, despite early trauma, to trust what is known, in the lexicon of Yr, as an "earth-one." Slowly this "veteran of many deceits" (Green, 1964, p. 224) learns to inhabit a middle ground between the within and without, the here and there, coexisting with the darker aspects even of the normative world.

It is saddening to note that the doctor herself, Frieda Fromm-Reichmann, after living such an exemplary life and having effected such a hard-won and rarefied outcome, died, according to her friend Martin Buber, of a broken heart (Rollo May, personal communication, 1983). "What you see can drive you crazy," wrote her knowing patient (Green, 1964, p. 175), referring to the dangers that inhere in overly prolonged immersion in the world's treachery and the resultant torment of its multifarious victims.

ALL SENTIENT BEINGS

There is a story out of Beckett (1934/1972), "Dante and the Lobster," in which the protagonist goes through his day pondering literature and existence. He purchases a lobster for his aunt that is attacked by a cat while he attends an Italian lesson and discusses the Florentine poet on the themes of pity and damnation. Arriving later at the aunt's, he unwraps the lobster and is mortified to find it mangled by the cat:

"They assured me it was fresh" said Belacqua.

Suddenly he saw the creature move, this neuter creature. Definitely it changed its position. His hand flew to his mouth.

"Christ!" he said "it's alive."

His aunt looked at the lobster. It moved again. It made a faint nervous act of life on the oilcloth. They stood above it, looking down on it, exposed cruciform on the oilcloth. It shuddered again. Belacqua felt he would be sick.

"My God" he whined "it's alive, what'll we do?"

The aunt simply had to laugh. She bustled off to the pantry to fetch her smart apron, leaving him goggling down at the lobster, and came back with it on and her sleeves rolled up, all business.

"Well" she said "it is to be hoped so, indeed."

"All this time" muttered Belacqua. Then, suddenly aware of her hideous equipment: "What are you going to do?" he cried.

"Boil the beast" she said, "what else?"

"But it's not dead" protested Belacqua, "you can't boil it like that."

She looked at him in astonishment. Had he taken leave of his senses?

"Have sense" she said sharply, "lobsters are always boiled alive. They must be." She caught up the lobster and laid it on its back. It trembled. "They feel nothing" she said.

In the depths of the sea it had crept into the cruel pot. For hours, in the midst of its enemies, it had breathed secretly. It had survived the Frenchwoman's cat and his witless clutch. Now it was going alive into scalding water. It had to. Take into the air my quiet breath.

Belacqua looked at the old parchment of her face, grey in the dim kitchen.

"You make a fuss" she said angrily "and upset me and then lash into it for your dinner."

She lifted the lobster clear of the table. It had about thirty seconds to live.

Well, thought Belacqua, it's a quick death, God help us all.

It is not. (Beckett, 1934/1972, pp. 21–22)

We have here a man of native psychological genius who had read very nearly everyone in sight right down to our own William James, understanding that there are no easy answers and, in a sense, no answers at all. Like Lao-tzu and others before him, Beckett (in Ackerley & Gontarski, 2004, p. 215) points relentlessly beyond certainty and schema while striving all the time for definition not essentially a matter of words: "My work is a matter of fundamental sounds . . . If people want to have headaches among the overtones, let them. And provide their own aspirin."

Yet Beckett lives an impeccable life from the ethical point of view. Visiting an ailing mother in Dublin when the World War breaks out in Europe, he returns to take part in the resistance, preferring France at war to Ireland at peace. There he might stay undisturbed in Paris were he to remain uninvolved. Yet "the Germans were making life hell for my friends . . . I couldn't stand with my arms folded" (in Ronsley, 1977, p. 220). Still, Beckett seems to have had no particular need for attention or acclaim and later dismisses his considerable risks as "boy scout stuff." When rumors begin to circulate that he may win the Nobel Prize, Beckett makes it clear that he desires neither distinction nor attention and later complains that notoriety has compromised his relationship to his work. The money received he gives away to struggling artists. With what remains he purchases a phone that can call out but cannot receive. The voices he wanted, it seems, were already there.

And so the modernist playwright is less bizarre than we had first surmised, and lives a life of uncommon decency during his finite sojourn on what Pozzo had called "this bitch of an earth" (Beckett, 1954, p. 121). Eschewing all talk of "closed systems" whereby one might escape "the contingencies of the contingent world" (Beckett, 1957, p. 168), Beckett finds, rather, an ethos in nothingness, "a coming and being and going in purposelessness" (Beckett, 1953, p. 47). It is a credo grounded in nullity, if you like, and the real message of Beckett's enigmatic example and code is what we are to make of it all. If our mortal lot is without preordained import or destiny, there is nonetheless the possibility of this-worldly decency and limited triumph, human immersion and sympathy, humility and care—this in spite of the fact that the writer's characters seem to fall, almost reflexively, into sadomasochistic patterns of relations. Beckett's (1934/1972, p. 21) terse and evocative language connoting form in movement is exquisite: "a little mercy to rejoice against judgment." "We are not saints," muses Vladimir, "but we have kept our appointment. How many people can boast as much?" (Beckett, 1954, p. 289)

WISE AND DISCERNING VOICES

Man desires a world where good and evil can be clearly distinguished, for he has an innate and irrepressible desire to judge before he understands. Religions and ideologies are founded on this desire. They can cope with the novel only by translating its language of relativity and ambiguity into their own . . . dogmatic discourse. They require that someone be right: Either Anna Karenina is the victim of a narrow-minded tyrant, or Karenin is the victim of an immoral woman; either K is an innocent man crushed by an unjust Court, or the Court represents divine justice and K is guilty.

This "either-or" encapsulates an inability to tolerate the essential relativity of things human, an inability to look squarely at the absence of the Supreme Judge. This inability makes the novel's wisdom (the wisdom of uncertainty) hard to accept and understand.

—Milan Kundera (1986, p. 7),
The Art of the Novel

"Know thyself" does not mean "observe thyself." "Observe thyself" is what the Serpent says. It means: "Make yourself master of your actions." But you are so already, you are the master of your actions. So that saying means: "Misjudge yourself! Destroy yourself!" which is something evil—and only

if one bends down very far indeed does one also hear the good in it,
which is: "in order to make of yourself what you are."
—Franz Kafka (1954/1991, pp. 20–21),
Blue Octavo Notebooks

Do you see how our native psychological geniuses point us relentlessly
back to nuance and self? Do you understand the place of will and intention
and the cautious integration of manifold elements? We have met both sinner
and saint, and she and he are surely we.

TROUBLE IN THE NEW WORLD

In Isaac Bashevis Singer's (1998) *Shadows on the Hudson*, a novel about
Holocaust-obsessed Jews in the New World of Manhattan during years immediately following the incinerators and jackboots of Auschwitz–Birkenau, a
man laments the hypocrisy even of the recently damned as he reflects upon
sainthood and fallenness. His interlocutor responds cynically:

> There are no saints. You're still clinging to outmoded notions. If you see
> someone ready to sacrifice himself for you, you ought to know that he
> gets the greatest pleasure from it. Try to stop him from sacrificing himself,
> and he'll stick a knife in you. (p. 40)

Skeptical to the core, the Yiddish master understood that it is all too easy to
leap over the fathomless entanglements of life in order to *prove* our virtue.
Vanity, taught Fromm-Reichmann (in Green, 1964), was the psychotherapist's greatest enemy after illness.

The point we are making pertains to the radical ambiguity of things—
our personal crimes and misdemeanors and those played out upon the
greater world stage. Our own collective disciplines are hardly immune from
scrutiny:

> I see Organization Men in psychiatry, with all the problems of deathlike
> conformity. Independent thinking by the adventurous has declined; psy-
> chiatric training has become more formal, more preoccupied with certifi-
> cates and diplomas, more hierarchical . . . . These are the preoccupations
> of young psychiatrists. There are more lectures, more supervision, more
> examinations for specialty status, and thus the profession soon attracts
> people who take to these practices. Once there were the curious and
> bold; now there are the carefully well-adjusted and certified.
> —Robert Coles (1995, pp. 9–10),
> "A Young Psychiatrist Looks at His Profession"

With Taoist intuition, the science fiction writer Philip K. Dick (in Sukin, 1995, pp. 278–279) discerns virtue, counterintuitively, in negative terms and in smallness:

> The authentic human being is one . . . who instinctively knows what he should not do . . . and . . . will balk at doing it . . . This, to me, is the ultimately heroic trait of ordinary people; they say no to the tyrant and they calmly take the consequence of this resistance. Their deeds may be small and almost always unnoticed, unmarked by history. Their names are not remembered, nor did [they] expect [them] to be . . . I see their authenticity in an odd way: not in their willingness to perform heroic deeds but in their quiet refusals . . . [T]hey cannot be compelled to be what they are not.

Psychologists would do well to recall those studies about too many people who turn up the voltage and look away from the pain, experiments that should have reminded us only of what we had already surmised about the many and the few and the just and forlorn—and, yet, even still, the biblical "still, small voice," an attendance upon grace.

In the waning pages of Singer's (1998) novel, a conversation occurs in which a struggling artist discusses morality and belief with an old friend:

> "I have abandoned Judaism. I am no longer a Jew," Anfang rapped out . . . Frieda felt as though her brain were rattling in her skull like a nut inside its shell . . . She had no idea what to say. "Why, exactly?" she finally managed to ask.
>
> "You're shocked, aren't you?" Anfang demanded. "I was reading, and the New Testament attracted me. There I found an answer to all my questions."
>
> "What does it say that cannot be found in our own sacred books?"
>
> "I don't know. But at least there is no brutality, and no animal sacrifice."
>
> Frieda's eyes filled with tears. "Perhaps not, but the Nazis exterminated six million Jews and the Christians were silent. The murderers carried out the slaughter and the priests looked on."
>
> "Those were not the true Christians."
>
> "Who exactly are the true Christians?"
>
> "We Jews."
>
> "Why should we call ourselves Christians? God isn't three persons and has no son."
>
> "It's all symbolism."
>
> "The Inquisition was no symbol."
>
> Anfang did not answer. Frieda looked at him. Through her tears his face seemed blurred, distorted, shapeless. He smiled weirdly. Frieda wiped her eyes. God in heaven, have compassion upon him, she prayed to herself. This poor man is in great anguish. (pp. 553–536)

AGAINST BREAKDOWNS IN COMMUNICATION

> Could a greater miracle take place than for us to look through each other's eyes for an instant? . . . I know of no reading of another's experience so startling and informing as this would be.
> —Henry David Thoreau (1854/1996, p, 13),
> *Walden*

> They presuppose their neighbor's bad disposition and their own good disposition. This presupposition, however, is inhumane, as bad as war and worse. At bottom, indeed, it is itself the challenge and the cause of wars, because . . . it attributes immorality to the neighbor and thus provokes a hostile disposition and act.
> —Friedrich Nietzsche (in Kaufman, 1954, p. 72),
> *The Wanderer and His Shadow*

> It is a state composed of the recognition of another, a fellow human being like one's self; of identification of one's self with the pain or joy of the other; of guilt, pity, and the awareness that we all stand on the base of a common humanity.
> —Rollo May (1969, p. 289),
> *Love and Will*

And, so, we begin to understand why so much is made, for example, in Eastern traditions about mindful thought and action yet without excessive attachment to results. It is interesting to note that Kafka (whose literature of menace, even torture, is now revered as starkly prophetic of our modern condition and globe) bore himself with remarkable gentility in his professional life as an attorney, once even going so far as to refer a man who had been wronged by a company for whom Kafka was to provide legal counsel to a prosecutor he knew would defeat him. Needless to say, this was done without self-aggrandizement, nor did photo opportunities or press conferences ensue.

THOUGHTS THAT COME ON DOVES' FEET GUIDE THE WORLD

One of the more heartrending considerations of humanity's dark side that I have encountered during my own finite sojourn on Pozzo's "bitch of an earth" has been engendered by my relationship with my patient Kristina, a dissociative identity. Early in our work together, "the Unseen"—a mysterious chorus of poetic voices within—sent me an epigrammatic poem entitled, simply, "God," echoing Kristina's childhood conjecture that God, who must surely have witnessed the torture inflicted on her, had wanted to help yet was not, apparently, powerful enough to do so:

> if there is a god
> maybe even he is
> so high
> he cannot see clearly
>   the unseen

One day Cara, Kristina's "inner guide," forwards a written dialogue she had completed during the course of a counseling session with her pastor. The cruelty of the normative world and the insufferable pain of her own daily existence have conspired to press her to the edge of suicide. We note that writing, rather than speech, has always been Kristina's preferred method of communication on matters of substance and gravity:

> Doctor,
> I send these session notes along to you because in some ways they remind me of how you and I so often spoke those first years in your office, when I felt separation from all that was around me yet a strange sense of peace about the entire thing. Knowing I wasn't quite right but knowing also that normality was a societal notion. And here we find ourselves once again. Today we mostly wrote to Pastor William and sometimes spoke. This time we said exactly what it was I was thinking despite the puzzled looks. And it's funny because I felt peace, as if I were being real for a moment in time. I made sense to myself at least. It was the first time in a long time. I know no one could tell me I was wrong because we're not.
>
> Some of this is very choppy because William is asking me questions or talking in between what I am writing. I will try to fill in his words for clarity . . .
>
> I want to leave the world. Inside I can cut myself to pieces. If we want we can kill ourselves a million times a day and it doesn't bother anyone.
>
> (He asks me what that imagining does for me.)
>
> Let's me be OK for a while. I'm not cutting on the outside where I get in trouble for it. So I'm OK for a while. Nobody can take that from us.
>
> (He asks again for me to clarify what it does for us.)
>
> It makes things feel less out of control. I want to live inside again. It's the only place we fit.
>
> (He wants us to try to live outside.)
>
> I tried.
>
> (He asks if it works at all.)

For a short space. It's not worth it though, not one part anymore.

(He tries to tell us that it is worth it.)

How can you define my universe? How can you tell me what is my truth? I just told you my truth and you disagree with me. How can you do that?

(He says he sees hope.)

Is it possible you are seeing what you need to see? Hope that we'll fit in someplace in your world.

(He says there must be hope.)

I've looked for it. We've tried to build it ourselves or take it from others. But it doesn't work in the end because it's fake.

(He can't believe our hope is fake.)

Hope is like a costume I put on for a play I really don't want to act in.

(He disagrees.)

You have to disagree with us because it's your role in the play. We want to kill ourselves. So we do that inside. What's so wrong with this? It works.

(He asks who told us this.)

God is more perfect inside. We can communicate better there. I'm OK just with him and myself. He says don't do what you hate, being part of a world that never worked for me.

(He says God makes the world work.)

God doesn't make the world work. People do. I can't though. I never have. With other people sometimes I'm not working well. That makes me unhappy.

(He says it doesn't have to be that way.)

You say "have to" or "not have to" when it just "is." You might not understand what I'm saying. I'm saying that when I'm with someone I get along with there's always a part of me that hates it. And I'm so unhappy with that part. Because I know I'm just pretending to get along well. Inside I'm saying, "What am I doing here? What is supposed to happen now?" I'm just confused all the time. And that hurts me. I just want to stop trying to make it work if it's so much trouble. Why can't I find someone who sees it my way and says, "Yeah, get out of here!" God sees my pain. He would want it to go away.

A poignant reverie on the darkness of the world and what Beckett (1931) had called the "suffering of being." Do you understand this? Can you see?

A CHORUS OF WISDOM TEACHERS
ON CHARACTER AND ETHICS

The child is an ever-attentive witness of grown-up morality—or lack thereof; the child looks and looks for cues as to how one ought to behave, and finds them galore as we parents and teachers go about our lives . . . showing in action our rock-bottom assumptions, desires, and values, and thereby telling those observers much more than we may realize.

—Robert Coles (1997, p. 5),
The Moral Intelligence of Children

"Most men are not wicked," said Kafka . . . "Men become bad because they speak and act without foreseeing the results of their words and their deeds. They are sleepwalkers, not evildoers."

—Gustav Janouch (1971, pp. 97–98),
Conversations with Kafka

Compassion is . . . that form of love . . . based on our knowing and our understanding each other . . . It is the awareness that we are all in the same boat and that we shall sink or swim together.

—Rollo May (1972, p. 251),
Power and Innocence

TEN COMMANDMENTS IN DOWNTOWN WARSAW

The Polish directors Krzysztof Kieslowski's most sublime work, arguably, is *The Decalogue* (1987), a series of 10 one-hour films originally made for Polish television, each corresponding loosely to one of the Ten Commandments. It is taken by students of film to be one of the masterpieces of world cinema, an illumined and chastened work. All of the episodes are shot in and around a single apartment complex, one of the more fashionable in Warsaw yet simple, even austere, by Western sensibilities and tastes. As we watch, we become increasingly aware of an eerie interplay of persons and events, protagonists in one film making fleeting appearances in some of the others—a "poetic universe of convergences." A man appears in all but one of the films, remaining always silent yet functioning as a witness of sorts who vigilantly observes all that occurs while influencing nothing at all. "His intense stare," Kieslowski (in Insdorf, 1999, p. 73) had said, "engenders self-examination." He is, perhaps, our collective sense of conscience, the "still small voice" quietly exhorting inward Kafkan trial, truer *jihad*.

As with Kafka (who Kieslowski revered) or Beckett or Fromm-Reichmann, we find here no grandiloquence or unified theory but, rather, steadfast awareness and cautious comportment—attributes premised on an awareness of the ubiquity of suffering in its endless variations and with its myriad concomitants, its defensive flights into would-be safety all too frequently at others' unsuspecting expense. The filmmaker (in Insdorf, 1999, p. 124) summarizes succinctly with a message befitting a Buddha: "If I had to formulate the message of my *Decalogue*, I'd say, 'Live carefully, with your eyes open, and try not to cause pain.'"

INNER VOICES

Only days after the September 11, 2001, destruction of the World Trade Center, Cara forwards a brief personal reflection written more for her own benefit, and mine, than as an attempt to engage a new arrival known only as the girl who whispers. The Whisperer, however, "hears" Cara writing or thinking from across intrapsychic walls or divides and promptly responds. Cara signs her initial remark; thereafter, the two voices alternate:

> Really difficult day. I'm so emotional. I can't think straight. There's a stabbing pain and I just can't focus. I'm probably distracted about all that is happening.
>   Cara
>
> I hear your world is so afraid.
>
> I see you want to talk again. Whose world? My world or the outside world?
>
> Maybe both.
>
> You're right. Much of the world is afraid, especially right now.
>
> Why?
>
> You want their answer or mine? They'd say because terrorists are trying to take away their freedoms. They're afraid that life won't be back to the way they knew it. I think that most people are really afraid of looking too deeply at themselves or even their world. They are also afraid of death. They are afraid of unknowns.
>
> Why?
>
> Because it's uncertainty. Most people cannot live with not knowing what is going to happen next. Life is very structured. We make meaning for ourselves even if it has no inherent meaning. Which is why most people cling to ideology, religion, politics, theories or systems.

Know that this is not simply madness. Do you understand this? Can you see?

INNOCENCE AS A BLINDER

On yet another evening in Tiburon that summer, a young woman who worked with me at a state prison some distance inland from the Bay Area where we studied and met, presented on *Power and Innocence,* May's (1972) inquiry into the roots of violence written, significantly, in response to the Vietnam War. Seminars would begin with the presenter commenting on the text she or he had been assigned, followed by Rollo's personal reflections and, finally, an opening up of the discussion to the larger group. The woman kept returning in her remarks to the inmate who administered the therapy wing at the prison, an infamous serial killer whose story remains, even now, widely known. She seemed to take odd delight in relating the gruesome details of this man's bloodcurdling acts and violent past, sharing macabre and graphic details of the many murders he had perpetrated and displaying proudly a gift he had given her.

May listened with interest. When the woman had finished, he commented, "Well, these are certainly gruesome things that this man has done. They send chills up and down our spines"; he paused and continued: "But I would say that each one of us is capable of doing such things." The wise sage looked at the young woman before him as she stared, dumbfounded, back in turn. He had caught her—indeed, perhaps all of us—completely off-guard. "You don't know what I am talking about, do you?" he inquired. "I will tell you what I mean. I have three children who I love very much, but sometimes I have dreams about murdering them." He did not elaborate at all, but this, nonetheless, is what one of our greatest humanists said.

In the book we discussed that night, one finds a chapter entitled "Innocence and Murder." May there reflected on Melville's Billy Budd and his "tragic flaw." "Innocence," he wrote with keen insight, "acts as a blinder," curtailing attunement with both humankind's "sufferings" and its "joys" (May, 1971, p. 210).

THREE OR FOUR PHILOSOPHERS
ON MADNESS AND NORMALCY

The evil that is in the world always comes of ignorance . . . . On the whole, men are more good than bad . . . . But they are more or less ignorant . . . the most incorrigible vice being that of an ignorance that fancies it knows everything . . . .There can be no goodness nor true love without the utmost clear-sightedness.

—Albert Camus (1948, p. 131)

No, the goal of humanity cannot lie in its end but only in its highest specimens.

—Friedrich Nietzsche (in Hollingdale, 1999, p. 102)

If we had to offer the briefest explanation of all the evil that men have wreaked upon themselves and upon their world . . . it would not be in terms of man's animal heredity, his instincts and his evolution: it would be simply in the toll that his pretense of sanity takes as he tries to deny his true condition.

—Ernest Becker (1973, pp. 29–30),
The Denial of Death

Do you see, then, why Nietzsche was determined to get beyond facile yet fatuous distinctions of "good" and "evil" and on to the work of inquiring more deeply into things? And why he railed against a psychology founded on expedience and error? "No longer 'cause and effect,'" he opined, "but the continually creative" (Hollingdale, 1999, p. 225).

PROFESSIONAL CONSCIENCE AND THE STILL SMALL VOICE

It is interesting to note that our sister professional organizations did not become entangled in the same way as ours in our nation's recent mishandling of Islamic detainees in Guantanamo Bay. Colleagues in related disciplines, nonetheless, are by no means immune to the need for ongoing scrutiny in matters of ethics closer to home. I suggest to Kristina that she share an excerpt from her journal so that a conventional yet hardly malevolent psychiatrist might be moved to consider, a little more earnestly, the depths of the young woman before him. Kristina responds with indignation and panache:

> You do not understand our relationship with Dr. K if you think I would even bother sharing with him any of my inner thoughts. I feel now that if I can make it through a session where he has not literally nodded off, I have made progress. What good is it to share yourself with that kind of person? He wouldn't have any clue of my depths. And while one supposes that a person in his profession would seek to know such things, quite the opposite is true. In fact, it is more a reality rampant among mental health professionals than someone with your sensitivities could possibly know. If the person is searching, you are delighted to help. In most cases the doctor would rather the patient not be searching so much as obeying orders and ground rules and taking their properly dosed medications.
>
> I have made these efforts with Dr K. I can describe it as trying to reach out and touch him, to see if he is real, to see if I am real when I am with him. I have no proof from him that I even exist. I have made efforts and have been thwarted at every turn. And I think, why is someone like me,

who craves (all the while being punished by the very desire for) relationships, so often rejected? I have been hurt so much by people who seem at first to offer a relationship and then at a moment's notice pull it away, like ripping a bandage off a healing wound. I figure it is because they do not have a relationship with themselves and can only go so far in having one with me. I have learned not to try to touch people. I have learned not to desire a sense of realness when I am around them. Unfortunately, Dr. K is one of these people.

And, indeed, the divide that remains between need and reality—Nietzsche's (in Hollingdale, 1999, p. 188) "pathos of nobility and distance"—is too great to fathom or ignore. ("A breakdown of communication," observes Dick, "there is the real illness.") We can be thankful, at least, that Kristina is so expressive in her remarks, though this can hardly obscure the fact that there are innumerable patients out there who, not so eloquent or aware, crave also a kind of genuine encounter that they are neither able to articulate nor, quite possibly, even recall if in fact they ever knew it at all. Professions and their minions get lost as people do. There is no code of ethics that can ever spell things out or summarily settle accounts. Therein patients like us must minister to ourselves.

ATONEMENT AND HIGH ASCENT

On a recent early autumn afternoon, only days after the Jewish Day of Atonement (a day of judgment no less than dress rehearsal for one thought by some to lie beyond), Kristina, who—now married with children and living far from here—grew up nearby in a wildly torturous, self-righteous, and fundamentalist home, paid me a visit. It was the first time we had seen each other in some years. Later that evening, she sent a message to her present psychotherapist:

> Saw Dr. Mendelowitz today. I haven't seen him in very long time. It was good to see him again. Made me sad, maybe. He saved my life when I was eighteen. Picked me up out of a ditch where people who didn't believe in me had thrown me. We dusted off the dirt, got through some bad times and had a lot of good moments. No one ever listened to me before that. No one believed. If I hadn't "found" him, I do not know what I'd be doing now and where I'd be. Not that I've "found myself," but he was a map and I was an arrow. And he was the first person to tell me that I could go anywhere I wanted.

Ditches, we may recall, are the places where those ramshackle characters out of Beckett are, when they are not bound to their writing tables, most apt to be found. It goes without saying that they did not simply slip. Deborah too, speaking on behalf of the world's casualties, writes, gravely, of "the oiling of the ancient wheels on which [we are] broken" (in Green, 1964, p. 181). This is by no means merely the madness of inmates.

We are, then, really meditating upon character after all, upon its myriad and often tortuous pathways on the way to what we might call awareness of self, world, and other as a pervasive and never-ending moral endeavor. It is instructive to note that the devil plays no significant part in the Hebrew bible and that a Satan there connotes a kind of provocateur or irritant, someone who crosses one's path unexpectedly and may well, if courageously met, effect salutary change. It may well be the simple things—listening more carefully, caring more deeply, attending more authentically the pause between stimulus and response wherein one may find the courage to say, more resolutely, "yes" or "no"—that are requisite to forestall complicity in the malfeasance of an often insensible world. At every point in our reverie upon humanity's dark side we turn insistently back upon ourselves: our shortcomings and exemplars, our failures and ideals, our inmost preoccupations and themes. By their fruits we shall know them, indeed.

There is a legend that when the Jews were sent into exile, the Shekina, the divine indwelling feminine essence, was exiled as well, hovering about and awaiting patiently invitation to return. Teshuvah, taken especially to heart during the Day of Atonement, connotes repentance, return, and high ascent. No one writes about such hallowed themes with greater obeisance and eloquence than Kafka. Let us close, reverently, then, with what we may take to be his, yes, essentially Hebraic sacred code:

> The way is infinitely long, nothing of it can be subtracted, nothing can be added, and yet everyone applies his own childish yardstick to it. "Certainly, this yard of the way you still have to go, too, and it will be accounted onto you."
>
> It is only our conception of time that makes us call the Last Judgment by this name. It is, in fact, a kind of summary court in perpetual session.
>
> —Franz Kafka (1954/1991, p. 27),
> *Third Blue Octavo Notebook*

It is a sobering, exhilarating, and devastating insight all at once: a lifetime spent in learning how to be human. Do you understand this? Can you see?

REFERENCES

Ackerley. C. J. & Gontarski, S. E., (2004). *The Grove companion to Samuel Beckett: A reader's guide to his works, life, and thought.* New York, NY: Grove Press.

Afterman, A. (1992). *Kabbalah and consciousness.* Riverdale-on-Hudson, NY: Sheep Meadow Press.

Becker, E. (1973). *The denial of death*. New York, NY: Free Press.

Beckett, S. (1931). *Proust*. New York, NY: Grove Press.

Beckett, S. (1953). *Watt*. New York, NY: Grove Press.

Beckett, S. (1954). *Waiting for Godot: A tragicomedy in two acts*. New York, NY: Grove Press.

Beckett, S. (1957). *Murphy*. New York, NY: Grove Press.

Beckett. S. (1972). *More pricks than kicks*. New York, NY: Grove Press. (Original work published 1934)

Camus, A. (1948). *The plague* (S. Gilbert, Trans.). New York, NY: Knopf.

Coles, R. (1995). *The mind's fate* (2nd ed.). Boston, MA: Little, Brown.

Coles, R. (1997). *The moral intelligence of children*. New York, NY: Random House.

Green, H. (1964). *I never promised you a rose garden*. New York, NY: Holt.

Hollingdale, R. J. (1999). *Nietzsche: Man and philosopher* (Rev. ed.). Cambridge, England: Cambridge University Press.

Hrabal, B. (1990). *Too loud a solitude* (M. H. Heim, Trans.). Orlando, FL: Harcourt Brace Jovanovich.

Insdorf, A. (1999). *Double lives, second chances: The cinema of Krzyzstof Kieslowski*. New York, NY: Hyperion.

Kafka, F. (1991). *The blue octavo notebooks* (E. Kaiser & E. Wilkins, Trans.). Cambridge, England: Exact Change. (Original work published 1954)

Kaufmann, W. (Trans. & Ed.). (1954). *The portable Nietzsche*. New York, NY: Viking Press.

Kieslowski, K. (Writer & Director), & Piesiewicz, K. (Writer). (1987). *The Decalogue*. Poland: Ryszard Chutkowski/Polish Television.

Kundera, M. (1986). *The art of the novel* (L. Asher, Trans.). New York, NY: Harper & Row.

Janouch, G. (1971). *Conversations with Kafka* (G. Rees, trans.) New York, NY: New Directions Books.

May, R. (1969). *Love and will*, New York, NY: Norton.

May, R. (1972). *Power and innocence*. New York, NY: Norton.

Mendelowitz, E. (2008). *Ethics and Lao-tzu*. Colorado Springs, CO: University of the Rockies Press.

Ronsley, J. (Ed.) (1977). *Myth and reality in Irish literature*. Waterloo, Ontario, Canada: Wilfrid Laurier University Press.

Singer, I. B. (1998). *Shadows on the Hudson*. New York, NY: Farrar, Straus, & Giroux. (Original work published 1957)

Sukin, L. (Ed.) (1995). *The shifting realities of Philip K. Dick: Selected literary and philosophical writings*. New York, NY: Vintage Books.

Thoreau, H. D. (1996). *Walden*. Cologne, Germany: Konemann. (Original work published 1854)

6

EVIL: AN EXPERIENTIAL CONSTRUCTIVIST UNDERSTANDING

LARRY M. LEITNER

Experiential personal construct psychology (Leitner, 1988) is a theoretical elaboration of George Kelly's (1955) personal construct theory approach to clinical psychology. This elaboration entails an understanding of the central importance of human connection in living a life that is rich and meaningful. Experiential personal construct psychology has been used to understand the experience and treatment of severe disturbances (Leitner & Celentana, 1997; Leitner, Faidley, & Celentana, 2000), symbolism in psychotherapy (Faidley & Leitner, 2000), resistance in constructivist therapy (Leitner & Dill-Standiford, 1993), constructivist notions of the unconscious (Leitner, 1999), creativity in psychotherapy (Domenici & Leitner, 2001; Leitner, 2001; Leitner & Faidley, 1999), among many other clinical phenomena. In this chapter, I address the reasons people commit horrendous acts and the treatment

I have changed names and other details to protect the identities of clients in all clinical material. An earlier version of this paper was presented as the Keynote Address at the 14th Australasian Personal Construct Conference, Wollongong, NSW, Australia, October, 2010. I would like to thank April Faidley for constructive comments on an earlier version of this paper.

DOI: 10.1037/13941-006
Humanity's Dark Side: Evil, Destructive Experience, and Psychotherapy, A. C. Bohart, B. S. Held, E. Mendelowitz, and K. J. Schneider (Editors)

implications of experiential personal construct psychology's position on "evil." To provide a context, I begin with an overview of experiential constructivism.

EXPERIENTIAL CONSTRUCTIVISM

Experiential personal construct psychology holds that the world becomes rich and meaningful for us to the extent we have invested deeply in relationships. We term such relationships *ROLE relationships* (Leitner, 1985; Leitner & Faidley, 1995), with ROLE in all caps to distinguish Kelly's definition of *role* from the more typical one. We invest deeply in others by exposing our most central ways of being to them as they expose their most central constructions to us. The mutual affirmation associated with such connections leads to the experience of wonder and richness in the world (Leitner & Faidley, 1995). However, others may not affirm us. Rather, they may take our most central ways of being and treat them callously and harshly. The fact that I can offer you *who I am,* my heart, my soul, and have you crush me makes ROLE relationships potentially terrifying. Thus, each of us weaves a path between deeply connecting with others (with attendant possibilities for richness and meaningfulness) and terror and consequent retreat from connection (with attendant possibilities for safety as well as meaninglessness and dread). Symptoms often are communications about our struggles with this dilemma. Experiential personal construct psychotherapy helps the client explore his or her relational choices and experiences and possibly decide again to risk connection or to extricate himself or herself from injurious connections.

Thus, experiential personal construct psychology explicitly is a relational theory of person. Inherently, we are relationship seeking; absent interconnection, life is empty and devoid of meaning. That being the case, the following questions ensue: How does experiential personal construct psychology explain our seemingly endless capacity to engage in inhumane acts against others? How would an experiential constructivist therapist engage someone who has committed such acts? Are there people who systematically engage in such acts to the extent that they might justifiably be called "evil"? This chapter represents my initial attempts to address these issues. To do that, I discuss issues of interpersonal injuries and structural arrest within experiential personal construct psychology.

DEVELOPMENTAL INJURIES AND STRUCTURAL ARRESTS

From an experiential constructivist perspective, we are born relationship seeking and meaning making. Not surprisingly, most of our early meanings come from interactions with our family and caregivers. These are the people we are close to and connected with from the moment we enter the world. Because they are among the first meanings we create, many of the meanings we form in our interactions with these others become the foundations of our personalities. They are the bedrocks upon which all subsequent meanings are built. If we suffer relational injuries early in our development, we can become psychologically wounded for the rest of our lives.

Leitner et al. (2000) discussed how these early relational injuries can freeze meaning making. Kelly (1955) used the term *suspension* to describe the process of holding in abeyance events that are too threatening to construe. Given that the meanings we develop in early childhood tend to be concrete and specific, they can be more easily disconfirmed (see Bannister & Agnew, 1977; Barratt, 1977; Klion & Leitner, 1985). These suspended events, then, lie at a low level of awareness, only vaguely or emotionally construed, yet still influencing our experience of the world. When this happens, the person cannot advance past a more simplistic and problematic way of construing the world. We called this early freezing *structural arrest* and detailed two types of structural arrests: *self–other permanence* and *self–other constancy*.

Self–other permanence, similar to object permanence, is the first developmental milestone leading to our ability to develop ROLE relationships. Self–other permanence is the ability to hold onto the reality of the other's presence over time. People deeply wounded early in life often do not have a sense of self–other permanence. If I have no sense of your permanence, you literally cease to exist when I am out of contact with you, making the long-term commitments necessary for relational intimacy impossible. Similarly, if I do not have a sense of my existence separate from yours, I cannot commit to intimacy. I cannot empathically resonate with the other's experience without losing myself as a separate person.

The next developmental challenge is self–other constancy. Self–other constancy is being able to integrate new experiences of self and other into a multidimensional understanding of persons. If I lack constancy, when I see you as nurturing, for example, I experience you as warm and wonderful and feel connected to you; when I see you as angry, I lose touch with your nurturing and experience you as dangerous and threatening. People who are traumatized a bit later in childhood often struggle with self–other constancy. Due to these early injuries, individuals can reach adulthood without the capacity to integrate all facets of an other into one coherent person. You can see here the experiential origins of idealization and devaluation. When all is well between us, I perceive you as wonderful without qualification. As soon as something is amiss between us, that positive construction disappears completely. Without being able to hold positive and negative construals simultaneously, a person cannot modify ecstatic love to stable, abiding love or transform rage to a milder anger or irritation.

When we experience either of these structural arrests (i.e., not developing self–other permanence or self–other constancy), our subjective growth occurs under the shadow of this limitation. In essence, meaning making, which in healthy persons should be characterized by multiplicity and complexity, can be frozen or severely limited, and subsequent development is stunted or misshapen. Thus, infants and children who are relationally injured as they are acquiring these concepts grow up to struggle in many ways. For example, psychotic symptoms may be one manifestation of a failure to develop self–other permanence. If neither I nor others have a permanence I can depend upon, my experiences and my sense of self may fracture into disconnected segments. Hallucinations can come and go randomly, not tightly connected to outside events. At one moment, the voice is present; at another, it is gone. At one moment, the voice is a male authority figure; at another, a passive whining female; at another, God. Similarly, many more "normal" or "neurotic" symptoms can be seen as struggles with self–other constancy. For example, depressive symptoms such as the depths of helplessness, hopelessness, and worthlessness may arise from criticism, rejection, or invalidation from another, which depressed persons are unable to mitigate with the supportive, positive interactions that have come their way at other times and from other persons.

In some ways, this conceptualization is overly simplistic, too black and white. It is true that some people are so severely mistreated and so badly injured that they are completely arrested in one of these early phases. However, it is probably safe to say that no person has received perfect relational nurturance in life. In other words, all of us have tendencies, strong or weak, toward such developmental arrests and their subsequent manifestation in our behaviors, thoughts, and feelings. Thus, each of us has a history of relational injuries and invalidations that leads us to experience some aspects of life from a position of structural arrest. I now turn to some of the ways in which these early relational injuries are manifested in adult life and to tying them more systematically to what is construed as evil.

ADULT MANIFESTATIONS OF INJURY

In this section, I discuss four particular manifestations of arrest that seem to be closely linked to the capacity to act inhumanely toward our fellow persons. These are, from my perspective, necessary conditions for the perpetration of acts of evil.

Objectification of Others

ROLE relationships by definition involve our being able to understand the innermost experiences of others. I cannot invest deeply in a reciprocal relationship with you unless I come to know your most central ways of being. Such knowing is absolutely essential in ROLE relationships (Leitner & Faidley, 1995). Early injuries that interfere with our ability to form ROLE relationships also limit our capacity to see the other as a subjective, meaning-making being. The objectification of the other, then, is one of the hallmarks of someone who has been deeply wounded and has globally retreated from ROLE relationships.

Objectification of others has a long history of association with what we may call "persons' inhumanity to persons." Robert J. Lifton is one of the great writers and theoreticians about some of the horrific acts of the 20th century. In an analysis of the genocide perpetrated by Nazi doctors in World War II, Lifton (1986) asserted that when people are put into a death-dominated environment, they *must* objectify the other so that they can disavow what the other does. When we objectify the other, we are not affected by his or her suffering (Hirigoyen, 2000). When the other is not a person, he or she does not have feelings, families, or friends. Furthermore, as a nonperson, the other is not entitled to basic human rights. Thus, a Nazi doctor could work in a death camp by day and still be a loving parent and spouse at night. The doctor dealt with "things" during the day and went home to "people."

Hirigoyen (2000) offered a profound portrait of systematic emotional abuse that easily could qualify as torture. In her discussion, she says, "One sees in abusers wild infatuations followed by brutal and irreparable rejection. People around them don't understand how someone can fall from grace in the blink of an eye for no apparent reason" (p. 132). I emphasize these points for two reasons. First, I think the extent of objectification can be seen. The other is not a person with strengths and weaknesses, desires and fears, frailties and virtues. Rather, the other is in total an object of infatuation or irreparable rejection. Second, I believe that the sudden shift of the other between these two poles is a beautiful illustration of a structural arrest. Something happens so minor that one person does not even notice, and in the eyes of the other, she is completely transformed from wonderful and cherished to worthless and rejected. In summary, objectification of the other can be a consequence of early injury and structural arrest; it also can lead to the ability to engage in violent acts toward others.

Denying Connectedness

With regard to the objectification of others, people who are struggling with ROLE relationships are not likely to experience a sense of connection with others. Again, the lack of experience of connection can be seen as a definition of the lack of ROLE relationship. People are more prone to perpetrate appalling acts toward others when they have little sense of connection.

When I experience a connection to you, you—in some ways—become a part of me. Therefore, I feel your feelings and the perpetration of deplorable acts toward you becomes inconceivable to me. By way of contrast, I only can engage in deeply wounding acts when I do not experience us as connected to one another.

Many thinkers have argued a similar point. Parker (1991), for example, described our destructiveness in terms of our wounded capacity to feel our connectedness to others and to the world, as well as to our diminished sensibility to the real presence of the other. He goes on to emphasize that if one is keenly aware of the real presence of another person, one is incapable of being destructive toward that person. Similarly, Hirigoyen (2000) showed how abusiveness arises from a "dispassionate rationality" (p. 7) combined with an incapacity to respect others as human beings. Lifton and Markusen (1990) described extraordinary evil in terms of "normal" psychic mechanisms like splitting, dissociation, or psychic numbing, all of which blunt affect, including the feeling of connection to others.

Numbing of Inner Experience

In this section, I look at the ways that when we numb our inner experience in general, we are more prone to perpetrate abhorrent acts. Experiential personal construct psychology holds that we are interconnected beings. In a ROLE relationship I extend myself, as an experiencing being, into your subjectivity. As a matter of fact, experiential constructivism holds that it is the very experience of extending myself into your subjectivity that makes me most alive. Thus, if I stop experiencing the other's distress, I simultaneously numb my own sense of subjective aliveness.

Given what we have said about the ways that objectifying others leads to the perpetuation of abhorrent acts, perpetrators have shut off access to their own experience. In essence, if I had a well-developed sense of subjective aliveness, I would be able to feel inside of me the pain I am causing you. Consider, for example, Hirigoyen's (2000) comment about the "dispassionate rationality" (p. 7) associated with systematic abuse in relationships. Certainly, "dispassionate rationality" does not describe a subjective experience of aliveness. Furthermore, the blunting of affect that Lifton and Markusen (1990) described involves not only affect toward others but also feelings about the self.

Inability to Introspect

ROLE relationships place demands on those who engage in them. One such demand is the struggle with responsibility (Leitner & Pfenninger, 1994).

Experiential personal construct psychology defines *responsibility* as being able to examine one's meaning-making system in terms of its implications for others. Such self-examination requires the ability to introspect. When someone has been injured early in life and struggles with ROLE relationships, the ability to introspect can be compromised.

Introspection can lead to guilt if I become aware of the ways in which my style of relating has been injuring to people I care for. Peck (1983), for example, argued that what made someone evil was not that they were sinful but that they could not acknowledge their sinfulness due to an "unwillingness to suffer the discomfort of significant self-examination" (p. 72; see also Klose, 1995). In other words, the inability or unwillingness to introspect can be tied to the perpetration of evil acts. Even relatively "normal" lack of introspection could put one at risk for unwittingly committing acts that seriously injure others. Furthermore, Lifton and Markusen's (1990) view that mechanisms such as dissociation and psychic numbing can lead to evil acts is related to the impact of these mechanisms on blocking introspection.

Other scholars have made a similar argument. Miller (1990) stated that an inability to introspect occurs when we are injured early in life. As I do, Miller believed that every person who engages in horrible acts was originally an innocent victim. Furthermore, Miller believed that if we repress the traumas affecting us, we wind up with little capacity for empathy and are trapped in a rigid unawareness of deep feelings. In other words, we have to be able to look openly at our own woundedness to disallow our early injuries from leading us to being perpetrators of deplorable acts against others. Miller argued that when we are utterly dependent on the person who has wounded us and this wounding person refuses to acknowledge his or her actions, we wind up repressing and, therefore, become prone to wounding others in turn.

The Net Result

In summary, experiential personal construct psychology holds that all people are born relationship seeking. Early injuries lead some people to freeze the process of meaning making at a very basic level. This developmental arrest can manifest itself in adulthood in many ways, including the experience of traditional symptoms of psychopathology. However, when it manifests itself through the four interconnected styles of objectifying others, denying our connectedness, numbing of experience, and the inability to introspect, we have the groundwork for a person who can commit acts of incredible destructiveness.

At this point, we can formally propose an experiential constructivist definition of evil: *Evil* is the perpetration of acts, out of our own woundedness, that injure the meaning-making process of the other. Because the other's process of meaning making is the very definition of life within experiential personal construct psychology, we are talking about acts that injure our subjective sense of aliveness. In other words, due to how our injuries have affected us, we wind up committing acts that devastate others. While this definition may seem very broad, we have chosen it to cover acts that range from the taking of lives to the psychological destruction of others.

TOWARD A BROADER UNDERSTANDING OF EVIL

Early injuries can lead people to engage in acts with terrible consequences. However, no person has parental figures who are 100% nurturing and affirming; all of us experience some early injuries, large or small. Thus, all of us have within us the ability to perform acts that injure others. In a similar vein, Klose (1995) suggested that none of us is ever totally free from some amount of self-deception. Therefore, we must engage in an inner dialogue in regard to our own capacities for evil. Katz (1993) made a similar point when he argued that we become comfortably misguided when we focus on extraordinary examples of evil such as the Holocaust. As we do that, we overlook the extent to which "ordinary sorts of people, using ordinary behavior, have contributed to extraordinary evil" (Katz, 1993, p. 138). Similarly, Kelly (1955) stated,

> People are threatened by 'evildoers.' . . . The 'evildoer' exemplifies what we might do if we dared, or what we might be if we behaved childishly, or what we would have been if we had not tried so hard to do better. (p. 505)

In this section, I focus on two aspects of this broader understanding of evil: the ways we all perpetrate appalling acts on others and the ways we perpetrate atrocious acts on the more-than-human world.

Evil Toward Others

All of us have our areas of blindness and limitations on our ability to reflect upon who we are. All of us have behaved in ways that have seriously injured others. (Please note that in all of the clinical examples in this chapter, I am referring here to what we might call "evil acts"; I am not saying the people who commit these acts are "evil.") Consider this example: Alexander had struggled with his attraction toward men for many years. He insisted that it was "all psychological" and that if he could gain insight into the roots of the attraction, he would be 100% heterosexual. Once, while out of town, he went to a location where gay men congregate. While engaged in a homosexual act, he was arrested by the police. When his behavior at the park became public, his wife and children felt extremely betrayed. His wife filed for divorce and subsequently struggled mightily with the issue of trusting any other man. His children, wondering in what other ways their father had misled them, began to act out at school. Thus, Alexander's unwillingness to seriously consider what his attraction meant led to people he cared for being badly injured.

The fact that we, like Alexander, unintentionally engage in actions that injure others in no way excuses us from the hard work of taking responsibility for them. I would argue that when we engage in an act that seriously injures a person to whom we are connected, we have to assume the responsibility of carefully and openly examining our meaning-making system. In so doing, we might be able to minimize the likelihood that we injure another person in such a way again. Should we fail to engage in the difficult and painful work of self-examination, we run the risk of continuing to commit injuring acts.

You can see this risk being played out currently in the mental health professions. There are clear data showing that the public has been misled with regard to both the safety and the efficacy of our biomedical treatments of psychopathology. The use of many of these treatments has been shown to have, at best, a short-term ameliorative effect on symptoms followed by a worsening of symptoms over time. They also are frequently associated with intolerable, brain-damaging "side effects." Furthermore, they often produce a situation where the withdrawal from the drugs actually causes the very disorder they were being used to treat. (See Whitaker, 2010, for a thorough discussion of these issues.) It is well documented that someone diagnosed with schizophrenia in a Western country has a worse prognosis than someone receiving the diagnosis in an undeveloped country. Furthermore, the pills we use to treat the "disease" result in the Western "schizophrenic" dying 15 to 20 years earlier than a counterpart not so diagnosed (see Boyle, 2002). However, the mental health profession has not bothered to acquaint itself with the raw data about these issues. Not all mental health professionals have engaged in the self-examination necessary to explain why we allowed (or actually facilitated) the public to be so misled.

Sometimes, we perpetrate evil acts because someone threatens us. If someone represents a part of ourselves that we despise, we may attempt to injure him or her, consciously or unconsciously. For example, Sally grew up in a home where she was physically abused by her mother. She learned to be very frightened of her own needs for closeness and nurturance. When she had a daughter of her own, the daughter's needs were upsetting to her because they gave her a felt sense of her own neediness. Acknowledging the legitimacy of her daughter's needs would painfully resurrect a dim awareness of the bottomless well of her own unmet needs. She felt that she had to "toughen up" her daughter, a notion that led to abuse. Because intimacy itself can be terrifying (see Leitner & Faidley, 1995), the most intimate other may become the object of the greatest abuse, as the abuser desperately defends against terror (see Hirigoyen, 2000).

I would like to turn to another aspect of our engagement in "evil" acts. Experiential personal construct psychology holds that the universe is fundamentally interconnected. Kelly (1955), for example, once famously stated that the actions of his hands typing a manuscript in Columbus, Ohio, would affect the price of yak milk in Tibet. The notion of an interconnected universe means that I am, in some ways, connected with all humanity on the planet (see Leitner, 2010, for a thorough explication of why this is the case). In this regard, we all bear some responsibility for whatever evil is perpetrated in the world, including things such as the abuses at Abu Ghraib in Iraq. In a similar vein, Klose (1995) astutely observed that the massacre in My Lai, Vietnam, was more than an evil act committed by the soldiers. Our society sent those soldiers over to Vietnam to kill. Thus, we all bear some responsibility for the act. As I write these words, a Private Manning is being held incommunicado by the U.S. military. Private Manning's crime was informing the media about a U.S. attack in the Middle East that killed 12 innocent civilians and no terrorists. I, along with every citizen, share some responsibility for his predicament.

To minimize our culpability for things like Abu Ghraib, we have to thoughtfully and intentionally resist our natural tendency to forfeit ethical judgments to leaders (Klose, 1995). When we do that, we abdicate our bit of responsibility for the shape and direction of the world. I believe we give our leaders such ethical power because the world, with all of its interconnections, seems too complex a place for individual action. Because we do not know all of the details about events happening across the world, we naturally assume that our leaders, who are supposed to know such details, have judged issues accurately. This tendency may be why we sometimes have entire cultures engaging in horrific acts like the Holocaust. The interconnected nature of the universe implies that we have an ethical obligation to be more aware of the specifics about what is happening elsewhere, as well as an obligation to work toward social justice both at home and abroad.

Toward a More Nuanced Understanding of Evil

Kelly's (1955) concept of the interconnected universe means more than the assertion that we are connected to all of our fellow persons. It also means that we are connected to the entire planet. Our inability or unwillingness to acknowledge this connection results in our perpetrating violence upon the earth. We already are aware of the ways in which our having ignored this connection is causing issues such as global warming, the greatest mass extinction of animals since the dinosaurs, the destruction of coral reefs and the ecosystems associated with them, the depletion of fisheries around the world, and the desertification of once-productive lands. If we continue to ignore this connection, we run the risk of making life on the planet unsustainable.

How, you might be thinking, does our damaging the more-than-human world square with our definition of evil? Let us go back to the four manifestations of structural arrest that I have proposed lead to evil: objectification of the other, numbing of experience, lack of introspection, and the denial of connectedness. As we exploit the planet for our own short-term benefit, we are using the entire world as a means to our own ends, certainly an objectifying tendency. We also are not considering our connection to future generations as well as the planet at large. Furthermore, we tend to continue on blithely unaware of the ways we are damaging the planet. Because the universe is a process unfolding over time (Kelly, 1955), we can speak of actions that lead to the issues mentioned above as damaging the process of the universe. Hence, we can speak of those acts as "evil."

This position means that all of us need to spend time introspecting about why we damage the planet in the ways we do. First, we may need to heighten our own awareness that our actions do affect the interconnected universe. Second, we need to become more thoughtful about the ways our own lifestyles affect the planet. For example, do I really need a new laptop or cell phone when the exotic materials needed for these devices leads to the extinction of animals in Africa? Am I willing to be a party to such extinction to get a few milliseconds of faster speed or a bit larger hard drive? How can I, as an American, do something about the fact that I live in a country with 4% of the world's population that consumes 30% to 50% of the world's resources? These sorts of questions will raise my awareness of ways I can be less violent toward the planet.

TREATING PERPETRATORS

People who have performed appalling acts often appear in therapy. This can be a difficult situation for a therapist. We naturally tend to be more empathic toward the victims than the perpetrators of abhorrent acts. Although the basic principles of therapy do not change when dealing with these perpetrators, the principles sometimes have especially important implications for the therapist and the therapy. From an experiential constructivist perspective, the relational connection with the therapist is vital for overcoming the traumas that have led someone to negate relating to others as a survival strategy.

This position is close to the position advocated by Peck (1983). He stated that it is in the realm of the "inter-human" that genuine healing of evil can occur. The inter-human means the establishment of a person-to-person relational connection, which, of course, is the foundation of experiential personal construct psychology. The client (to say nothing of many, many psychotherapists—perhaps all of us at certain moments and times), however, will be severely limited in establishing this connection until he or she can deal with these tendencies to objectify, numb, and not introspect. The very interpersonal issues that lead to the commitment of horrible acts will interfere with the therapist establishing a ROLE relationship with the client, providing both an impediment and an opportunity for the therapist. Similarly, Miller (1990) focused on understanding the original injuries that led to the development of the client's characterological style. Miller works on helping the client forgive the person or persons who originally injured him or her because such forgiveness can help the client become free from the deadening effects of psychological numbing.

Optimal Therapeutic Distance

Optimal therapeutic distance (Leitner, 1995) is one of the hallmarks of good experiential personal construct therapy. Optimal therapeutic distance is a blending of connection with and separation from the client. Experientially, I am optimally distant when I am close enough to my client to feel what the client is experiencing inside of me yet distant enough to recognize these experiences as the client's feelings, not my own. Optimal therapeutic distance implies, therefore, that the therapist has to be able to access the parts of himself or herself that could experience the world in the same way and engage in the same actions as the client.

For example, if I am seeing someone who has been diagnosed "schizophrenic," I cannot feel what it is like to be my client without having access to the parts of me that can be so terrified, confused, overwhelmed, and alone that I, too, could have hallucinations. If I cannot go to that scared and vulnerable spot, my understanding of the client's pain is an intellectual understanding, not an emotional one. Similarly, if I am seeing someone who has committed appalling acts, I have to access the parts of me capable of engaging in such inhumanity. Viktor Frankl (1963) made a similar point at the end of his classic work, Man's Search for Meaning, when he stated that people are both so evil they can send fellow human beings into the ovens of Auschwitz and so noble that they can walk into those ovens with a prayer on their lips. All of us have the potential for acts of evil, and a therapist must find that potential within himself or herself. Obviously, this places unusual demands on the therapist. Nevertheless, a therapist who is incapable of gaining access to her or his own capacity for violent destructiveness will not be of much help to a client who has actually acted on that capacity.

Let me illustrate from a case I have used on other occasions (Leitner, 2010). Bill presented with classic posttraumatic stress disorder symptoms. He was haunted by an event in Iraq when, as the lead vehicle in a convoy, he had driven over an Iraqi child in order to protect his convoy against a possible insurgent attack. It was known that the insurgents enlisted children to delay convoys in just this way, and Bill was following specific orders to not let his soldiers be so entrapped. Bill was plagued by the implications of what he had done; it signified to him that he was capable of reprehensibly evil actions. Bill's actions also presented a special challenge for me. I could not tell him that he had orders to do such a thing or that he was doing what he thought was best to protect himself and his fellow soldiers. Bill intellectually knew those justifications; indeed, he had been told such things frequently by others to no avail. I had to find a way to resonate with his experiences such that my words could make a difference for him. Specifically, I had to find the part of me that would do such a thing and use that experience to understand Bill's. At one point, I said, with great emotion, that I could really understand why he was struggling with what he had done. I only could do that with such emotion when I had accessed my capacity for engaging in such an act. David Winter (e.g., 2007), a constructivist scholar, described being able to connect in such a way with a serial killer in the United Kingdom.

Find Woundedness

Experiential personal construct psychology holds that every person who perpetrates an evil act has wounds that led to their willingness to do so. Miller (1990) agreed by holding that every evil person was once an innocent victim. If I can look past the acts themselves and how they repulsed me to see the injured person behind the acts, I can find a greater capacity for empathy. Furthermore, accessing the client's wounds gives me the moral authority to eventually challenge my client to be something more than someone who responds out of his or her places of deepest injury.

For example, with Bill, I was able to find out about how he had lost a friend in Iraq from an improvised explosive device. I also found out that he had lost his father in a traffic accident while a child. Such injuries certainly make someone even more fearful of death than most of us. As I resonated with what it would be like to have such wounds (optimal therapeutic distance), I was able to say to Bill that being haunted by what he did had some implications about who he was as a person. Who would you rather have as a friend—someone who was haunted by such an act or someone who could run over a small child and not be haunted by it? As we explored that question, I eventually could raise the issue that one of the challenges in life is to learn to live with the parts of ourselves that have done things we are ashamed of. Was there some way that Bill could live with the parts of him that had committed this act—recognizing that he was more than just the person who committed the act?

Tendencies to Objectify, Numb, and Not Introspect

The therapist must find ways to confront the client's tendencies to objectify, numb, and not introspect. As described above, these tendencies lead to the client being able to perpetrate acts that are deeply injurious to others. Therefore, the client needs to be made aware of tendencies in these areas. The therapist can start by gently wondering what the other person must have been feeling in a given situation. The therapist also can use the therapeutic relationship to help the client learn about another's internal subjectivity in the session by having the client wonder about what the therapist feels about the topic. When the client does not know, the therapist can then wonder what it is like for the client to be in situations where he or she does not know what the other is feeling. If it is genuine, the therapist can express surprise that the client is lacking in this basic aspect of human connectedness, as such an emotional reaction from the therapist can make the void in the client's life more salient. As the client develops an understanding of the limitations this creates for effective living, the therapy can move to exploring how it came to be that the client evolved a style that stopped him or her from feeling the intersubjective experience of genuine connection. Such questions often can lead the therapist to the client's greatest wounds.

Similarly, the therapist can wonder about the lack of emotionality the client brings into the room. I have, for example, found it useful for clients who have been around very young children to contrast the spontaneous emotionality of a young child with the lack of emotionality my client shows. I then can wonder what happened to transform them from that natural spontaneity to someone to whom emotions seem forbidden. For example, Susan was referred because she had viciously abused her son. When we were discussing her lack of emotionality, we found out that when she was young, her parents ridiculed any tender and vulnerable emotions she might show. She learned not to express such emotions. The rage she felt toward her parents for this ridicule (as well as other things) was the only emotion she could experience. As we discussed these dynamics, I eventually could say to her, "Wow. It will take a great deal of courage to share tender and vulnerable emotions with me. I look forward to the time you feel ready to do that." This intervention was helpful in her reconstruing emotional pain and neediness as something that could be courageously shared in relationship, not as an invitation to be humiliated.

Likewise, the inability to introspect can be confronted. When Susan described her son's actions as indicative of his being a "snot-nosed, spoiled little kid," I asked her what her response to his actions said about her. This was followed by a stunned silence, as she had not considered the question. As we looked at why she had never considered the question, I was able to tell her that many answers to life's problems lie within us if we have the courage to explore our inner experience.

Denial of Responsibility

Tied to a lack of introspection, people who commit appalling acts often deny responsibility for the acts. As I mentioned earlier, Leitner and Pfenninger (1994) defined responsibility as the willingness to examine our meaning making in terms of its implications for others. Obviously, I cannot examine my meaning-making system if I lack the ability to introspect. Not surprisingly, then, one often sees people who commit atrocious acts denying responsibility for their behavior. A skilled therapist must find ways to help such a person begin the process of accepting responsibility for his or her behavior.

Let's consider Susan again. As she was experiencing the world at the start of therapy, her son had caused her to beat him by acting in such a "snot-nosed" manner. As we discussed this, I asked why her partner had not beaten their son. This question led to a discussion that she had a *choice* in how she responded to her son's "snot-nosed" behavior. In other words, she responded violently because of what the behavior signified to her, not because of any intrinsic characteristics of the behavior. Furthermore, if she had chosen to behave violently, she could choose other ways of being in response to his behavior.

Real Guilt

Therapy for someone who has committed horrific acts often results in the client experiencing guilt. Within constructivist psychology, *guilt* is the awareness that you are acting against your most central meanings. I am calling the guilt experienced here "real guilt" as it is something other than the sort of guilt often seen in depressed people. Rather than having meanings that I am not living up to because they are unrealistic (e.g., I should be nice to every person all the time), the guilt experienced here is the guilt we feel when we have done real wrongs to real others. It also is the guilt we feel when we recognize that we have lived most of our lives betraying ourselves through denying our basic relational nature. Not uncommonly, the client becomes depressed as he or she experiences this guilt.

Here, the therapist must provide some perspective. Guilt in this situation is a sign of growth. The client is beginning the process of assuming some relational responsibility. A component of assuming such responsibility means grieving the ways he or she has injured others and has deprived the self of relational life. As such, the guilt, and the resulting depression, should be nurtured and cherished by therapist and client. It would be a therapeutic mistake to try to remove the guilt and depression prematurely through cognitive or chemical interventions. There will be time later to help the client feel less guilty about these issues. However, in my experience, some residual guilt always remains, and I believe that such residual guilt is healthy as it reminds the client of what happened and why he or she should avoid that path again.

For example, Susan spent several months feeling depressed and guilty as she realized and internalized the things she had done to her son. After we had sat with her depression for a while, I was able to say, "You know, all of us have done things we are ashamed of. The bigger issues are whether, on balance, you can do more good than bad in your life and what you might do to help your son continue to grow." This intervention accomplished three things. First, it told her that all of us wind up doing things that can be construed as evil, as none of us have perfect self-awareness. Second, it gave Susan a long-term perspective to consider as she integrated the "evil part" of her into her total personality. Finally, it introduced the idea that she could discover ways she might help her son for his sake as well as hers.

TREATING VICTIMS

Therapy with victims of appalling acts necessarily raises different issues. Most therapists find it much easier to deal with people who have been victims of obvious and overt horrors than to deal with those who perpetrated the horrors. However, I believe that many therapists find it difficult to deal with victims of violence that has been more subtle, culturally prescribed, or presented to the therapist in unusual ways (as in hallucinations). Too often, the therapist can inadvertently compound the client's wounds in the latter situations.

Walk With the Pain

The concept of optimal therapeutic distance means that the therapist has to be willing to experience the deep pain and devastation the client feels when atrocious acts have been perpetrated upon him or her. Sometimes therapists are too scared to stay with the pain and try to medicate it or otherwise take it away. However, pain, grief, and depression are understandable reactions to having horrific events happen to you. The therapist must be willing to help the client understand that the painful feelings are understandable and, in many ways, a healthy reaction to terrible events. Therapists uncomfortable with bearing the internal upheaval of distress should forgo such clients.

For example, elsewhere I have described a case involving a woman whose mother acted tenderly toward her only when she was giving her bubble baths. She then recalled, in horror, that the bubble baths actually were precursors to her stepfather sexually abusing her. I had to be able to simultaneously experience what that must have been like as well as prepare us for doing something with it. Because she could tell that the revelation had an emotional effect on me, she was able to describe the events with greater detail and specificity. After I had walked with her distress for several sessions, I was able to say, "Ultimately, you know, you have to decide whether you want to have the two of them continue to rule your emotional life." However, if I had said this prematurely, my client would rightly have sensed that I was saying it to distance us both from the horrors of her experience. That would have been a therapeutic mistake of the first magnitude.

Responsibility

Many victims of violence and abuse struggle with the issue of responsibility. Particularly when we are small children, we are often placed in the terrible position of depending on parents who fundamentally are unreliable. The net result is that we have to either face the overwhelming anxiety of being dependent on people who will not protect and nurture us or foster the feeling that their failures are somehow our fault. If we could just do it right, they would love and protect us. So, for example, when my client was sobbing about the sexual abuse after the bubble baths, she wailed, "Why did this happen to me?" As I listened to her, I felt a combination of horror, betrayal, pain, and, quite unexpectedly, guilt. I then gently said to her, "There is a way you blame yourself for this, isn't there?" The tears started to really flow as she dealt with her feeling that the sexual abuse was her fault. Eventually, I was able to say, "We need to look concretely and specifically about what it was you think you did to bring this on. Personally, I have no doubt that we will find out that you were nothing other than an innocent victim."

Indirect Presentations of Victimhood

Many clients have been injured in more subtle ways, or their injuries were incurred as others behaved in culturally acceptable ways. For example, Janice presented with deep and uncontrollable depressions. These depressions came "out of the blue" for no reason. However, as we explored her life, I found out that she was raised in a conservative, traditional home in which she was denied educational opportunities readily made available to her less intelligent brothers. Because the entire culture embraced the belief that women did not need an education, no validation of her experience of being injured was provided by her family. Her injuries emerged through her depressions, and I was the first person to validate the fact that she had been injured by her family and her culture. Too often, therapists are blinded by their own cultural lenses and fail to affirm these culturally based injuries. To take just one example of this blindness, consider the ways the profession prescribes antidepressants. As even a brief perusal of the literature will show (see, e.g., Caplan, 1995), depression is a gendered disorder with women getting most of the "treatment" with antidepressants, sometimes resulting in a lifetime dependency on the drugs (see Whitaker, 2010).

George is another example of a wounded person presenting his wounds in indirect ways (Leitner, 2007, 2009). George believed that his body was rotting. Such "delusional thinking" had gotten him diagnoses like "paranoid schizophrenia" as well as "treatments" on brain-disabling neuroleptics. Neither the diagnosis nor the treatments associated with it had been helpful to George. As we explored his life, we found out that his childhood was dominated emotionally by the experience of being locked in a closet for extended periods of time, sometimes as long as a week. During those times, his father told him that he could not urinate or defecate in the closet or he would be in "real trouble." George became convinced that the holding in of feces was poisoning and rotting his insides. By being open to the idea that his symptom had *meaning* and was not just a random manifestation of a brain disease, we were able to uncover the basis of his "delusional thinking." George was eventually able to give up his "delusion" as he experienced and understood the distress behind the symptom.

Forgiveness

People who have been seriously damaged by others often struggle with forgiveness. Within experiential constructivism, *forgiveness* is defined as the reconstruing of self and other such that previous injuries do not continue to cause you to retreat from relational connection (Leitner & Pfenninger, 1994). We note that there is nothing in the definition that implies that the victim must become friends with the perpetrator or even stop hating him or her. The work of forgiveness has to do with the internal work necessary to come to terms with and resolve the wounds and violence perpetrated against the victim. As long as the injuries the other has caused continue to interfere with living a rich and meaningful life, the victim continues to be determined by the past. Thus, forgiveness is absolutely necessary for the victim to go on.

However, forgiveness is a process; some clients, and some therapists, attempt to preempt the process by forgiving prematurely (Leitner et al., 2000). In essence, one cannot forgive until one has had time to understand exactly what the injuries were as well as mourn the life that was lost when one had been wounded. People often believe they have forgiven as a way to avoid the hard and painful work of looking at the injuries up close and grieving the loss of the person they might have been. To be helpful, therapists need to help the client become aware of such tendencies. The first thing the therapist needs to do in such situations is to convince the client that the therapist is ready to hear about and feel the client's wounds.

People who hang on to injuries and do not forgive often confuse forgiveness with letting the perpetrator off the hook. The therapist and client must be clear that forgiveness, as defined within experiential personal construct psychology, has nothing to do with absolving the perpetrator from responsibility for his or her actions; rather it has to do with allowing the victim to be able to lead a meaningful life despite being injured. For example, Joan had been systematically abused by her husband prior to her divorce. After years of therapy, she and her therapist became aware that she could not do the work of forgiveness because she wanted some acknowledgment from the world that she had been damaged by him. Without that acknowledgment, she felt that her pain and devastation were not viewed as legitimate by others. The therapist and Joan then arranged a "ceremony" where some of her friends could listen and acknowledge the validity of her distress. After this ceremony, Joan was able to go on with her life.

After we have walked with the client's pain, we have the chance to help the client forgive in the manner described by experiential constructivism. With the bubble bath example above, I gently challenged my client by asking how long she wanted her mother and stepfather to control her life. The client eventually decided that, because she no longer had any relationship or contact with her mother, she was going to make me her mother and take what she needed to learn about relationships from me. In so doing, she was able to overcome some of the effects of the abuse on her and begin to live a life more filled with richness and meaning.

EVIL PEOPLE?

Now we are left with a final question. Could someone be so damaged so early in life that he or she might wind up being an "evil" person? From an experiential constructivist perspective, evil acts cannot be perpetrated absent the relational injuries and the adult manifestations described earlier. Thus, no person is born evil. Rather, we all are born relationship seeking and suffer injuries leading to behavior that can be termed evil. However, might the tendencies to objectify others, deny connectedness, numb experiences, and not introspect (and therefore not assume responsibility) be so pervasive that they essentially completely and totally define the person? If so, we could talk about a person being "evil," without any redeeming properties whatsoever. Furthermore, if they were so defined, it would mean there was no hope for redemption.

Experiential personal construct psychology would hold that if a person suffered only relational invalidation in early life, the person would die. Thus, all of us who have survived infancy have experienced some affirmation. Therefore, a part of every person has been affirmed that has felt the healing balm of interpersonal nurturance. Every person has the potential to overcome the demons from the past and to reestablish a life of connection and richness. However, our present knowledge concerning ways of being with people may not allow for healers to know the ways by which they can help some people who have been so devastatingly damaged. Furthermore, our own individual limitations as therapists might mean that we cannot be present with certain types of people. The net result is that certain people would look incorrigible. However, as therapists and scholars, we always must keep in mind that incorrigibility speaks more to our personal and professional limitations than to unique characteristics of the client. As we continue to develop our understandings of the ways connection can transform lives, we will see the day that more and more "untreatable" people can be helped.

REFERENCES

Bannister, D., & Agnew, J. (1977). The child's construing of self. In J. K. Cole & A. W. Landfield (Eds.), *Nebraska symposium on motivation* (pp. 99–125). Lincoln, NE: University of Nebraska Press.

Barratt, B. B. (1977). The development of peer perception systems in childhood and early adolescence. *Social Behavior and Personality, 5,* 351–360. doi:10.2224/sbp.1977.5.2.351

Boyle, M. (2002). *Schizophrenia: A scientific delusion?* New York, NY: Routledge.

Caplan, P. J. (1995). *They say you're crazy: How the world's most powerful psychiatrists decide who's normal.* Reading, MA: Addison Wesley.

Domenici, D. J., & Leitner, L. M. (2001). Utilizing artistry in a therapy relationship. *The Humanistic Psychologist, 29,* 114–125. doi:10.1080/08873267.2001.9977010

Faidley, A. J., & Leitner, L. M. (2000). The poetry of our lives: Symbolism in experiential personal construct psychotherapy. In J. W. Scheer (Ed.), *The person in society: Challenges to a constructivist theory* (pp. 381–390). Gieben, Germany: Psychosozial-Verlag.

Frankl, V. E. (1963). *Man's search for meaning: An introduction to logotherapy* (I. Lasch, Trans.). New York, NY: Washington Square Press.

Hirigoyen, M.-F. (2000). *Stalking the soul: Emotional abuse and the erosion of identity.* New York, NY: Helen Marks.

Katz, F. E. (1993). *Ordinary people and extraordinary evil: A report on the beguilings of evil.* New York, NY: SUNY Press.

Kelly, G. A. (1955). *The psychology of personal constructs.* New York, NY: Norton.

Klion, R. E., & Leitner, L. M. (1985). Construct elicitation techniques and the production of interpersonal concepts in children. *Social Behavior and Personality, 13*, 137–142. doi:10.2224/sbp.1985.13.2.137

Klose, D. A. (1995). M. Scott Peck's analysis of human evil: A critical review. *Journal of Humanistic Psychology, 35*, 37–66. doi:10.1177/00221678950353003

Leitner, L. M. (1985). The terrors of cognition: On the experiential validity of personal construct theory. In D. Bannister (Ed.), *Issues and approaches in personal construct theory* (pp. 83–103). London, England: Academic Press.

Leitner, L. M. (1988). Terror, risk, and reverence: Experiential personal construct psychotherapy. *International Journal of Personal Construct Psychology, 1*, 251–261. doi:10.1080/10720538808409398

Leitner, L. M. (1995). Optimal therapeutic distance: A therapist's experience of personal construct psychotherapy. In R. Neimeyer & M. Mahoney (Eds.), *Constructivism in psychotherapy* (pp. 357–370). Washington, DC: American Psychological Association. doi:10.1037/10170-015

Leitner, L. M. (1999). Terror, numbness, panic, and awe: Experiential personal constructivism and panic. In E. M. Stern & R. B. Marchesani (Eds.), *Awe and trembling: Psychotherapy of unusual states* (pp. 157–170). Binghamton, NY: Haworth Press.

Leitner, L. M. (2001). The role of awe in experiential personal construct psychotherapy. In R. B. Marchesani & E. M. Stern (Eds.), *Frightful stages: From the primitive to the therapeutic* (pp. 149–162). New York, NY: Haworth Press.

Leitner, L. M. (2007). Theory, technique, and person: Technical integration in experiential constructivist therapy. *Journal of Psychotherapy Integration, 17*, 33–49. doi:10.1037/1053-0479.17.1.33

Leitner, L. M. (2009). Theory, therapy, and life: Experiential personal construct psychology and the "desert places" of a therapist. In R. Butler (Ed.), *On reflection: Emphasizing the personal in personal construct theory* (pp. 361–374). London, England: Wiley.

Leitner, L. M. (2010). The integral universe, experiential personal construct psychology, transpersonal reverence, and transpersonal responsibility. In J. R. Raskin, S. R. Bridges, & R. A. Neimeyer (Eds.), *Studies in meaning: Exploring constructivist psychology* (Vol. 4, pp. 227–245). New York, NY: Pace University Press.

Leitner, L. M., & Celentana, M. A. (1997). Constructivist therapy with serious disturbances. *The Humanistic Psychologist, 25*, 271–285. doi:10.1080/08873267.1997.9986886

Leitner, L. M., & Dill-Standiford, T. J. (1993). Resistance in experiential personal construct psychotherapy: Theoretical and technical struggles. In L. M. Leitner

& N. G. M. Dunnett (Eds.), *Critical issues in personal construct psychotherapy* (pp. 135–155). Melbourne, FL: Krieger.

Leitner, L. M., & Faidley, A. J. (1995). The awful, aweful nature of ROLE relationships. In G. Neimeyer & R. Neimeyer (Eds.), *Advances in personal construct psychology* (Vol. III, pp. 291–314). Greenwich, CT: JAI Press.

Leitner, L. M., & Faidley, A. J. (1999). Creativity in experiential personal construct psychotherapy. *Journal of Constructivist Psychology, 12*, 239–252. doi:10.1080/107205399266091

Leitner, L. M., Faidley, A. J., & Celentana, M. A. (2000). Diagnosing human meaning making: An experiential constructivist approach. In R. Neimeyer & J. Raskin (Eds.), *Constructions of disorders: Meaning-making frameworks for psychotherapy* (pp. 175–203). Washington, DC: American Psychological Association. doi:10.1037/10368-008

Leitner, L. M., & Pfenninger, D. T. (1994). Sociality and optimal functioning. *Journal of Constructivist Psychology, 7*, 119–135. doi:10.1080/10720539408405073

Lifton, R. J. (1986). *The Nazi doctors: Medical killing and the psychology of genocide*. New York, NY: Basic Books.

Lifton, R. J., & Markusen, E. (1990). *The genocidal mentality: Nazi holocaust and nuclear threat*. New York, NY: Basic Books.

Miller, A. (1990). *Banished knowledge: Facing childhood injuries*. New York, NY: Doubleday.

Parker, R. (1991, January). *Sin and salvation*. The annual Loomer Lecture, Berkeley, CA.

Peck, M. S. (1983). *People of the lie: The hope for healing human evil*. New York, NY: Simon & Schuster.

Whitaker, R. (2010). *Anatomy of an epidemic: Magic bullets, psychiatric drugs, and the astonishing rise of mental illness in America*. New York, NY: Crown.

Winter, D. A. (2007). Construing the construction processes of serial killers and other violent offenders: 2. The limits of credulity. *Journal of Constructivist Psychology, 20*, 247–275. doi:10.1080/10720530701347902

7

WHEN PEOPLE DO BAD THINGS: EVIL, SUFFERING, AND DEPENDENT ORIGINATION

JOHN BRIERE

Our world is filled with stories of horrendous crimes and criminals—of rapists and killers, sex traffickers, terrorists, genocidal dictators, sadists, and psychopaths. When faced with such people and what they have done, many in society invoke a powerful explanation: that of *evil*. Evil people are thought to be divorced from the human condition, morally corrupt or perverse, and, from a Western theistic perspective, acting against the will of God (e.g., Gen 2:18). Implicit is the notion that some individuals are different from the rest of us: They operate outside the normal bounds of human compassion, and, by virtue of their inhumanity, are able to do horrible things without compunction. They are, in a sense, alien: the antithesis of everyone else.

The specific criteria for evil are not always easy to determine. Some acts, such as child rape, genocide, or serial killing, are thought to be the sole domain of evil people. However, the exact point at which something transitions from mere garden-variety meanness or violence to the assumed product

DOI: 10.1037/13941-007
Humanity's Dark Side: Evil, Destructive Experience, and Psychotherapy, A. C. Bohart, B. S. Held,
E. Mendelowitz, and K. J. Schneider (Editors)

of evil is not always clear (Neiman, 2002). In fact, given the complexity of defining evil on the basis of acts alone, the actor's intention is usually considered as well. If a soldier kills people during war, it will matter whether his or her intent is to protect the homeland, to follow military orders, or just to kill people. He or she might be labeled a hero in the first two instances, and in the last, a bad or perhaps evil person. In fact, the word *atrocity* can be defined as killing during war that is not for rule-bound, military reasons, but rather for personal gratification.

The context of violence is also relevant. If an act is perpetrated on someone who is viewed as "good," we view it as more evil than when the victim is "bad." In movies, for example, the average hero appears to be able to kill many bad people—in the absence of any jurisprudence or self-reflection—without being seen as bad himself or herself. In such cases, justice, not evil, is assumed to have been committed by the killer.

Finally, we generally do not assign a label of evil to people who are not able to stop themselves from doing unacceptable things; in most cosmologies, the conduct of evil requires free will (e.g., Hick, 1966; Neiman, 2002). Yet, independence of action is a complicated notion. Since we believe that human behavior generally arises from specific causes and influences (a central premise of the behavioral sciences), when is one's bad behavior actually freely chosen? For example, a repeated finding in psychology is that childhood maltreatment can lead to a variety of later outcomes, many of which are thought to adversely influence human behavior. Although our culture stresses accountability, independence, and free will, the fact that early life can affect later behavior makes it difficult to decide when, and to what extent, the behavior of a previously victimized person is under his or her control.

ANOTHER ANALYSIS

Although commonly applied, the concept of evil may be more socially useful than empirically accurate. This label allows us to avoid an equally frightening possibility: that outrageous acts of inhumanity are, ironically, a regular part of the human condition. If this were true, there may be no need to resort to a special type of person to explain very bad things. We need only look within ourselves for the causes and conditions—now and in the past—that can lead us toward harming others. In some ways, it would be helpful if evil existed, because then we could find it and stop it (in some social narratives, kill it) and be reassured that the problem resides elsewhere—not in our homes, our history, or our culture. On the other hand, if we can accept that each of us is potentially capable of doing very bad things to others, albeit perhaps only under specific circumstances (Goldstein, 2010), it may be possible to intervene in what we otherwise tend to externalize. In the remainder of this chapter, I call on aspects of Buddhist philosophy—and my own experience as a trauma psychologist who has worked for years with victims and perpetrators—to outline this alternative view.

ON BAD BEHAVIOR AND FREE WILL

The idea of evil resides in the notion that people can freely choose to do things that they otherwise should not. In other words, evil is thought to arise independently, operating as its own First Cause (Aristotle, 1941). The evil man committed an atrocity and did so just because he wanted to; he could have not engaged in the act, but he chose to do so anyway. If it turns out that he was psychotic, however, he is less likely to be seen as evil, and may even be judged as not guilty by reason of insanity. If he killed (bad) people out of some need for vengeance or retribution, we can perhaps understand why he did what he did, and, again, he is unlikely to be seen as evil. If there is a logical *why*, a cause, or mitigating factor, evil is a less common attribution.

Yet, an extensive psychological literature indicates that human behavior is influenced by a range of phenomena that are generally not under the individual's control, including genetics, biology, mental illness, the effects of childhood experiences, and socialization to view things in certain ways and respond accordingly. In this regard, it may be useful to consider the Buddhist notion of *dependent origination* (also known as *dependent arising*) in our examination of evil as an independent entity.

Dependent origination, simplified, refers to the idea that all things arise from concrete conditions and sustaining causes, which, themselves, arise from other causes and conditions (Bhikkhu Bodhi, 2005). In other words, all events occur because of the effects of previous events: No event occurs independent of causality. This view accords with the basic principles of Western psychology: that people do things because of the influence of other things. Dependent origination and modern behavioral science suggest that attributions of self-arising behavior (e.g., of intrinsic evil) may be due to insufficient information: If we could know about the brain tumor, childhood terror, or psychosis experienced by a schoolyard sniper, we would no longer assume that he or she fully, independently, chose to kill those children. The acts would be horrible, but he or she would not be evil.

Of course, this view is subject to debate. For example, per quantum mechanics and chaos theory, not all events are, in fact, predictable on the basis of prior events (Bishop, 2009; Kellert, 1993). More problematic for Western culture, a fully determined cause-and-effect model is incompatible with the notion of free will (Kane, 1996; Sartre, 1943/1993). Notably, most Buddhist and Western psychologies, although acknowledging some level of determinism, also endorse the notion of freely chosen behavior (e.g., Gier & Kjellberg, 2004). Indeed, Buddhism holds that the individual can intervene in dependent origination by gaining wisdom, ultimately attaining freedom from suffering (nirvana). As various writers have suggested, this seeming contradiction may be due, in part, to the ways the debate is framed and conceptualized (e.g., Baer, Kaufman, & Baumeister, 2008). It may also reflect the limitations of the human mind in grasping a universe where free will and determinism are both true, depending on perspective, just as light can be viewed as either a wave or a particle, depending on how it is observed.

However apportioned, dependent origination suggests that humans (and other beings) are embedded in a complex web of reciprocating conditions, actions, and reactions, across time, such that any given behavior may be influenced by a wide range of causes and conditions. Thus, it may not be just obvious phenomena (e.g., severe mental illness, brain dysfunction) that are implicated in bad behaviors, but also unloving parents, abuse, loss, racism, oppression, poverty, insufficient education, or the effects of growing up in an authoritarian or avaricious culture. As many clinicians working with violence will attest, individuals who commit horrific crimes are rarely Hannibal Lecters (Harris, 1991), reveling in their murderous behavior and laughing at the rest of us. More typically, they are very unhappy, often previously maltreated, and/or seriously marginalized people, many of whom suffer from significant psychological difficulties, if not frank mental illness. Even the small minority who can be diagnosed as "true" psychopaths are now believed to suffer from neurologic pathology, operating from aberrant brain circuitry that prevents the development of empathy, normal anxiety, inhibition of anger, or a capacity to learn from negative experiences (Blair, 2008).

The fact that bad behavior is unlikely to be metaphysical in nature does not subtract from the horror of what we humans can do to one another. As a trauma specialist in an urban environment, I encounter victims of rape, abuse, assaults, shootings, and other forms of violence on a regular basis. I have spent time with more than a few torture survivors and sex-trafficked women. What has been done to them, often repeatedly, sometimes defies description. I have also met batterers, rapists, pedophiles, and killers; they often belong to "victim" categories as well, although it is hard to see that when confronted with the cruel things they have done.

Presented next is an example of a relevant case, combining aspects of several individuals who were assigned the death penalty for especially repellent murders. As is true for another case presented later in this chapter, details have been disguised to prevent identification.

A. M.

A. M. is a 26-year-old woman, recently found guilty of smothering her two young children. Court documents indicate that she had fallen in love with a colleague at work and had decided that the only way he would have a relationship with her was if she were free of dependent children. In the trial, the prosecutor described A. M. as a psychopath who felt no remorse about what she had done. The innocence of the children, both under 5, was emphasized repeatedly, as was the evil of a mother who not only did not protect her children but willfully caused them excruciating deaths.

In the penalty-phase hearing, evidence indicated that A. M. had been neglected and harshly punished as a child, as well as repeatedly sexually abused by her father until late adolescence. Medical records indicated that she had been treated for psychotic depression following the birth of each of her children. Prior to the crime, she discovered that she was pregnant again, and obtained an abortion. According to the defense psychologist, she subsequently developed a delusion that killing her children would allow her to marry a man who, in actuality, hardly knew her. The forensic psychologist noted that he found her distant but almost cheerful during interviews, seemingly unaffected by what she had done. When asked about her feelings regarding her dead children, she stated, "It's alright. I can have more."

The point at which dependent arising differs from an "evil" analysis is not in discounting the damage done or the anger we often feel when seeing the results of violence. The difference resides in how we explain such behavior and what we do about it. An "evil person" perspective localizes and externalizes the cause to a single individual, a "bad seed," who willfully acts in isolation. From that perspective, the solution is to find such people and lock them up or do away with them, so that no further bad acts will occur. Since evil has no cause, but rather emerges from free (albeit malignant) will, the intervention can be limited to law enforcement, detection, and punishment.

A dependent origination analysis offers another option. It suggests that the notion of freely chosen "evil" gets us off the hook by making us, and the world we create, by definition, not the problem. Attributions of evil also block compassion for those who commit bad acts, as well as discouraging attempts to remediate, rehabilitate, or psychologically treat them. In contrast, dependent origination directs our attention to (among other things) ourselves, as inevitably interdependent with the perpetrator and his or her acts—asking, for example, what our part is in the "badness" of others, directly or indirectly, whether by acts of commission or omission. For example, to the extent that we allow politicians to reduce funding for child abuse prevention programs, services to the mentally ill, antipoverty initiatives, and postincarceration support programs, are we complicit in the crimes of those who might have been assisted by these interventions?

This approach suggests that "bad" people are stuck in a predicament, one that is injurious both to themselves and to others. Based on prior negative experiences, some people who do violent or abusive things may suffer from intense anger, hatred, resentment, and other destructive emotions (Dalai Lama & Goleman, 2003) that are easily triggered in interpersonal contexts and, once activated, not easily controlled (Briere, 2002). Such people may have come to false conclusions about, for example, the uncaring or hurtful nature of people, the treatment they deserve, and the benefits of aggression (Anderson & Huesmann, 2003; Beck, 1999). In many cases, they have a limited repertoire of nonviolent responses available for dealing with negative internal states or provocations by others (e.g., Pollock et al., 1990).

If this view has merit, a significant literature should be available on the prevalence of negative early experience and current dysfunction among those who have committed extreme violence against others. In fact, this is a common finding, internationally: Those who commit sexual or physical assaults against children, beat their partners, rape people, engage in serial killings, or commit atrocities are more likely to have childhood histories of emotional neglect, psychological maltreatment, sexual or physical abuse, exposure to parental domestic violence, and, in some countries, being forced at an early age into militias (e.g., Ea & Sim, 2001; Giannangelo, 1996; Glasser, Campbell, Glasser, Leitch, & Farrelly, 2001; Klevens, Duque, & Ramírez, 2002). Furthermore, a number of studies indicate that those who commit violent crimes are more likely than others to suffer from serious mental disorders and cognitive impairments (e.g., Friedman, 2006), a finding that is especially obvious in studies of death row inmates (e.g., Lewis, Pincus, Feldman, Jackson, & Bard, 1986).

Yet, even injury-based models of bad behavior are not always enough. Although there are many famous examples of especially cruel and violent individuals, some of the most horrendous acts in history occurred in the context of "normal" society. Hitler, for example, may have suffered from whatever dysfunction and disturbance that led him toward a Holocaust, yet he would not have been successful but for the complicity of many thousands of ordinary citizens. The banality of their contributions to the deaths of millions highlights a stark contention: Humans, in significant quantity, are capable of acts of extreme cruelty—absent mental disorder, brain tumors, and other individual phenomena, sometimes all that appears to be required for "good" people to do bad things is underlying dissatisfaction or anger, tapped or channeled by charismatic leadership, nationalism, or a cultural story line about ancient enemies or unacceptable groups. The German people could not all have been evil, as typically defined; they were, instead, human, in the same way that Americans were human over the several hundred years that they supported and participated in the violent enslavement of African people (Segal, 1995). Although this chapter focuses on the etiology of bad behavior by individuals, the human capacity to engage in hurtful and destructive behavior en masse should not be overlooked. In fact, it may be strong proof that it is not the special case of evil that engenders cruelty and violence, but rather natural characteristics of the human race, given proper conditions.

In summary, and paraphrasing Buddhist psychology, "evil" behavior may arise from some combination of suffering (within which we can include hatred), misunderstanding about the state of reality and one's actual needs, and not knowing better ways to approach well-being. This disturbance and confusion are easy to miss, especially when our own anger and outrage are triggered by seemingly inhuman behavior by individual persons. In fact, when we are exposed to such violence, our own first inclination is often violent as well, pointing to the ubiquity of the problem. In this regard, for example, it may be difficult for cultures that embrace capital punishment or foreign wars of retribution to foster the conditions that allow widespread compassion and nonviolence.

IMPLICATIONS FOR INTERVENTION

To the extent that people who hurt or exploit other people are unlikely to be intrinsically evil, but rather responding to adverse biology, history, or societal dynamics, intervention to decrease behaviors we consider evil may be possible. Equally important, exploration and understanding of the reasons for bad behavior may be helpful in the victim's psychological processing of the trauma that he or she has undergone.

Social Interventions

Most immediately, the dependent origination of bad acts brings our attention to social and cultural supports for violence and maltreatment. Social psychology suggests that persons holding certain culturally transmitted beliefs regarding (a) the lesser value and entitlements of certain groups of people (e.g., women, children, people of color, gay men and lesbians) or (b) the acceptability of exploitation, domination, and interpersonal violence to meet one's needs are considerably more likely to engage in violent or hurtful behavior than persons without such beliefs (e.g., Anderson & Huesmann, 2003; Burt, 1980; Clement & Chamberland, 2007). Such data highlight the functional utility of making our society more kind and accepting, and less harsh and oppressive, as a direct way to decrease individual acts of violent behavior and discourage large-scale violence in political or social contexts. If our culture did not discriminate against minorities and others with lesser social power, if it actively confronted poverty, and if it intervened in social phenomena that reinforce hurtful or uncaring actions, "evil" behavior seemingly would be far less common. Similarly, to the extent that social, educational, and early intervention programs could prevent childhood abuse and neglect, the "downstream" effects on later crime, violence, and specific horrendous acts would disappear. In this sense, although law enforcement interventions and harsh punishment of individuals may produce a sense of satisfaction that justice has been served, they are post hoc activities—they do not prevent the crime that triggered forensic involvement, nor do they address the etiology of the problem. Because such interventions are often violent as well, they may increase, not decrease, violence in others (e.g., Staub, Pearlman, Gubin, & Hagengimana, 2005). In the words of the 14th Dalai Lama, "Through violence, you may 'solve' one problem, but you sow the seeds for another."

Intervening in Individual Suffering That Leads to Bad Behavior

If an important antecedent to hurtful behavior is personal suffering, interventions that address sustained psychological distress or dysfunction in those who are at special risk of hurting others would likely be helpful. This may occur at two levels, chronologically: intervening as a way to prevent initial bad behavior and assisting those who have already committed bad acts so that they will not commit more of them. Relevant interventions might include improving those conditions described above, such as poverty, social discrimination, and the likelihood of childhood victimization. In addition, psychotherapy for abuse victims and survivors that targets anger, aggression, and trauma-related reenactment might decrease the likelihood of future violence. In this way, working to reduce suffering is not only humanitarian, it may be an important way to break the victim-to-perpetrator cycle that transmits pain from person to person and from generation to generation.

Spiritual Change

Finally, from a spiritual perspective, activities that increase compassion for others (e.g., meditation, prayer), insight (e.g., discernment), and good intentions (e.g., vows) also are likely to decrease bad acts against others. Importantly, this does not mean that involvement in religion, per se, is protective against maltreating behavior, given the many cruelties that have occurred throughout human history in the name of deities or credos.

DEPENDENT ORIGINATION AND THE VICTIM OF BAD ACTS

We have considered above the utilitarian notion that knowledge of the suffering underlying some very bad behavior can inform us about how to decrease such acts. But the goal is not just prevention; we are also obviously concerned with the effects of such acts on victims. As will be suggested here, it may be that misattributions of evil also affect survivors of horrendous crimes.

People who have been hurt by other people are typically affected in multiple ways. The direct impacts of having been assaulted, exploited, betrayed, belittled, or degraded can be profound, including posttraumatic stress, severe and lasting anxiety or depression, and an inability to trust or form meaningful relationships with others (Briere, 2004). Having been hurt by another also can encourage extreme anger, if not hatred, and a desire for vengeance, which are associated with their own negative psychological effects (e.g., Chida & Steptoe, 2009; Field & Chhim, 2008), and can discourage compassion for oneself and one's victimizer—cognitive–emotional states that have been linked to psychological well-being (Gilbert, 2009; Staub et al., 2005).

The effects of trauma vary, to some extent, according to how the victim understands what was done to him or her. In general, those who attribute greater intentionality (and therefore, potentially, more evil) to a perpetrator, or greater responsibility to themselves, tend to suffer more severe impacts (Briere, 2004).[1] If someone tumbles down a flight of stairs, it will matter psychologically whether he or she tripped or was pushed. In a more extreme example, torture and rape may be associated with so many psychological effects because both appear especially intentional; they were done on purpose—in fact, the perpetrator may have enjoyed inducing pain or humiliation. From the other side of the injury, those victims of interpersonal violence who experience self-blame and deservingness of maltreatment, in other words, those who take responsibility for an event actually outside of their control, tend to suffer more extreme effects than those who do not blame themselves (Whiffen & MacIntosh, 2005).

Implications for Psychotherapy

To the extent that attributions of perpetrator intentionality (including evil) or victim responsibility compound the psychological injury associated with

---

[1]As might be expected, natural disasters generally produce fewer psychological effects than does interpersonal violence (e.g., Briere & Elliott, 2000). See Neiman (2002), however, for an account of the Lisbon earthquake of 1755, with its thousands of casualties. This disaster came to be viewed by many as God's punishment of evildoers (e.g., Kendrick, 1956), thereby adding intentionality to the mix. This conflation had subsequent impacts on European models of good, evil, and the intentions—or even existence—of a beneficent God (e.g., Kant, quoted in Breidert, 1994).

having been hurt by another, psychological interventions that consider dependent origination may be helpful for victim recovery. In many cases, this is a "hard sell," since it implies that the perpetrator, like the victim, is prey to causes and conditions, in many cases even victimization of his or her own. If actions arise from current and prior circumstances, so do those of rapists or killers.

Importantly, this does not mean that the victim should immediately "forgive" (let alone forget) what the perpetrator has done, especially to the extent that doing so implies nonentitlement to intensely negative feelings and thoughts. In fact, social or personal pressure to block negative internal states associated with trauma may inhibit the normal psychological processing necessary to recover from negative experiences (Briere, 2002). It is "normal" to be very angry, and, in some circumstances, to feel hatred toward those who have hurt one or one's loved ones. A concentration camp survivor, parent of a murdered child, or victim of a hate crime surely is entitled to extremely negative feelings and aggressive impulses toward the person who did these things.

Yet, a central tenet of some spiritual traditions, both East and West, is that the continuing experience of hate and deep resentment is bad for people, and that being less involved in these states improves mental well-being (Dalai Lama & Goleman, 2003). From this perspective, letting go of angry cognitive–emotional states is not for the benefit of the perpetrator alone, but more importantly, for the benefit of the victimized.

But, how can this be accomplished?

Supporting Awareness of Dependent Origination

Whether called *forgiveness* or some other term, the capacity to (over time) not hate or hold extreme resentment against someone who has done grievous harm may be, for some, an important aspect of complete recovery—not necessarily because the perpetrator "deserves" this process, but because the survivor does. Although there are no doubt many paths to reduced hatred of the perpetrator, I have found that processing trauma in the context of dependent origination, during psychotherapy or elsewhere, is an important one.[2] In most cases, this involves a stepwise process (see Briere, 2012; and Briere & Scott, 2012, for more detail):

> 1. *Slow but sustained processing of painful emotions and cognitions, with acceptance and, to the extent possible, nonavoidance of distress.* This usually involves the traumatized client carefully (and safely) revisiting the painful event or events over time, allow-

---

[2]Suffering social systems also may undergo similar processing of adverse experience, such as the Truth and Reconciliation Commission activities of postapartheid South Africa, acknowledged by most (but not all) as having reduced subsequent vengeance-based violence.

ing herself or himself to feel the feelings and think the thoughts that naturally arise from such memories. During this time, the clinician works to validate the client's experience and helps him or her to see that "bad" feelings from trauma are not, in fact, bad, but rather a normal and healthy part of recovery. It is important that the clinician not push for premature closure or "forgiveness" at this point: expressions of hatred, disgust, and a desire for retribution reflect understandable, human response to unfair and hurtful experiences.

2. *Detailed cognitive exploration of the facts of the trauma.* This includes the specific details of what happened and the conclusions the survivor formed about himself or herself and the perpetrator at the time of the event, including self-blaming cognitions that may have arisen. The clinician does not attempt to make interpretations or offer his or her own conclusions: The goal is for the client, after enough emotional processing has occurred, to engage in relatively unencumbered analysis of the experience and the validity of what he or she concluded at the time.

3. *Support for awareness of dependent origination.* As the client explores his or her thoughts, feelings, and reactions, the clinician provides nondirective opportunities for the client to consider the *whys* of the event: Why did he or she come to the conclusions that he or she did? Why did the perpetrator do what he or she did? In fact, *were* there reasons (not justifications), or was the perpetrator intrinsically evil? Why do people do what they do?

   When this occurs in the absence of pressure from the clinician to decide on one version or attribution versus another, in the context of noncontingent acceptance and support, and typically over time, the client's detailed analysis may lead to *cognitive reconsideration* (Briere & Scott, 2012): a slow transition (a) from a view of self as having deserved or somehow caused the event to that of a person who was not responsible for what happened, and (b) from a view of the perpetrator as intrinsically evil to that of someone whose behavior arose from of his or her own predispositions, difficulties, and adverse history. This process may occur relatively rapidly for some individuals and not at all for others. Importantly, it should be seen as an evolutionary progression arising from growing awareness, not as a specific state that the therapist induces in or demands from the client.

4. *Development of compassion*. For those who can access a sense of dependent origination, ideally in the context of a supportive other, it is not uncommon for a growing sense of caring for self to arise, as well as, in some lucky cases, greater appreciation of the suffering of the perpetrator. This is a form of *compassion*, which can be defined as awareness and appreciation of suffering in oneself and others as an inevitable part of the shared human condition, with associated nonjudgmental, sometimes even caring feelings for all concerned. Thus, compassion rests both on the realization of dependent origination as existent for all, as well as forgiving states generated by this awareness: the notion that we humans are all in the same predicament, and all struggling the best we can given the hand we've been dealt. This view is not limited to Buddhism. For example, the Trappist monk Thomas Merton (1968) noted in his final lecture that "compassion is based on a keen awareness of the interdependence of all these living beings, which are all part of one another, and all involved in one another" (p. 292). The effects of compassion are both psychological and neurobiological (e.g., Pace et al., 2009). They do not appear to be solely due to the termination of hate and the lessening of anger but also due to the impacts of positive emotionality, arising, in part, from activated neurobiological systems thought to be devoted to human attachment and connection (Briere, 2012; Gilbert, 2009).

Ultimately, then, awareness of dependent arising can reduce emotional responses associated with seeing the perpetrator as intrinsically bad, which, in turn, can lessen injurious thoughts and feelings and foster cognitive–emotional states that facilitate recovery, perhaps even psychological growth. From this perspective, attributions of evil may represent societal externalizations that, in fact, do ill themselves, as well as potentially inhibiting the survivor's broader recovery from horrendous acts. Furthermore, such attributions may engender aggressive behaviors that not only cause further harm but also may lead to even more of the same from others.

H. L.

H. L. is a 52-year-old man who escaped the Pol Pot regime in 1979. Now in the United States, he describes the death of family members and friends in the killing fields of Cambodia and his own torture in a "reeducation" camp, reportedly for being a CIA agent. He states that, as a Buddhist, he no longer blames the Khmer Rouge. He notes that they were less fortunate than he, because they were unable to keep from doing ill, and because their behavior made them even more insane and unable to have a good rebirth.[3]

The brief way in which awareness of dependent origination and the development of compassion have been described in this chapter may erroneously imply that the process is easy. In fact, the emotional (and sometimes physical) pain associated with violent victimization is so intrinsically personal that it is hard to move beyond the obvious frame. As Gilbert (2009) noted, in fact, traumatized or abused people (and, I would suggest, cultures) sometimes have a difficult time accepting compassion for themselves, let alone the perpetrators. And attributions of evil toward those who have caused harm are more immediately logical and seemingly satisfying than a perspective that suggests otherwise. In fact, on some occasions, clinicians or others who suggest dependent origination too early, or without sufficient nuance, may be seen as uncaring of the victim or in denial about the severity of the situation.

Ultimately, a dependent origination/compassion view can only arise if the survivor's situation allows it; awareness of interdependence is, itself, dependent on current conditions and prior causes—including, in many cases, the opportunity to suffer, rage, and process outrageous circumstance in the context of safety, support, and caring. Whether in therapy, in spiritual practice, or at a societal level, the development of this perspective is both lucky and the result of hard work, since it goes against the stream of typical belief. When it occurs, however, appreciation of the reciprocating interconnectedness and causality of experience, as opposed to a belief in independent badness, may be salutary to both the victim of violence and our culture at large.

REFERENCES

Anderson, C. A., & Huesmann, L. R. (2003). Human aggression: A social–cognitive view. In M. A. Hogg & J. Cooper (Eds.), *The handbook of social psychology* (rev. ed., pp. 296–323). London, England: Sage.

Aristotle. (1941). Physics. In R. McKeon (Ed.), *The basic works of Aristotle* (pp. 689–926). New York, NY: Random House.

---

[3]An authority on the treatment of victims of the Khmer Rouge notes that although she has seen similar outcomes, they are uncommon due to the extremity and breadth of the violence perpetrated during the Pol Pot regime (S. Megan Berthold, personal communication, March 28, 2011).

Baer, J., Kaufman, J. C., & Baumeister, R. F. (2008). *Are we free? Psychology and free will.* New York, NY: Oxford University Press.

Beck, A. T. (1999). *Prisoners of hate: The cognitive basis of anger, hostility, and violence.* New York: Harper-Collins.

Bhikkhu Bodhi. (2005). *In the Buddha's words: An anthology of discourses from the Pali Canon.* Somerville, MA: Wisdom.

Bishop, R. (2009). Chaos. *Stanford encyclopedia of philosophy.* Retrieved from http://plato.stanford.edu/entries/chaos/

Blair, J. R. (2008). The cognitive neuroscience of psychopathy and implications for judgments of responsibility. *Neuroethics, 1,* 149–157. doi:10.1007/s12152-008-9016-6

Breidert, W. (Ed.) (1994). *Die Erschütterung der vollkommenen welt* [A world-shattering earthquake]. Darmstadt: Wissenschaftliche Buchgesellschaft.

Briere, J. (2002). Treating adult survivors of severe childhood abuse and neglect: Further development of an integrative model. In J. E. B. Myers, L. Berliner, J. Briere, C. T. Hendrix, T. Reid, & C. Jenny (Eds.), *The APSAC handbook on child maltreatment* (2nd ed., pp. 175–203). Newbury Park, CA: Sage.

Briere, J. (2004). *Psychological assessment of adult posttraumatic states: Phenomenology, diagnosis, and measurement* (2nd ed.). Washington, DC: American Psychological Association. doi:10.1037/10809-000

Briere, J. (2012). Working with trauma: Mindfulness and compassion. In C. K. Germer & R. D. Siegel (Eds.), *Wisdom and compassion in psychotherapy: Deepening mindfulness in clinical practice* (pp.265–279). New York, NY: Guilford Press.

Briere, J., & Elliott, D. M. (2000). Prevalence, characteristics, and long-term sequelae of natural disaster exposure in the general population. *Journal of Traumatic Stress, 13,* 661–679. doi:10.1023/A:1007814301369

Briere, J., & Scott, C. (2012). *Principles of trauma therapy: A guide to symptoms, evaluation, and treatment* (2nd ed.) Thousand Oaks, CA: Sage.

Burt, M. R. (1980). Cultural myths and support for rape. *Journal of Personality and Social Psychology, 38,* 217–230. doi:10.1037/0022-3514.38.2.217

Chida, Y., & Steptoe, A. (2009). The association of anger and hostility with future coronary heart disease: A meta-analytic review of prospective evidence. *Journal of the American College of Cardiology, 53,* 936–946. doi:10.1016/j.jacc.2008.11.044

Clément, M., & Chamberland, C. (2007). Physical violence and psychological aggression towards children: Five year trends in practices and attitudes from two population surveys. *Child Abuse & Neglect, 31,* 1001–1011. doi:10.1016/j.chiabu.2007.04.005

Dalai Lama & Goleman, D. (2003). *Destructive emotions: How can we overcome them? A scientific dialogue with the Dalai Lama.* New York, NY: Bantam Books.

Ea, M.-T., & Sim, S. (2001). *Victims and perpetrator? Testimony of young Khmer Rouge comrades.* Phnom Penh, Cambodia: Documentation Center of Cambodia.

Field, N. P., & Chhim, S. (2008). Desire for revenge and attitudes toward the Khmer Rouge Tribunal among Cambodians. *Journal of Loss and Trauma, 13*, 352–372. doi:10.1080/15325020701742086

Friedman, R. A. (2006). Violence and mental illness—How strong is the link? *The New England Journal of Medicine, 355*, 2064–2066. doi:10.1056/NEJMp068229

Giannangelo, S. J. (1996). *The psychopathology of serial murder: A theory in violence.* Westport, CT: Praeger.

Gier, N., & Kjellberg, P. (2004). Buddhism and the freedom of the will: Pali and Mahayanist responses. In J. K. Campbell, O'Rourke, M., & Shier, D. (Eds.), *Freedom and determinism* (pp. 277–304). Boston, MA: MIT Press.

Gilbert, P. (2009). Introducing compassion-focused therapy. *Advances in Psychiatric Treatment, 15*, 199–208. doi:10.1192/apt.bp.107.005264

Glasser, M., Campbell, D., Glasser, A., Leitch, I., & Farrelly, S. (2001). Cycle of child sexual abuse: Links between being a victim and becoming a perpetrator. *British Journal of Psychiatry, 179*, 482–494. doi:10.1192/bjp.179.6.482

Goldstein, E. (2010). Mindfulness and trauma: An interview with John Briere, Ph.D. Retrieved from http://blogs.psychcentral.com/mindfulness/2010/03/mindfulness-and-trauma-an-interview-with-john-briere-ph-d/

Harris, T. (1991). *Silence of the lambs.* New York, NY: St. Martin's Press.

Hick, J. (1966). *Evil and the god of love.* London, England: Macmillan.

Kane, R. (1996). *The significance of free will.* Oxford, England: Oxford University Press.

Kellert, S. (1993). *In the wake of chaos.* Chicago, IL: University of Chicago Press.

Kendrick, T. D. (1956). *The Lisbon earthquake.* London: Methuen.

Klevens, J., Duque, L. F., & Ramírez, C. (2002). The victim-perpetrator overlap and routine activities: Results from a cross-sectional study in Bogotá, Colombia. *Journal of Interpersonal Violence, 17*, 206–216. doi:10.1177/0886260502017002006

Lewis, D. O., Pincus, J. H., Feldman, M., Jackson, L., & Bard, B. (1986). Psychiatric, neurological, and psychoeducational characteristics of 15 death row inmates in the United States. *The American Journal of Psychiatry, 143*, 838–845.

Merton, T. (1968). Address to a conference on East–West monastic dialogue, quoted in *Religious Education* (1978), *73*, 292.

Pace, T. W., Negi, L. T., Adame, D. D., Cole, S. P., Sivilli, T. I., Brown, T. D., . . . Raison, C. L. (2009). Effect of compassion meditation on neuroendocrine, innate immune and behavioral responses to psychosocial stress. *Psychoneuroendocrinology, 34*, 87–98. doi:10.1016/j.psyneuen.2008.08.011

Pollock, V. E., Briere, J., Schneider, L., Knop, J., Mednick, S. A., & Goodwin, D. W. (1990). Childhood antecedents of antisocial behavior: Parental alcoholism and physical abusiveness. *The American Journal of Psychiatry, 147*, 1290–1293.

Sartre, J. P. (1993). *Being and nothingness.* New York, NY: Washington Square Press. (Original work published 1943)

Segal, R. (1995). *The Black diaspora: Five centuries of the Black experience outside Africa*. New York, NY: Farrar, Straus & Giroux.

Staub, E., Pearlman, L. A., Gubin, A., & Hagengimana, A. (2005). Healing, reconciliation, forgiving and the prevention of violence after genocide or mass killing: An intervention and its experimental evaluation in Rwanda. *Journal of Social and Clinical Psychology, 24*, 297–334. doi:10.1521/jscp.24.3.297.65617

Whiffen, V. E., & MacIntosh, H. B. (2005). Mediators of the link between childhood sexual abuse and emotional distress: A critical review. *Trauma, Violence, & Abuse: A Review Journal, 6*, 24–39. doi: 10.1177/1524838004272543

8

THE UBIQUITY OF EVIL—
AND MULTIMODAL COGNITIVE
TREATMENT OF ITS EFFECTS

ARNOLD A. LAZARUS

Little progress can be made by merely attempting to repress what is evil;
our great hope lies in developing what is good.

—Calvin Coolidge

Is anyone who performs evil deeds ipso facto an evil person, or is he or she merely an individual who carries out wicked acts? This question may seem like something that might be posed to a high school class, but it has in fact been a subject of debate for many years among and between secular scholars and theologians. Google, in response to the word *evil*, shows the vast complexity of the term. The wide range of definitions, etymological origins, religious opinions, philosophical positions, and ethical proposals is daunting. Legal scholars are apt to argue about differences between *malice* (the intent to harm) and *sadism* (wherein a person derives pleasure from inflicting pain on another). Knowing the details of these profound issues is not necessary when designing a logical rationale for therapeutic techniques. For this purpose, one may simply state that evil is the antithesis of good. Evil is a deliberate action that harms an object or creature. The intent to do harm is its essence. Yet

DOI: 10.1037/13941-008
Humanity's Dark Side: Evil, Destructive Experience, and Psychotherapy, A. C. Bohart, B. S. Held,
E. Mendelowitz, and K. J. Schneider (Editors)

157

deliberate acts known to be harmful would not be considered evil if they were done in self-defense or in defense of another.

Our proclivity for evil is largely due to the fact that *Homo sapiens* are aggressive creatures. Few (if any) other members of the animal kingdom take positive pleasure in the exercise of cruelty upon another of their own species. As the British psychiatrist Anthony Storr (1968) stated:

> We may like to believe that the guards in the German concentration camps could be classified as abnormal, but many seem to have been ordinary men whose taste for cruelty had only to be reinforced by training and example for them to become accustomed to the daily, wanton infliction of abominable pain and humiliation. . . . Of course there are shining instances of human beings who, at the risk of their own lives, refused to participate in barbarity. (p. 98)

Thus, evil may be ubiquitous, yet there are those among us who are essentially kind, loving, empathic, concerned, and gentle—but the pickings are slim. What's more, as is the case with many human attributes, it is important to consider the difference between a state (i.e., an uncharacteristic, specific, and temporary phenomenon) and a trait (i.e., a stable, defining, and enduring characteristic). Thus, some "good" people are capable of isolated acts of evil, and some "evil" people are capable of great kindnesses.

CONCEPTUALIZING EVIL

Perceptions of good and evil are so extensively divergent that what is considered the height of evil by some is seen as exceedingly good by others (e.g., a suicide/homicide bomber is reviled by most civilized people yet revered by his extremist brethren). Hence, universally agreed-upon definitions of good and evil seem impossible to achieve since diverse societies, religions, and cultures have such widely different views. One of the most famous phrases in the entire history of the Supreme Court was in reference to "obscenity" (Wikipedia Encyclopedia): "I may not be able to define it, but *I know it when I see it*," coined by Justice Potter Stewart in 1964. Perhaps the same may be said of evil.

Like most phenomena, evil falls on a continuum from mild to extreme. In his book *On Evil*, Terry Eagleton (2010) presented a theological argument to support the contention that evil transcends ordinary human wrongdoing and means more than merely inflicting harm on one's fellow human beings. To debate when a deliberate and vicious act of harmfulness on another human being is an evil deed or merely an example of wrongful and very bad behavior would take us into the realm of ontological conundrums. As a practicing clinician, I am content to leave these ponderous issues to the philosophers. Let us take a hypothetical example. "A" held a grudge against "B" for refusing to help him change a tire on his car. Under cover of darkness he deliberately and willfully damaged "B's" car engine so that when he tried to set out for work the next morning, his car would not start. "A" was fully aware that his little act of sabotage would cost "B" considerable inconvenience and expense. What he did not realize is that "B" was expected at an important staff meeting. "B" owned no other vehicle and hired a taxi, which took a long time to arrive. The CEO of the company was extremely displeased by his lateness. "B" feared that this would cost him a promotion. Had "A" realized the total consequences of his deed he might have restrained his anger and not meddled with "B's" car. Be that as it may, "A" had confessed his misdeed to a respected confidant, who said to him it suggests that he is fundamentally an evil and vengeful person. Many clinicians and counselors deal with hundreds of these petty issues—most clients present as guilt-ridden, conflicted, anxious, and depressed individuals. Counselors and clinicians who work in high-security prisons will encounter problems that fall at the opposite end of the continuum—dealing with the perpetrators of armed robbery, assault, and murder will be their daily fare.

EVIL AND THERAPY

Therapists who work with cases of child abuse usually have a heartbreaking and difficult time trying to remove the scars. I consider the perpetrators of child abuse to be exceedingly evil. I have treated many adults who were victims of child abuse. It was impossible to make significant inroads with many of these unfortunate individuals. What makes these cases so difficult to treat is that flashbacks to the atrocities they had endured often erupt unexpectedly, like epileptic seizures. Nightmares tend to disrupt their sleep, untoward images cascade through their minds, and negative sensations besiege them. Many had received psychotherapy, hypnosis, and medication, to no avail. The scars ran too deep.

I have no special expertise in understanding or treating people whose levels of aggression and lack of empathy and concern for others make them capable of hideous and barbaric cruelty. Very few of my clients were perpetrators of evil; the vast majority were victims of evil. For more than 50 years, most of the people I have treated would be considered "oversocialized." Their needless guilt often led them to see themselves as "evil." In these cases, Albert Ellis's views about unconditional self-acceptance (USA) and unconditional other acceptance (UOA) can serve as powerful antidotes for their toxic ideas. Readers unfamiliar with Albert Ellis and the tenets of his school of psychotherapy, rational–emotive behavior therapy (REBT), will find a wealth of information on Google. REBT rests on the principle that most of our emotional problems are based on irrational beliefs. The position Ellis adopted that pertains to evil is that we are all fallible. If someone performs a stupid or nasty act or says something really foolish or mean and is chastised and called a "stupid fool," he would be coached to say and believe, "I'm a fallible human being. I'm not a stupid fool, and I am working on becoming less fallible." The same applies when using UOA—one avoids imposing pejorative labels on others for displays of their shortcomings.

Despite my prior comment about the therapeutic value of USA and UOA, Ellis, in my opinion, goes too far: His thinking becomes a reductio ad absurdum when he stresses that "Hitler, Stalin, Genghis Khan are never bad people and if you condemn them you're going to condemn yourself, when you are bad." (Go to Google and search for "Albert Ellis Interview + Heery.") I have discussed and debated this view with Ellis and several of his followers. They all stuck steadfastly to this belief. This seems like "absolutistic think-ing" (which Ellis strongly criticized) because they are claiming that there are absolutely no evil people—merely people who carried out evil deeds. Ellis frequently stressed that as a result of his philosophy he did not even feel upset by Hitler: He did not hate Hitler, but rather hated what he had done. Ellis's problematic distinction and the logic that follows from it strike me as fatuous; I cannot discern any heuristic benefits by adopting it. When dealing with the hypersensitive people we see so often in our practices, the ones who rant and rave about minor infractions, oversights, displays of vulgarity, and similar pedantries, separating the deed from the person can be helpful. "Nellie is such an evil person. She is always gossiping and spreading rumors. I hate her." A therapist might find some value in stating something to the effect that perhaps Nellie is a very insecure person and her untoward behav-ior is her way of mitigating her own feelings of inadequacy and depression. Maybe if we knew more about her, we would feel sorrow for her rather than hatred. The opening sentence of this chapter raises these considerations. I reiterate that there is a point at which deeds of horror transcend the line of thought that the deed should be separated from the person. For instance, I contend that the doctors in Nazi death camps who performed atrocious and inhuman operations on people in the name of scientific investigation were unspeakably evil individuals. Rationally speaking, surely there needs to be a cutoff beyond which "this is a fallible human being doing bad deeds" becomes "this is a bad person." (See the state-versus-trait distinction noted above.)

A CASE EXAMPLE

I don't know how many clients Ellis treated who were beyond what I am calling the "cutoff point," whose antisocial personality disorders (I still prefer the terms *psychopath* and *sociopath*) led them to perform acts of torture, murder, rape, child molestation, and other behaviors that most members of our society would consider barbaric. Given that Ellis's vast writings covered mainly anxiety, depression, sexual disorders, marital problems, social inhibitions, anger, and obsessive–compulsive and posttraumatic stress disorders, it can be argued that his thinking and methods were most suited to what used to be called the "run-of-the-mill neurotic." Not that these people are necessarily easily changed for the better. A case in point may clarify some significant issues. This case example is about a young woman who suffered from the belief that she was evil and subject to eternal damnation. It shows how easily a guilt-prone individual can be pushed into self-destructive false beliefs that emanate from tenets of Judeo–Christian religions applied by a rigid and fault-finding minister. The treatment called for a broad-based but personalistic approach.

"Sheila," a single woman, age 28, described herself as "exceedingly evil and consumed by guilt." Some 10 years earlier, her parents had joined an extremely conservative church and pressured Sheila into doing likewise after she graduated from college. She had majored in fine arts and obtained a job at a museum. Sheila had no siblings and felt especially close and beholden to her parents. Interestingly, a couple of years after Sheila had joined that church, her parents became members of a different religious group, but Sheila remained at the original one. Sheila said she had tended to be somewhat uptight and oversensitive as far back as she could remember, but her pervasive guilt had been ignited by a charismatic minister of her church who preached on "rules of decency" that were extremely strict. Women were encouraged to use no makeup, dancing was permitted only between spouses, masturbation was a sin, and even lascivious thoughts could land one in the eternal fires of hell. Her only sexual encounters had been with a young man who was a classmate in college. At that time she had no idea she was "going against God's will." Nevertheless, the minister informed her that her name in the Book of Judgment now had a smear against it. Every night she obsessively ran through the litany of events that she had experienced that day to ascertain that her sins (if any) were minimal. She was obsessed with fears of being evil and kept herself under constant vigilance and tension to ensure that she was feeling, doing, and thinking the "right things" because God was observing her at every second. She had also developed various medical issues that her doctors called "psychosomatic."

Sheila had consulted several therapists. She first met with a counselor at her church who, from what I inferred, endeavored to persuade her that the minister's strict views and taboos were debatable. She then consulted a therapist who allegedly told her that she was suffering from deep masochistic tendencies that required careful exploration. He supposedly made much of the fact that Sheila did not use the opportunity to leave that church with her parents but had elected to stay with the minister, a punitive father figure, with whom she had bonded. She had very little rapport with or confidence in this therapist, so she consulted a third professional who came recommended by friend in whom she had confided. From Sheila's account it seemed that she (the therapist) attempted to persuade her that a belief in a personal deity is like believing in Santa Claus. She tried to reeducate Sheila by challenging other irrational and fallacious beliefs, but Sheila was not ready to make the changes and said she found that her therapist strongly reminded her of a strict teacher she had at high school. She next found her way to my office in a rather fortuitous manner. She overheard two visitors at her museum discussing therapy and therapists, and she came away with "Lazarus in New Jersey." She gravitated to the name *Lazarus* because of its strong biblical connotations. When she arrived home from work she promptly Googled "Lazarus + New Jersey + Psychologist" and tracked me down.

Our initial session was devoted mainly to rapport building: I listened attentively to her issues and complaints and asked nonthreatening questions. I also provided a brief explanation of my theories and treatment methods. I often asked, "How does that sound to you?" In describing my multimodal therapy orientation, I emphasized that I would assess not only three or four areas of function but would focus on seven interactive processes: her behaviors, thoughts, feelings, sensory reactions, mental images, interpersonal relationships, and biological factors (which might require input from a physician). She volunteered that she liked the sound of my "no stone left unturned" approach and asked if I would recommend something for her to read on the subject. I loaned her a copy of Corsini and Wedding's (2008) *Current Psychotherapies* and recommended that she read my chapter "Multimodal Therapy" (Lazarus, 2008). I also inquired whether she would be willing to take home a 15-page *Multimodal Life History Inventory* (Lazarus & Lazarus, 1991) and complete it at her leisure. The inventory covers developmental history, main problem areas, and interpersonal relationships, and it has various questionnaires—for example, irrational beliefs, emotional difficulties, and family background—to mention a few of the issues traversed. Sheila was a cooperative client. The mainstay of my interventions focused on what I considered to be many toxic beliefs, interpersonal issues (mainly unassertiveness and social skill deficits), and bodily tension that resulted in acute pains in her neck and shoulders (for which she found relaxation skills, the use of calming mental imagery, diaphragmatic breathing, and weekly massages from a certified massage therapist most helpful).

Some 3 months into the therapy, Shelia's parents expressed a desire to meet me, and Sheila willingly gave permission to them and to me to set up a meeting. Her parents were pleasant people, both deeply concerned about their daughter. They concurred that she was doing much better, mainly as reflected by the fact that she seemed less uptight and was no longer attending what I had dubbed "that evil church" so regularly. (When I felt that the degree of rapport between Sheila and me was strongly positive, I began speeding up matters and took the liberty of teasing her good naturedly—hence my reference to "that evil church," which became our little joke, except I was being quite serious.) When I asked her parents what had drawn them to that church initially, Sheila's mother said that there was one minister who gave excellent sermons, the choir was outstanding, the décor was attractive, and she had no idea that the one preacher would have such a debilitating effect on Sheila. I told them that when the time was right, I intended to go full force to persuade Sheila to leave that church and asked them whether I had their permission to do so. (It is not uncommon to find parents who undermine a therapist's efforts, and I wanted to get a feel for whether I might run into parental opposition.) The father said that if and when this was achieved, he would give me a bottle of red wine he had been storing for 5 years in his wine cellar, despite the evil preacher's proscription on alcohol. I jokingly suggested that when the time came perhaps we could all sit down and drink a toast so that the licensing board could not accuse me of bribery.

Not long after this meeting, Sheila arrived at my office in a very upset state of mind. We did some relaxation exercises, deep breathing, and imagery (picturing herself in peaceful places). We also discussed her "buttons"—issues over which she still upset herself. After calming down she then confessed (and I use that word advisedly) that she had masturbated and was now surely rated by God as so evil that she was doomed to hell. Given my sense that we had an excellent level of rapport, I decided to deploy one of my "nuclear weapons." I told her,

> You are insulting God. Here is the architect and builder of the universe which is so vast and so extensive that our mortal minds cannot even begin to fathom it. Here is this divine force, this omnipotent power that right now might be contending with a collision of two enormous galaxies, many times larger than our Milky Way, and billions of light years from our earth. The explosions and cosmic chaos are so powerful and widespread that they are far beyond our ability to even begin to imagine. At the same time, billions of light years in another direction, there are other huge cosmic events and disruptions that only God could deal with. And you make the Lord sound like a petty, narrow-minded clergyman! There are big enough troubles on our earth—bombing, torture, killing, raping, theft, and political skulduggery, to mention but a few evils—yet this is but the tiniest drop in the ocean compared to the gargantuan matters that God has to settle and judge. Do you really believe that such a superpower has the slightest interest in whether you rub your clitoris, whether or not you pray to him, and obey asinine commands that are man-made? Do you think that God really cares whether Hymie Goldberg

keeps his head covered in Temple, while Chris McTavish takes his hat off in church? What do you really believe, Sheila? Surely God is not going to enforce silly narrow-minded prohibitions and punish those who break them. Won't God be interested in such matters as whether one is honest, trustworthy, sincere, kind, helpful, caring and loving, and be utterly indifferent to people who put words into his mouth calling for strictures, restraints, pedantry and minutiae?

Sheila looked at me intensely as I was delivering this monologue. In truth, I am a skeptic and do not believe in mysticism or superpowers (unless we are referring to a tornado). But I was speaking her language. There would be no point in trying to cast doubt on the existence of God, as one of her other therapists had done. When I inquired how she felt about what I had said, she replied, "I think you have a point." Our session ended on that note.

At our next session Shelia seemed in a cheerful mood and began by accurately paraphrasing the soliloquy I had delivered at our previous meeting. "It's now so obvious to me that God Almighty would not be petty or small minded," she said. I noticed that she was wearing a shade of pink lipstick that matched her blouse, and she also had a touch of rouge on her cheeks. We had never discussed the pros and cons of wearing makeup. A few sessions before, we had done some role playing to help her ask her boss if her work hours could be shortened, but this was no longer necessary because she had received a substantial salary increase. She then mentioned that she had been doing a lot of reading on Buddha and Buddhism and found these ideas most congenial. She asked how familiar I was with Buddhism, and I said I knew the main tenets and found them to be closer to my own way of thinking than would be true of most religions. We then chatted about the Dalai Lama. At the end of our meeting I suggested it was probably time for her to take a vacation from therapy and she agreed.

I next heard from Sheila by phone 5 or 6 weeks later. She was dating a man 3 years her senior who headed a humanitarian organization. She wondered if it would be a good idea for the three of us to meet so I could determine whether he is the "right man" for her. I said I had no objections to such a meeting, but that I was not a mind reader: If she tactfully found out everything she could about him and respected her own gut feelings, she would have a very good idea whether marriage should or shouldn't be in the cards. I ended the call by saying that as time passed, if she felt unsure or conflicted, I'd be entirely willing to bat the pros and cons around with her, and if necessary, meet the man in question. Intermittent calls and e-mails were exchanged with Sheila. Things were going well, and she was still dating "Bob."

Not too long thereafter, I received a wedding invitation that Sheila had wanted to come as a surprise. In deference to her parents, the wedding took place in the church where they were members. I attended the event, and at the reception, Sheila's father came to my table with a smile on his face and a bottle of red wine and two glasses in his hand.

CONCLUDING COMMENTARY

Our world is not a gentle, kind, safe, and loving haven. Evil is ubiquitous. Whether the degree of evil takes the form of serial killers torturing and murdering innocent and defenseless people or stems from far less traumatic matters as in the case of Sheila, the net result is pain, suffering, and unhappiness. It is no trivial matter to live with the belief that one is evil, and to fear eternal damnation. A helpful intervention depends on the client's readiness for change and undergoing a phenomenological shift. This calls for the therapist to facilitate a modified cognitive pattern that is compatible with the client's fundamental belief system. It is my view that to endeavor to convince Sheila to incorporate and embrace a secular, agnostic outlook had little chance of success.

REFERENCES

Corsini, R. J., & Wedding, D. (Eds.). (2008). *Current psychotherapies*. Belmont, CA: Thompson Brooks/Cole.

Eagleton, T. (2010). *On evil*. New Haven, CT: Yale University Press.

Lazarus, A. A. (2008). Multimodal therapy. In R. J. Corsini & D. Wedding (Eds.), *Current psychotherapies* (pp. 368–401). Belmont, CA: Thompson Brooks/Cole.

Lazarus, A. A., & Lazarus, C. N. *Multimodal life history inventory*. Champaign, IL: Research Press.

Storr, A. (1968). *Human aggression*. New York, NY: Atheneum.

9

VIRTUE AND THE ORGANIZATIONAL SHADOW: EXPLORING FALSE INNOCENCE AND THE PARADOXES OF POWER

MAUREEN O'HARA AND AFTAB OMER

The world is filled with both good and evil—was, is, will always be. Second, the barrier between good and evil is permeable and nebulous. And third, it is possible for angels to become devils and . . . for devils to become angels.

—Philip Zimbardo, *The Lucifer Effect*

Nearly all of contemporary political philosophy adheres, explicitly or implicitly, to an optimistic image of humanity. It concentrates on facilitating the "good", while ignoring the necessity to make strenuous efforts to confront and disempower evil.

—Yehezkel Dror, *The Capacity to Govern*

I call it cruel, and maybe the root of all cruelty, to know what occurs but not recognize the fact.

—William Stafford, "A Ritual to Read to Each Other"

A renowned psychiatrist once advised a colleague who was about to take a job at a leading psychology graduate school where he had once taught[1] to "beware the vipers and backstabbers," explaining that before he had finally left, he had been so undermined and demonized on a regular basis that he

---

[1]Case stories are fictionalized, participants disguised, and elements from different situations combined.

DOI: 10.1037/13941-009
Humanity's Dark Side: Evil, Destructive Experience, and Psychotherapy, A. C. Bohart, B. S. Held, E. Mendelowitz, and K. J. Schneider (Editors)

had to self-medicate to go to faculty meetings. He reported that the school consistently undermined its leaders. The mission proclaims a dedication to "new ways of thinking and acting," and the brand boasts that its faculty are leaders in transformational practice. Nevertheless, over the institution's history many good people have found themselves victims of conduct that is far from transformational. Unable to respond to the inevitable conflicts of organizational life in ways that are consonant with its stated values, when disagreements or disappointments have occurred, in place of a transformative response, the "off with their heads" approach was more like Alice's "Red Queen." Over its history, directors, presidents, vice presidents, deans, and other high-level administrators had been unceremoniously ousted for reasons that in a mature organization would have been handled through respectful dialogue, dignified feedback, or at the most extreme, a well-designed succession plan. Instead, interviews with former leaders and people who have remained reveal a legacy of deep hurt, chronic open wounds, and an inability of the institution to come to terms with its past. One former program director describes his experience of the way he was discharged as a form of posttraumatic stress.

Though abuse of power of all kinds is common in organizations, what makes this case striking and so painful for those targeted is the dissonance between the institution's view of itself as benign and enlightened and its malevolent conduct. As we hope to show in what follows, it is in this gap between espoused theory and actual practice that evil gains entry into virtuous organizations.

This chapter examines everyday harmful behavior that occurs in organizations involved in efforts to bring good to the world. It is based on case material gathered over two decades of inquiry into organizations dedicated to social services, social change, and education that engage in cruel and unjust treatment of their members and sometimes their clients. A virtuous organization may cohere around a myth of its own innocence. The maintenance of this myth through actions, attitudes, and values counter to the organization's stated view of itself can lead to harmful and sometimes devastating consequences. Situated within an American culture that historically has mobilized powerful defenses against the awareness of its own propensity for and perpetration of evil, well-meaning organizations often fall into similar patterns of false innocence and the perpetration of cruelty while aspiring to virtue. Some principles and practices that enable organizations to foster reflexive awareness are suggested to prevent and to remedy these harmful dynamics and to assist psychotherapists working with victimization.

We have struggled with how to characterize these institutions since they include social service groups, universities, psychotherapy training programs, professional organizations, and spiritual groups. What they have in common is their transformational missions and their aspirations to operate at a higher level of consciousness than "mainstream" groups. We have settled on the term *virtue-driven organizations* for this discussion.

CASES

A savvy entrepreneur, seeking to do something to help humanity after he had made his fortune with an Internet start-up, was hired to lead a nonprofit eldercare organization whose culture was grounded in Quaker ideas about governance by consensus and group spirit. The organization felt it needed some new direction, and the new director's energetic approach, so effective in his rapid action hi-tech start-up, had appealed to the board of trustees, who were also from the business world. He frequently commented to staff that his philosophy was to "ask forgiveness, not permission" for his initiatives. The effects of his style were a shock to the prevailing, somewhat contemplative culture, which was not used to dealing with difference. This created considerable friction that destroyed the group's capacities for deliberative collective action. What had been a well-honed and delicately attuned community group found itself confronting paranoia, conflict, and betrayal. Within a year the organization had collapsed amidst a maelstrom of blaming, scapegoating, and recrimination.

A social service agency whose mission was committed to empowerment, social justice, and progressive cultural transformation condoned behavior among its staff that was so toxic it drove one of its managers to suicide. Days before she took her life, the manager had begged leadership to intervene in the relentless harassment only to be told that her emotional intensity and instability were "cause for concern."

A college committed to interdisciplinary work at the boundary between spirituality, alternative education, and social justice imploded after a faction moved against the president. The innovative and educationally successful school had been surviving on the margins of higher education for more than 30 years, supported by donations, grants, and a dedicated staff willing to work for less than market salaries in exchange for fulfilling their vocation as change agents. Values at the school were explicitly countercultural, and over time unorthodox fiscal measures aimed at financial survival had become routine. These were justified in the school as "necessary subterfuges." In addition, to save money, people filled multiple roles in which reporting structures were unclear and personal relationships often got out of hand. When challenged on the ethics of such activities by a group within the school, leadership became defensive and reactionary, prompting the disaffected faction to report the school to the accreditation agency in retaliation. Within months the president was gone. Though officially a resignation, he had been threatened that if he did not resign he would be fired "for cause" and therefore would be ineligible for severance, continuing health insurance, and the pension plan. As the school unraveled, accusations of misconduct extended to a wider group until they reached a fever pitch, with various subgroups squared off against others. Shortly thereafter, the school lost its accreditation and closed, leaving staff and faculty unemployed and their dreams and reputations in tatters.

We begin our inquiry by affirming authentic innocence and virtue. We have worked as teachers, psychotherapists, leaders, and organizational consultants in higher education, arts organizations, nongovernmental organizations, social service agencies, health care, and spiritual communities that embrace authentically transformative missions. We work in them and for them because we share their aspiration to transform society. These groups are composed of good people, and they do good work. In our view, such organizations constitute an important cultural resource providing practical hope in challenging and cynical times. And we are not alone. Communities across the globe are experiencing a Cambrian explosion of groups dedicated to worthy causes, with more created every day in which socially minded entrepreneurs seek to combine doing good works with making a living (Hawken, 2007). The value and urgency of this work and our experience of how often such aspirations unravel into harmful situations in which people get badly hurt prompt this inquiry.

EVIL AND CULTURE

In the debate between humanistic psychologists Rollo May and Carl Rogers (Greening, 1984) about whether the capacity for evil is intrinsic to the individual, lying "just below the surface" ready to be unleashed, as May argued (p. 17), or is the result of damage inflicted by an injurious world on an "essentially constructive prosocial person," (p. 12) as was Rogers's conviction, both consider evil as an aspect of the individual human psyche. Some studies have supported May's view and suggested that intrinsic to all of us is a sadistic impulse to enjoy inflicting pain on the powerless, which, though ordinarily inhibited by prosocial group norms, can, if it becomes disinhibited, make monsters out of any of us (Baumeister & Campbell, 1999). Others have countered this damning view by pointing out that even in situations of mass frenzy, such as the massacre at My Lai, not everyone fired their weapons; some hid from the rampage, and still others chose to intervene at the risk of their own lives (Dutton, 2007). But overall, experimental studies of misbehavior in groups strongly point to the conclusion that serious psychological derangement aside, focusing on individual actors does not adequately account for the "banality" (Arendt, 1963/1994) of most evil. Sherif's Robbers Cave experiment (Sherif, Harvey, White, Hood, & Sherif, 1961), Zimbardo's Stanford Prison experiment in 1971 (Zimbardo, 2007), and many subsequent studies have established that groups can create circumstances in which ordinarily good people can be moved to commit extraordinary evil acts. In reflecting on the events at the Abu Ghraib prison in Iraq, where prisoners were humiliated, degraded, and tortured, Zimbardo concluded that certain contexts create forces that may make devils out of angels and angels out of devils and named this phenomenon the *Lucifer effect* (Dutton, 2007; Staub, 1989; Zimbardo, 2007).

We readily acknowledge a difference between the group psychosis in Jonestown, for instance, and the chaotic psychological violence in an alternative college; it would be absurd to blur the distinction. So why should we call these events "evil" and not just bad management or organizational dysfunction? This is no trivial matter because, as some of our friends have said, if we call every bad thing "evil," then we run the risk of normalizing real evil. We agree, but as we interviewed people who had been the victims of virtue-driven institutions, they used the word *evil* as the only word that went far enough to express how extreme their experiences were. Despite their surface banality, the traumatic impact of these events stems from the way in which the actions strike at the psychic core of the organizations and individuals involved. People we interviewed described intense suffering. They spoke of humiliation, degradation, suicidal despair, cognitive disintegration, financial ruin, professional failure, loss of their homes, failed marriages, incapacitating rage, and psychic terror. These experiences fit Herman's (1997) description: "traumatic reactions [that] occur when action is of no avail. When neither resistance nor escape is possible, the human system becomes overwhelmed and disorganized" (p. 34). Organizations may also show symptoms of trauma and may struggle to recover from the chaos caused by institutional evil for years, and some of them do not make it at all (Hormann & Vivian, 2005). We retain the use of the word *evil* because we sense that as a culture we are becoming increasingly numbed to the dehumanization that has become business as usual in many aspects of our lives. Use of less-loaded words such as *dysfunction* or *shadow* runs the risk of contributing to our collective denial of the harm we who work and live in mission-driven organizations that wish to do good can do to each other. As the wider culture becomes incoherent and lines blur between competing value systems, the moral consensus unravels and no longer provides unambiguous guidance as to acceptable and unacceptable conduct even to those who would be virtuous. Immoral action becomes normalized (MacIntyre, 1981).

For anyone wanting to go deeper into definitional complexities of the concept of evil, we refer to the work of moral philosopher Susan Neiman (2004) for an accessible contemporary exploration. Like her, we do not argue that people are intrinsically evil. We do not know people's intentions. Our discussion is based in a view that regards as evil human acts that do great harm to others and are not justified by the acts of the victims and are beyond explanation through accepted shared narratives within which participants' lives are ordered.

The mass graves in Flanders, the mile upon endless mile of white grave markers recording the deaths of young soldiers, do not suggest to most visitors that evil or an otherworldly dark force was at work. These graves present no threat to psychological coherence because they are recognizable within a warrior culture. One day attitudes about warfare might change, but as of 2011, sadly, most human beings are raised in cultures that see warfare and the death of young men (and now women) not as evil, but as "noble"; their deaths not slaughter or murder, but sacrifice. The martial narrative that frames battlefield carnage can account for lost lives, no matter how many, without having to change in any fundamental way. These are the graves of our fallen heroes.

As horrific as so many deaths are, they do not threaten the sense of cosmic order. Acts cross the line and become evil when there is no way to make sense of them within the existing conceptual order upon which people rely to live creative and fulfilled lives. Six million innocents dead in the Holocaust, one million butchered in Rwanda, 3,500 dead in the World Trade Center, eight dead and eaten by Jeffrey Dahmer, or five thrill kills by U.S. soldiers collecting body parts as souvenirs in Iraq are considered evil not because they are any more deadly or more horrific but because the circumstances of these deaths shock the civilized world out of its sense of virtue and innocence. The dissonance between what we believe ourselves to be—moral, humane, and rational—and what we experience when innocents are slaughtered and raped so challenges our sense of a benignly ordered universe that we must find ways to psychologically distance ourselves. As long as these acts can be labeled aberrations, they can be kept at arm's length existing outside the narratives we own as "ours." As long as they remain attributed to "others," they present no challenge to our sense of cosmic order.

To understand why some acts evoke the specter of "evil" while others may not, we must look to the larger context within which human consciousness forms—what O'Hara (2010) called the *psychosphere* and others may refer to as *culture*.[2] No individuals exist or can exist outside of culture. Even those

---

[2]O'Hara proposed that the term *culture* is not adequate because by most definitions it speaks to realities external to the consciousness of individuals. The term *psychosphere* refers holistically to the complex of interconnected, dynamically interpenetrated system of narratives, symbols, images, language, metaphors, patterns of life, values, epistemologies, cognitive habits, rituals, religions, sports, forms of commerce, metaphysics, art, and technologies that are the products of human creativity and together provide the field out of which collective and individual consciousness emerges. In this discussion, the words *narrative*, *culture*, and *psychosphere* are used interchangeably.

who are irredeemably alienated are alienated from some culture. We derive our identity, our sense of existential meaning and expectations of each other, and our conceptual landscape from within particular cultures. Our cultures are in us as much as we are in our culture. Acts that affirm identity, belief, attitudes, values, and taken-for-granted assumptions within a given culture and that reassure participants of its stability are prized. By contrast, acts that undermine these givens are fiercely resisted (Argyris, 1992; Heine, Proulx, & Vohs, 2006). To maintain coherence, organizations mount a defense against awareness of acts that fall outside the known psychosphere. Defenses are mobilized at psychological levels through an array of mechanisms and publicly through cultural practices such as governance structures, law, ritual, entertainment and the arts, and now social media. The more cohesive the culture, the more vigorous will be the defense of its core.

SACRED COMMITMENTS

For many who work in virtue-driven organizations, their involvement is not "just a job" but represents something far more psychologically important. Drawing from the work of Rank, Goffman, and Reich, Ernest Becker (1975) provided a useful framework in proposing that human beings build cultures to avoid facing their existential fears and to meet their most vital psychological needs. Like Rank, Becker proposed that the fear of death drives us to seek engagement with something heroic—an immortality project—that extends beyond us as physical beings (Becker, 1973). Dedicating one's life—even just some of it—to a cause we expect to continue after we depart represents a primal commitment and addresses our existential need to transcend death. In this frame, choosing to dedicate one's life to an altruistic organization involves a surrendering of one's individual being in exchange for a greater meaning in the interbeing[3] of a virtuous collective endeavor. It is a sacrifice of self—a sacred act—in exchange for some kind of eternal life. Working in a Zen hospice may offer a sense of expanded life through caring for the frail and dying and perhaps expiation of survivor guilt. In his examination of evil, Becker (1975) also proposed that even more terrifying to us than mere extinction—which as he pointed out is the inevitable fate of all of us—is the possibility of "extinction with insignificance" (p. 4). Cultures grant significance to individual human lives through acknowledging, remembering, and honoring people's presence among us. This is why in many societies

---

[3]*Interbeing* is a term offered by Buddhist thinker Thich Nhat Hanh to describe the state of connectedness and interdependence of all beings.

sanctified land is set aside for cemeteries and headstones carry individual names, and why invading armies go to lengths to destroy them, condemning the vanquished not only to subordination but to oblivion. It is also why to the ancients banishment and exile were fates worse than death. Whatever strengthens the sense of immortality removes the specter of oblivion, provides meaning and expanded life, and so binds members at deep levels of being.

Participants in virtue-driven groups characteristically become fiercely loyal, protective, and passionately invested in their missions. Many identify with their organization so passionately that even the smallest details become their concern. Someone proposes a change in the logo and everyone wants input; a curriculum change must be endlessly debated; a new hire must be approved by everyone; rewriting mission statements becomes a community endeavor. Likewise, whatever betrays a core value inevitably generates intense and sometimes extreme responses. Paranoia, rage, and terror are readily evoked by any threat to the coherence of the group's identity. The variously attributed quip about academic politics—"the reason they are so vicious is that the stakes are so small"—could not be further from the mark. Universities and scholarly disciplines are altruistic virtue-driven organizations to which talented individuals "profess" their dedication. In our view, the intensity of emotional involvement in such organizations should be read as a reflection of just how huge the stakes are.

IDENTITY AND ORGANIZATIONAL DEFENSE

The organizational shadow represents those elements in the group's psychosphere that are at odds with the authorized and accepted version of who they are (Bowles, 1991). Cultures create strong barriers against the intense feelings triggered by activities that bring to the surface what has been suppressed. Military groups cherish bravery and honor and defend against displays of cowardice, for instance. Heroes are ceremoniously honored, and someone who falls short is discharged "dishonorably." Scientists defend against the nonrational, pouring public scorn on those who cross the line; religious men and women defend against reports of sexual abuse of children; and virtue-driven groups defend against anything that casts doubt on their claims of innocence. The defenses against guilt and shame—the normal responses to failing to meet the espoused standards—involve elaborate cultural practices that, as we will discuss, provide a gatekeeping function to maintain a collective sense of virtue. The responses often include doing damage to innocent individuals.

A pervasive ideology of collective innocence has been a feature of American identity since the first colonies were established and is still a dominant theme of the American mythology (Spector, 2010). To preserve its sense of purity, American culture has mobilized powerful defenses against awareness of its own capacity for and perpetration of evil acts. To reduce the anxiety associated with proximity to that which is taboo, Americans have projected unrecognized impulses onto selected "others." This founding construction of Americans as innocent—a people chosen by destiny to drive out sin and corruption and bring a purer, utopian way of life to the world, and the attribution of wickedness to "others"—remains a strong theme in the American narrative. Indeed, it is core to American culture's immortality project itself. And it is especially strong in the psychosphere of American groups that seek to do good work.

Groups have many defensive strategies they can use to avoid facing the shame and guilt that arise when conduct associated with the organization's shadow occurs (Pauchant & Mitroff, 1992). These defenses are psychological in the sense that they may operate below the level of perception (Banaji, 2001), but they are also cultural—built into conceptual, narrative, and institutional practices such as leadership, governance, policy, and law that structure the norms and values of how we live (Dror, 2001; Koortzen & Cillers, 2002; Michael, 1997; Pauchant, 1994). The most common defenses are simple lies, distortions of fact, or spin. An organization in which an anonymous smear poisoned the chances of an insider's promotion, for example, sent out an announcement denying that the campaign had any effect on the outcome. What started as an attempt to calm the waters set off a vicious cycle of injury that ended by seriously wounding the victim and generating significant organizational pain. Not only did the target lose out in the promotion—loss number one, but because of the official denial he was left to handle the injustice and reputational damage alone—loss number two. This was followed by interpretative violence: The victim's anger was regarded by leaders attempting to convey the impression of empathy as "understandable disappointment that he didn't get the position." Thus, in an attempt to hide its complicity, the institution invalidated the employee's experience, alienated him from his colleagues, and made him look like a sore loser. The perpetrators, on the other hand, were rewarded by accomplishing their goal, and the institution learned nothing about the toxic effect of false witness or about its own complicity. The innocence narrative was restored, the victim has been silenced, and evil has been enabled.

Silencing victims and eliminating evidence help evil thrive. "Gag orders," "executive sessions," "confidentiality policies," and "strategic communications" all serve to sustain the narrative of innocence in the wake of cruel or unjust actions and undermine attempts at resistance. When a weekend coup removed a successful executive director from his post, members of the institution asked the board for evidence of wrongdoing. This was refused purportedly "to protect the E.D." In exchange for a severance settlement, a gag order was imposed that prevented the executive director from making any public or private statements that might reveal the circumstances of his departure or portray the institution in any negative light whatever. Conversations with colleagues and friends about his removal were forbidden by the order, and potential supporters were warned not to discuss the situation among themselves on penalty of dismissal. Silencing was aimed at preserving the organization's innocence narrative. But by preventing the victim from openly discussing his experience and the community from working through the shocking events, it lessened the organization's capacity to learn from its mistakes, gain closure on the organizational rupture, and further victimized the executive director.

In religious groups, denial of the shadow may show up as a "spiritual bypass." After injurious acts, injured parties are often urged to "seek the higher truth" or told to "let go." A hospice grief counselor who received an unjustified excoriating performance review from a supervisor with whom she had clinical differences was instructed by her director to "forgive." When she was unable to do this on schedule, she was dismissed (a secondary victimization) on the grounds that she was "spiritually unsuitable" for hospice work. In a cruel and crazy-making irony, a letter of support from her colleagues that referred to her "compassion and kindness" was considered divisive by the center's director and as further demonstration of her unsuitability for hospice work.

Guilt by innuendo—the "no smoke without fire" approach—and deliberate misinformation also serve to keep the myth of innocence intact. After a policy disagreement with an inexperienced president, the chief finance officer of a close-knit social service agency was publicly ordered to hand over his keys, his e-mail account was blocked, and he was "perp-walked" out of the building that had been his home for a decade. Stunned colleagues were left to wonder what he could possibly have done that was awful enough to necessitate such drastic measures. When they sought explanation, they were told, "We can't tell you, because if it came out it would be too damaging." Caught between genuine concern for the victim and an implied threat from remaining leadership, ordinarily actively involved and compassionate people acted as "innocent" bystanders.

Cover-ups are an essential element of false-innocence strategies. A senior employee at an institution had committed suicide after having been hounded and harassed by two colleagues with whom she had philosophical differences; in the month following her death, her husband and friends were invited to attend a memorial for her at the institution, where she was to be "honored" by the same people who had terrorized her.

Blame shifting is another common strategy for maintaining the narrative of innocence. If it can be shown that someone subjected to abuse by a group contributed to his or her own victimization in some way, then perpetrators can deny culpability (Ryan, 1971). In many institutions, including virtue-driven ones, blame shifting has been institutionalized as a standard form of "crisis management." Strategic communication, once called propaganda, has become a regular course in MBA programs, where leaders learn how to create campaigns to spin events in line with the organization's innocence narrative. Websites offering "spin templates" are readily available on the Internet. Strategic communications use sophisticated group psychology research to ensure that all members of an organization receive the desired narrative before the victims have time to mount any defense. When gag orders against victims are used in conjunction with spin by the crisis managers, a "reality" can be constructed that absolves the organization of any need to examine its conduct. Strategic communications almost never admit wrongdoing and despite frequent references to "transparency" are overwhelmingly aimed at obscuring the truth and restoring faith in the group's innocence.

Revisionism and erasure serve to sustain the false innocence of those who remain. As minority scholars have amply demonstrated, the official past and future are usually concocted by those with the power to do so. Virtue-driven groups, especially those in which the therapeutic frame is prominent, are often proud of their commitment to fairness, empathy, nonjudgment, and "seeing things from both sides." The shadow of this openness shows up as reluctance to follow rules of due process and evidence gathering, to take a stand against bad behavior, or to challenge the veracity of claims made by the different sides. By accepting official accounts at face value and listening to hearsay, distortion, and spin, the history of actual events becomes reduced to a matter of "whom do you believe?" Into this gap those with the most power to spin the information can construct the narrative that best suits their purposes.

Key to maintaining the official history and the innocence narrative intact is discrediting or erasing evidence of any positive contributions made by the people who have been targeted. Erasure often begins while they are still in the organization, as the dynamics of shame and embarrassment about what is taking place take over. The "dead man walking" treatment shows up as averted eyes, failure to inform individuals about important meetings, and subtly (and sometimes not so subtly) handing over authority and responsibility to the replacement-in-waiting. In one institution a communiqué about a (forced) resignation referred to the departing leader not by her name but simply as "the former president" and praised the talents of the incoming interim, who had played a significant role in the demise of the leader. Community members left dazed and terrified, asking, "If she can be vaporized, then who's next?" The erasure of the outgoing president's contribution was not an oversight but was deliberate, part of a planned strategic communication campaign designed by the school's attorney and the board chair that continued for years. In the case described in which the manager committed suicide, 2 years after her death, several of the projects she had been responsible for were being attributed to others. In yet another example, on a website recounting the century of accomplishment of a religious organization, the years during which a leader who was forced out was at the helm were represented by a gap.

The most pernicious of all defenses against the collective shadow is projection of the unacceptable aspects of the psyche onto a scapegoat. As the history of slavery, racism, sexual subordination, anti-Semitism, Islamophobia, homophobia, and xenophobia in America amply demonstrates, projecting unacceptable shadow elements onto reviled "others" has been an effective and noxious strategy by which to maintain the American myth of innocence. In virtuous organizations the scapegoat is often someone who is seen as "other"—not quite one of us, somehow set apart. Nothing qualifies a person for "otherness" more easily than being more talented, more courageous, more outspoken, or more sensitive to the interests of those whose voices are seldom heard. Those who suffer the deepest wounds from organizational misconduct are most often those who have been selected as the scapegoat. We shall have more to say about this later.

Bystander dynamics further add to the likelihood that harmful acts will go unopposed (Darley & Latané, 1969). During organizational crises, particularly if leadership is being attacked, diffusion of responsibility and fear for their own safety can lead nonparticipants to unwitting complicity. Strategic communications in the form of tailored announcements to different subgroups are designed to spread uncertainty, to exploit the inevitable ambiguity, and to generate bystander dynamics among those who might otherwise come to the defense of the victim.

BUILDING A REFLEXIVE ORGANIZATION

Harmful acts that cannot be explained and normalized from within the psychosphere of those affected terrorize us not because the actual injuries inflicted are necessarily so heinous but because the acts rupture the cultural coherence within which our sense of cosmic order and existential hope for immortality are contained. And because such acts transgress culture-sustaining narratives, people caught up in these events become disoriented, with no culturally aligned and sanctioned ways to act to reduce harm and heal their pain. In contrast to a crime, for which legal remedies can be employed, when an organization that claims to champion the oppressed oppresses its own members or when a group that espouses compassion treats someone inhumanely and is impervious to their entreaties for fairness, the contradiction can be bewildering. If this is followed up by cover-up behavior that further violates collective understandings, the cruelty spirals and may become intolerable.

We have suggested that virtue-driven groups cohere around a myth of their own innocence, which is falsely maintained by denying actions, attitudes, and values that are counter to their stated view of themselves. This compulsively enacted false innocence results in mistakes that can escalate into cover-ups and leave organizations vulnerable to repetition of similar mistakes. Organizations are caught in a double bind—if injustice is acknowledged, the collective myth of innocence unravels and the specter of annihilation looms. If it is suppressed, the injustice remains, individuals continue to be harmed, and no learning is possible. As with an individual who seeks the aid of a therapist to grow past such impasses, some kind of safe and disciplined practice akin to organizational therapy may be needed to permit resolution of the bind. In what follows, we suggest some principles and practices that enable organizations to develop a reflexive awareness that both prevents and remedies harmful dynamics.

DIFFERENCE AND RESPECT

The mission and sustaining narratives of organizations carry their cherished values. It is common to hear members of virtue-driven groups speak with pride of their alignment, harmony, and adherence to their values and cultural norms. But the alignment has its shadow. Defense of these values can act like a purification filter, keeping the group true to its values but excluding awareness of vital differences. Organizational dynamics (e.g., values, structures, practices) that entail denying, disavowing, repressing, suppressing, trivializing, and merely tolerating differences reduce a group's capacity for wise action (Omer, 2005). For differences to be recognized and engaged, they must first be seen as an asset worthy of more than tolerance or token presence—that is, as an element of a group's potential to see the world more fully and more clearly. Respect is the precondition and evidence of objectivity, hence not itself contingent on objectivity.

Those who have more power and privilege in a culture are often blind to key differences that need to be perceived in order to avoid harm. In the organization earlier described, in which a manager committed suicide in the face of persistent harassment by coworkers, the source of friction was a deep epistemological difference between the victim, who favored qualitative hermeneutic assessment, and the department head, who dismissed qualitative methods as "merely preliminary." Not only did the victim suffer harassment, the whole organization was diminished as it was unable to appreciate the added resource that qualitative methods might have represented for them.

Much behavior in organizations is unavoidably conflicted because competing interests are often pursued, leading to mixed signals and crazy-making. Taking the time to tease out these differences and to see them through the eyes of respect takes discipline and effort but when successful permits a fuller grasp of any situation and supports more creative options.

Group cohesiveness also has a downside. Though much valued in many mission-driven groups, the degree to which an organization is coherent and in alignment about its core values and maintains a symbiotic relationship between the members and their psychosphere is the degree to which it resists engagement with perspectives external to the organization. Its coherence becomes its liability, and groupthink (Janis, 1972) becomes a real threat. The diversity of perspectives—so crucial to providing corrective feedback in multiply determined processes—is diminished, and unintended harmful consequences become much more likely. When things go wrong, multiple vantage points enable the perception of distinct aspects of what actually happened. Groups of highly educated individuals such as academics or those who consider themselves more enlightened are especially prone to overestimating their openness to difference and underestimating their vulnerability to groupthink.

Practices that support creative conflict within an organization bring to the surface key differences that can serve to expand an organization's capacity for problem solving and wise action. When diverse perspectives are solicited, encouraged, and engaged, in place of a false solidarity built on unexamined consensus, an authentic consensus open to novelty and growth can emerge. Any difference that makes a difference may be significant. The differences in race, gender, positional power in the organization, and history within the group, if respected and engaged, offer the opportunity of creative synergy. In our experience, altruistic, virtue-driven organizations have difficulty emerging from a false consensus once established without the benefit of the perspectives from those who stand outside the group. This is where an informal or formal consultant who is not a participant in the group can make a substantial difference.

SHAME AND CULTURE

As cultures degrade under difficult circumstances (e.g., war, famine, recession), cultural practices that sustain respect diminish. The more numb to shame we become, the more disrespect becomes normalized. For example, contemporary commentators and interviewers in the media are far more disrespectful in their conduct than was the case 20 years ago (Brooks, 2009). As the wider culture becomes exhibitionistic about its shamelessness, with popular media subjecting us to a relentless exhibition of despicable behavior as entertainment, we are becoming numb to the everyday violations of human dignity. So it becomes more difficult for any organization to rely on shame awareness as a guide to disrespectful behavior, either from a perpetrator or a victim. For instance, calling security to escort a leader out of the building, shutting off access to e-mails, and banning him or her from reentering the building, all in the name of risk management, inflict wounds to dignity that go far beyond the loss of employment. For a person whose identity and sense of belonging are aligned with his or her group, as it is for many who serve virtue-driven organizations, the loss of face and humiliation can be excruciating, not infrequently leading to despondency and despair. As such disrespect becomes institutionalized, it becomes ever easier to handle conflicts without engaging with difference. Organizations that tolerate this kind of behavior, even when directed to do so by their attorney, are complicit in its violence. To counter, they need effective shame-discerning awareness and social processes that can renew a once common healthy sense of shame to provide a guide to their collective conduct. If not, degrading actions will become "the way things are," rationalized as "risk management," and not seen for the cruelty that they actually are, and the corrosive effect on the entire organization will go unnoticed.

POWER AND SCAPEGOATING

Virtue-driven organizations are frequently suspicious or at least ambivalent about hierarchy and power, setting the stage for scapegoating and attacks on leadership when things go awry. The role of the scapegoat is to provide an explanation for problems within a group that creates the illusion that they have been addressed (Colman, 1995). Though anyone can be selected by a group to serve as its scapegoat, within virtue-driven organizations, those in roles of high importance such as leaders or movers and shakers are often singled out. The erosion of support for the leadership function and the normalization of the scapegoating of leaders results in (a) leaders and leadership teams closing themselves off from necessary feedback and creative engagement with those who hold different perspectives and (b) organizations where leaders and leadership teams are disrespected. Such organizations become dangerous places for everyone. On the other hand, values and organizational practices that protect leaders and leadership teams from being scapegoated enable those with institutional power to remain open and continue to be learners. A key role for boards of trustees is to ensure that leaders do not become demonized or scapegoated.

Undermined or openly attacked leaders create an ambiguous context with respect to responsibility. "Bystander dynamics" are more common where responsibility is unclear (Darley & Latané, 1968). When the leadership function or the leaders themselves are attacked, it becomes less and less likely that any-one will feel safe enough to exercise leadership in the difficult work of engag-ing differences. Individuals and subgroups at the periphery of organizations are prone to attacking those at the center (the "center" being where governance/leaders are located), because contemporary culture manifests a profound fear of power—and for good reason (Omer, 2005). Thanks to a generation of criti-cal analysis of the abuses of power from feminists and critical theorists, and as a result of queer studies and other outsider studies, members of virtue-driven organizations have become reluctant to exercise power themselves, and so are often inept in its healthy practice. This abdication of the use of necessary force reinforces the bystander dynamic and leaves a power vacuum into which abu-sive and manipulative forms of power emerge. The most effective antidote to scapegoating in our view is the skillful exercise of the power of leadership.

POWER, COMPETENCY, AND ACCOUNTABILITY PRACTICE

Virtue-driven organizations are also often ambivalent about account-ability. Some of this can be traced to the extension of therapeutic values into organizational spaces, which results in demands for accountability being seen as an unwelcome authoritarian intrusion into authentic relationships (Bellah, Sullivan, Swidler, & Tipton, 1985; Lasch, 1978). Freedom from judgment and "shoulds" is valid as a therapeutic stance but when applied as a social practice quickly turns into malignant disengagement in which individual subjective opinions are given as much weight as collective agreements and obligations. This opens the door to personal grudges, smears, and rivalries. Sure of their own individual innocence, members of virtue-driven organiza-tions may consider themselves beyond the need for the kinds of conven-tional constraints on their beliefs and behavior that less "enlightened" groups require. Following through on promises; honoring contracts and due process; following clear policies and procedures; and providing clarity with regard to roles, responsibilities, and communication practices are commonly dismissed as burdensome and unnecessary. Such organizational narcissism can lead to a sense of entitlement, arrogance, and exceptionalism that mask uninten-tional cruelty and cause real harm (Duchon & Drake, 2009). Accountability practices, instead of stifling innovation, may in fact restore and revitalize relationships among members of virtue-driven groups by making real their commitment to fairness. Through painstaking application of such practices, a reflexive, shame-discerning awareness can arise that can in turn transform political games into a search for real justice. A shared hermeneutic discipline may be cultivated that enables all members of a community to collaborate in articulating a shared narrative about troubling events that incorporates the diverse meanings at play (Omer, 2003). Scapegoating and punitive blaming entail interpretive violence. The antidote is a respectful collective inquiry that seeks out and engages the various perspectives. Practices that provide a context for expressing difference are needed in all organizations, but none more than those that aspire to social transformation.

To be authentically accountable entails being accountable for the impact of one's choices, not just for one's intentions. Virtue-driven organizations and virtue-driven people typically identify with their intentions ("That's not what I meant, that wasn't my intent") and pseudo-innocently deny the impact of their choices on others (May, 1972, p. 24). Everyday evil may be understood as the refusal to be accountable for the harmful impact of one's choices.

The recent emphasis on transparency, though aimed at reducing opportunities for covert institutional wrongdoing, has its shadow, too. As long as we remain pseudo-innocent (particularly with respect to the power we have to affect others negatively), transparency may constitute a denial of the complexities and impact of well-intended actions. It is rarely possible for organizations to be totally transparent: Responsible stewardship of organizational power entails discretion about facts and even intentions. Because their innocence is an illusion, only the pseudo-innocent can claim to be fully transparent and sanctimoniously pontificate for full transparency.

CULTURAL LEADERSHIP PRACTICES AS A RESPONSE TO CULTURAL GATEKEEPING

During stable periods, the center of any culture—even a small organization's culture—is dense with rules, norms, taboos, and with what is generally known and taken for granted. Organizations maintain their continuity and coherence through the dynamics of cultural gatekeeping, where transgressions are punished or resisted and conforming is rewarded. During transformative periods, the center of a culture loses some of its power to impose its norms and so becomes more spacious—with expanded room for diversity, novelty, creativity, and heresy. During these periods, the creative periphery is in dynamic interaction with the center of the culture (Omer, 2005). Though such periods generate significant anxiety and dread, if handled effectively they can also lead to creative growth. The quality of cultural leadership makes the difference. When leadership responds to its own anxiety by acting to stifle and suppress the emerging disorder, communities become deadened and despotism becomes a possibility. But if leadership has the capacity to engage the edge of chaos, despite the dread that evokes, the center may expand and transformation is possible.

Finally, a word about psychotherapy. In efforts to make sense of their experience and ease the crushing pain that sometimes drags on for years in the event of cover-ups and post hoc spin, victims may seek psychotherapy. What they often find is that many therapists are ill prepared to work with victims of abuse at the hands of virtue-driven organizations. We spoke to individuals who reported being retraumatized by therapists who seemed unwilling to consider that real victimization had occurred in such institutions. Thus, victimization by virtue-driven organizations frequently leads to self-blame. For the cosmic order to make sense, someone or something must be responsible. As innocence narratives are constructed to shield perpetrators from blame, victims of organizational abuse become easy prey to their own doubts. One informant described how his already battered self-esteem had been further undermined by a well-meaning therapist who had hinted that his depression was a sign that he had deeper abandonment issues that he needed to work through. A woman who was relentlessly confronted for months for "not being person-centered enough" in a person-centered training group, until she suffered an emotional breakdown, was urged by a therapist to "re-story her victimization into a heroic choice story." As feminist and critical psychologists have pointed out, it is often easier for victims of abuse and relational trauma to look for the cause of their abuse within themselves than to acknowledge the helplessness and powerlessness that comes with victimization at the hands of those whom they have loved or admired (Herman, 1997).

CONCLUSION

In our view, when embraced authentically, without cynicism or guile, virtue is a worthy organizational aspiration. The groups who yearn for a more humane future and are willing to dedicate their lives to realizing this dream need to be celebrated and supported. But, as William Stafford (1960/1993) concludes the poem "A Ritual to Read to Each Other," which we quoted at the opening, "the darkness around us is deep." In our darkening times, if virtue-driven groups are to fulfill their missions, they will require more than aspiration—they will require taking a long, hard look at the ways they unintentionally and (usually ignorantly) violate their own values, thereby becoming not the virtuous change they seek but the everyday dehumanization they seek to transform. They must develop and use transformative organizational practices that reflect their deeper values to learn from mistakes, heal the damage wrought, prevent future evils, and incorporate what they learn into better theories of virtuous action. In our view, when leaders have the courage to acknowledge that they are lost in a crumbling cosmos, such transformative practice can be developed in any group. What is most likely to hamper these efforts will not be the availability of effective transformative practices but the human willingness to use them. As long as false innocence clouds self-awareness and defends against news of our inescapably flawed humanity, evil is given an opening.

Social psychologist Donald Michael, friend of Rollo May and the authors, concluded after a lifetime of reflecting on the shadow of organizations that if groups are to do more good than harm, they must first become realistic and humble about their missions and about the blindness caused by pseudo-innocence. Organizations, their members, and their leaders must develop the courage to acknowledge their "vulnerability and finiteness, both [their own] and [their] projects . . . because," as Michael said, "we are unavoidably ignorant and uninformed about the outcomes—the consequence of the consequences of what we do." He ended the last written work before he died with the admonition that "the blind must lead the blind" (Michael, 2010, p. 111).

REFERENCES

Arendt, H. (1994). *Eichmann in Jerusalem: A report on the banality of evil*. New York, NY: Penguin. (Original work published 1963)

Argyris, C. (1992). *On organizational learning*. Malden, MA: Blackwell.

Banaji, M. (2001). Ordinary prejudice. *Psychological Science Agenda, 14*, 8–11.

Baumeister, R. F., & Campbell, W. K. (1999). The intrinsic appeal of evil: Sadism, sensational thrills, and threatened egotism. *Personality and Social Psychology Review, 3*, 210–221. doi:10.1207/s15327957pspr0303_4

Becker, E. (1973). *The denial of death*. New York, NY: Simon and Shuster.

Becker, E. (1975). *Escape from evil*. New York, NY: The Free Press.

Bellah, R. N., Sullivan, W. M., Swidler, A., & Tipton, S. M. (1985). *Habits of the heart*. Berkeley, CA: University of California Press.

Bowles, M. L. (1991). The organization shadow. *Organization Studies, 12*, 387–404. doi:10.1177/017084069101200303

Brooks, D. (2009, July 7). In search of dignity. *New York Times*, p. A23.

Colman, A. D. (1995). *Up from scapegoating: Awakening consciousness in groups*. San Francisco, CA: Chiron.

Darley, J. M., & Latané, B. (1968). Bystander intervention in emergencies: Diffusion of responsibility. *Journal of Personality and Social Psychology, 8*, 377–383. doi:10.1037/h0025589

Darley, J. M., & Latané, B. (1969). Bystander "apathy." *American Scientist, 57*, 244–268.

Dror, Y. (2001). *The capacity to govern*. Portland, OR: Frank Cass.

Duchon, D., & Drake, B. (2009). Organizational narcissism and virtuous behavior. *Journal of Business Ethics, 85*, 301–308. doi:10.1007/s10551-008-9771-7

Dutton, D.G. (2007). *The psychology of genocide, massacres, and extreme violence: Why "normal" people come to commit atrocities.* Westport, CT: Praeger Security International.

Greening, T. (Ed.). (1984). *American politics and humanistic psychology.* San Francisco, CA: Saybrook.

Hawken, P. (2007). *Blessed unrest: How the largest movement in history is restoring grace, justice, and beauty to the world.* New York, NY: Penguin.

Heine, S.J., Proulx, T., & Vohs, K.D. (2006). The meaning maintenance model: on the coherence of social motivations. *Personality and Social Psychology Review, 10*, 88–110. doi:10.1207/s15327957pspr1002_1

Herman, J. (1997). *Trauma and recovery.* New York, NY: Basic Books.

Hormann, S., & Vivian, P. (2005). Towards and understanding of traumatized organizations and how to intervene in them. *Traumatology, 11*, 159–169. doi:10.1177/153476560501100302

Janis, I.L. (1972). *Victims of groupthink.* Boston, MA: Houghton Mifflin Company.

Koortzen, P., & Cilliers, F. (2002). The psychoanalytic approach to team development. In R.L. Lowman (Ed.), *Handbook of organizational consulting psychology* (pp. 260–284). San Francisco, CA: Jossey-Bass.

Lasch, C. (1978). *The culture of narcissism.* New York, NY: Norton.

MacIntyre, A. (1981). *After virtue.* South Bend, IN: University of Notre Dame Press.

May, R. (1972). *Power and innocence.* New York, NY: Norton.

Michael, D.N. (1997). *Learning to plan and planning to learn.* Alexandria, VA: Miles River Press.

Michael, D.N. (2010). *In search of the missing elephant: Selected essays by Donald N. Michael.* Axminster, England: Triarchy Press.

Neiman, S. (2004). *Evil in modern thought: An alternative history of philosophy.* Princeton, NJ: Princeton University Press.

O'Hara, M. (2010). Another inconvenient truth and the developmental role for psychology in a threatened world. *The Humanistic Psychologist, 38*, 101–119. doi:10.1080/08873267.2010.485915

Omer, A. (2003). Between Columbine and the Twin Towers: Fundamentalist culture as a failure of imagination. *ReVision, 26*, 37–40.

Omer, A. (2005). The spacious center: Leadership and the creative transformation of culture. *Shift, 6*, 30–33.

Pauchant, T.C. (Ed.). (1994). *In search of meaning: Managing for the health of our organizations, our communities and the natural world.* San Francisco, CA: Jossey-Bass.

Pauchant, T.C., & Mitroff, I.I. (1992). *Transforming the crisis-prone organization.* San Francisco, CA: Jossey-Bass.

Ryan, W. (1971). *Blaming the victim*. New York, NY: Pantheon.

Sherif, M., Harvey, O.J., White, B.J., Hood, W.R., & Sherif, C.W. (1961). *Intergroup conflict and cooperation: The Robbers Cave experiment*. Norman, OK: University of Oklahoma Book Exchange.

Spector, B. (2010). *Madness at the gates of the city: The myth of American innocence*. Berkeley, CA: Regent Press.

Stafford, W. (1993). West of your city. In *The way it is* (p. 75). St. Paul, MN: Greywolf Press. (Original work published 1960)

Staub, E. (1989). *The roots of evil: The origins of genocide and other group violence*. New York, NY: Cambridge University Press.

Zimbardo, P. (2007). *The Lucifer effect: Understanding how good people turn evil*. New York, NY: Random House.

III

BROADER IMPLICATIONS: IS PSYCHOLOGY A MORAL ENDEAVOR?

INTRODUCTION: BROADER IMPLICATIONS: IS PSYCHOLOGY A MORAL ENDEAVOR?

In this section, three authors consider what could be called *metatheoretical issues* and their relationship to human destructiveness and its remediation. They focus on whether there is a moral dimension to psychology that could contribute to how psychology relates to human destructiveness.

David Livingstone Smith (Chapter 10) is a philosopher who has written a recent book on human destructive tendencies (Smith, 2011). Smith writes from the standpoint of psychoanalytic theory. Psychoanalytic theory has been thought to have subversive implications for morality: It is thought to undermine the idea that humans can act in moral or immoral fashions or be held morally accountable. Smith considers the following five claims for this reasoning: psychoanalysis describes human nature as essentially evil, psychoanalysis is deterministic, moral judgments are caused by unconscious processes, regression is pervasive, and psychoanalytic theory conceives of the person as an aggregate of subpersonal mechanisms. Smith argues that the first three claims are inconsistent with Freudian theory. However, the final two merit serious consideration. Smith concludes by discussing the implications of the final two claims for clinical practice, arguing that the psychoanalytic attitude of neutrality is a necessary concomitant of conceiving of psychological processes occurring at the subpersonal level in particular. This helps in determining how the analyst views the client who has acted in an "evil" or destructive fashion.

Ronald B. Miller (Chapter 11) argues, in contrast to Smith but in accord with Hollis in his earlier chapter, that considering questions of evil and the dark side leads to a more basic issue, which is that the practice of psychotherapy is a fundamentally moral enterprise. He questions what he sees as psychology's adoption of a "natural science" perspective, as if therapy were merely a matter of technological, evidence-based intervention. He argues that we have "sanitized" our language by using terms that cloak the moral nature of what we are doing. He argues there is a heavy price to pay for psychologizing evil and sanitizing the language. He notes that we must practice from a moral framework, even though we should not confuse this with moralizing to our clients. He particularly focuses on the role of moral emotions, noting how many of the emotions we deal with in therapy are fundamentally moral in nature: disappointment, betrayal, shame, guilt, righteous anger, jealousy, disgust, pride, and being horrified at evil. He observes that by ignoring the moral element of what we do, we overlook how our clients are suffering, not merely from "psychological disorders" but from wounds inflicted by larger organizations in the form of social injustice, including those inflicted by our own profession.

Barbara S. Held (Chapter 12) has been one of the leading critics of the positive psychology movement (Held, 2004, 2005). Held asks, "When did feeling bad turn into being bad?" She notes that this equation did not begin with the positive psychology movement. However, some leaders of that movement may have inadvertently promoted that equation under the mantle of science. In her chapter, Held (a) argues that within aspects of the positive psychology movement there lurks the implicit logic that to feel bad is to be unvirtuous; (b) explores the (historical) basis and detrimental ramifications of this belief; and (c) links this belief to evil in terms of its ironically postmodernlike denial of the daunting, and sometimes horrific, realities of human existence, or what she calls the "perils of personhood." Compatible with other chapters in the book, her position entails the consequences of putting a forced "smiley face" on negative experience, which can be personally destructive and can cause those who cannot feel happy about their circumstances to feel bad about themselves.

REFERENCES

Held, B. S. (2004). The negative side of positive psychology. *Journal of Humanistic Psychology, 44*(1), 9–46. doi:10.1177/0022167803259645

Held, B. S. (2005). The "virtues" of positive psychology. *Journal of Theoretical and Philosophical Psychology, 25*(1), 1–34. doi:10.1037/h0091249

Smith, D. L. (2011). *Less than human: Why we demean, enslave, and exterminate others.* New York, NY: St. Martin's Press.

10

BEYOND GOOD AND EVIL: VARIATIONS ON SOME FREUDIAN THEMES

DAVID LIVINGSTONE SMITH

Like many other students of human nature before and after him, Freud argued that moral pretensions are often a cover-up for other less praiseworthy and more self-serving intentions. However, there are reasons to think that psychoanalysis has far more subversive implications for morality. My task in this essay is to consider what these skeptical implications might be, and to evaluate their plausibility. I discuss the theoretical claims of psychoanalysis and some of the entailments of those claims, but not questions about their truth or falsity. In other words, I ask what of moral significance follows from the supposition that psychoanalytic claims are true. I confine myself to Freud's work, both because of its foundational status and because of its philosophical sophistication. In any case, psychoanalytic theory has ramified so extensively in the 60-odd years since Freud's death that discussing even the most significant variants in appropriate detail and depth would be impossible within the

The author thanks Dr. Barbara Held and Dr. David Mandel for their helpful comments on an earlier draft of this chapter.

DOI: 10.1037/13941-010
Humanity's Dark Side: Evil, Destructive Experience, and Psychotherapy, A. C. Bohart, B. S. Held, E. Mendelowitz, and K. J. Schneider (Editors)

confines of a single chapter. So the reader should bear in mind the fact that the specifics that I address may not apply, or do not apply with the same force, to other theories coming under the broad umbrella of psychoanalysis. The reader should also be aware that limitations of space restrict the number of topics that I can discuss and the thoroughness with which I can discuss them.

I confine myself to considering five claims about the ethical implications of psychoanalysis, the first three of which, although frequently invoked, are mistaken and can be discarded. The remaining two are more substantial and raise profound questions, not just for psychoanalysis but for psychology in general. Finally, I gesture toward the clinical significance of Freud's theoretical views about evil.

This essay should be thought of as an introductory one. Anyone interested in pursuing the subject more deeply can turn to the literature on psychoanalysis and ethics (e.g., Lear, 1990; Reiff, 1961; Wallwork, 1991) as well as the relevant philosophical literature dealing with metaethics and moral psychology.

PEOPLE ARE ESSENTIALLY EVIL

The first interpretation that I consider (with the brevity that it deserves) is that psychoanalysis proposes that our behavior is driven entirely by self-serving sexual and aggressive urges and therefore that morality is merely a deceptive façade. This interpretation of Freudian theory is mistaken. Freud did not claim that moral sentiments and motives are nothing more than defenses against primitive biological drives. It is true that he argued that morality is, in large measure, derived from sexual and aggressive drives, but to say that A is *derived* from B is a far cry from saying that A is *reducible* to B. In Freudian theory, hedonistic motives provide the developmental platform for the emergence of other-regarding attitudes. They are at the beginning of a maturational trajectory that culminates in the development of a capacity to reflect upon, evaluate, and, when necessary, condemn one's own antisocial desires. To claim that Freud regarded morality as nothing but a cover-up for something deeper and darker is to fundamentally misconstrue his concept of human development.

The idea that Freud regarded human nature as basically "bad" is so wildly inaccurate and so easily refuted by recourse to his writings that believing anyone could give it credence is difficult. However, there are people who do. For instance, Martin Seligman (2002) offered a version of this thesis in his book *Authentic Happiness*. Seligman talked about what he called the "rotten-to-the-core dogma" (p. xii), which he defined as "the belief that happiness (and even more generally, any positive motivation) is inauthentic" (p. xii). According to Seligman,

Freud dragged this doctrine into twentieth century psychology, defining all of civilization (including modern morality, science, religion, and technological progress) as just an elaborate defense against basic conflicts over infantile sexuality and aggression. We "repress" these conflicts because of the unbearable anxiety they cause, and this anxiety is transmuted into the energy that generates civilization. So the reason I am sitting in front of my computer writing this preface—rather than running out to rape and kill—is that I am "compensated," zipped up and successfully defending myself against underlying savage impulses. (p. xii)

Among other errors in this passage is the claim that psychoanalysis treats all "positive" motivations as inauthentic. This is simply untrue, and it is a charge Freud explicitly addressed and rebutted on numerous occasions. For example, he wrote in a 1915 essay, "It is not our intention to dispute the noble endeavors of human nature, nor have we ever done anything to detract from their value." He went on to say that he placed "a stronger emphasis on what is evil in men only because other people disavow it and thereby make the human mind not better, but incomprehensible" (Freud, 1915/1957, pp. 146–147). This statement is consistent with the picture of human nature that is implicit in Freud's writings. Even in *Civilization and Its Discontents*, which contains one of his most somber assessments of the human condition, he pointed to the coexistence of both:

> The element of truth . . . which people are so ready to disavow, is that men are not gentle creatures, who want to be loved, who at the most can defend themselves if they are attacked; they are, on the contrary, creatures among whose instinctual endowments is to be reckoned a powerful share of aggressiveness. As a result, their neighbor is for them not only a potential helper or sexual object, but also someone who tempts them to satisfy their aggressiveness on him, to exploit his capacity for work without compensation, to use him sexually without his consent, to seize his possessions, to humiliate him, to cause him pain, to torture and to kill him [all italics added]. (Freud, 1930/1961a, p. 69)

Psychoanalytic theory neither states nor implies that human nature is essentially bad. So, we can set this aside and move on to an interpretation of Freud that, although equally erroneous, is far more interesting.

FREUDIAN PSYCHOLOGY IS DETERMINISTIC; THEREFORE, IT IS NIHILISTIC

The next four arguments that I consider state that psychoanalytic theory is inconsistent with moral agency and that therefore either psychoanalytic theory is false or nothing is morally right or wrong.

The first of these arguments turns on the implications of determinism. *Determinism* is the view that everything happens for a reason or, more formally, that every event is caused by prior events. We take determinism for granted in our everyday dealings with the material world; when something happens, we assume that something made it happen. For instance, if you try to start your car, but the car fails to start, you assume that something caused the car not to start (perhaps a dead battery). The hypothesis that there is no cause for the car's failing to start seems out of the question, and rightly so.

The doctrine of determinism notoriously brings a worry in its wake. If *everything* that happens has a prior cause, then everything that happens in our minds, including every one of our choices, has a prior cause as well. So, if determinism is true, then your choice to read these words was caused by prior events. Suppose that you decided to read this chapter because someone told you that it is interesting. If determinism is true, then their telling you that it is interesting was caused by prior events as well, and all of these events were also caused by prior events, and so on. Like every other event, your choice to read these words is but one link on a causal chain that extends indefinitely far into the past. It follows from this that, given the laws of physics and the state of the physical universe, say, 10 billion years ago (the number is arbitrary), your sitting right here right now reading exactly these words was fixed. The future simply could not have unfolded in any other way.

Those who are disturbed by this picture take it to imply that nobody is free and responsible for their actions. Obviously, we have no control over things that happened billions of years before our birth, so if all of our choices are the outcome of causal chains extending back long before our birth, then it seems to follow that we have no control over our own choices and the actions that flow from them. Our choices and actions are therefore not free because we could not have chosen otherwise, and we are not responsible for them because they are not under our control (van Inwagen, 1986).

If this reasoning is correct, then determinism has important implications for moral agency. It is generally accepted that people cannot have moral obligations that are impossible for them to fulfill—that is, it must be *possible* for you to do what you ought to do (the slogan is, "'ought' implies 'can'"). Suppose someone were to tell you that you have a moral obligation to travel back in time and assassinate Hitler. It would be reasonable to reject this injunction on the grounds that time travel is impossible. Now, some people think that if determinism is true, then *everything* that we do not do is analogous to traveling back in time to assassinate Hitler, because nothing that one does not do is something that one *can* do. Suppose that you are deliberating about whether to perform a certain act, and you decide to refrain from performing it. If determinism is true, then it was simply *impossible* for your deliberations to have issued in any other conclusion. Given the causal factors at play, your decision to refrain was as inevitable as the falling of the final domino in a row of falling dominos. In precisely those circumstances, with exactly those forces at play, you could not have chosen to perform the act. Given the principle that one cannot have a moral obligation to do the impossible, and given the principle that it is *physically impossible* to choose to do anything other than what one has chosen, it seems to follow that nobody has a moral obligation to choose any course of action other than the one that they have chosen—that is, that nobody is subject to moral obligations. I refer to the view that nobody is subject to moral obligations as *moral nihilism*.

Freud emphasized that psychoanalysis is premised on the truth of determinism (e.g., Freud, 1916–1917/1961c; 1920/1955c). That is, psychoanalysis would not make sense if determinism were false. So, if determinism entails moral nihilism, then if psychoanalysis is true, so is moral nihilism. Psychoanalysts, it seems, have to embrace the claim that nobody ever does anything that is morally wrong.

The idea that if determinism is true then nobody is free is known as *hard determinism*. The intellectual motivation for this position is the assumption that if choices are caused by prior events then they are not free. But those philosophers known as *compatibilists* think that this is a mistaken conception of freedom. Normally, when we talk about freedom, we contrast it with constraint and coercion. We hold that people act freely if they are not forced to act or prevented from acting otherwise, and we hold them responsible for their actions if they choose to perform them, irrespective of whether their choices were caused by prior events. Compatibilists accept this conception of freedom. They are full-blooded determinists, but they do not think that there is any contradiction between an act being free and its being determined. If this seems odd, or perhaps even incoherent, consider the following example. Suppose you decided to have lunch, and your decision was brought about by your being hungry. You decided to have lunch because you were hungry and if you had not been hungry you would not have chosen to have lunch. Now, suppose that while lifting a sandwich to your mouth it occurred to you that the decision to eat lunch was *caused* by your being hungry. Would this suggest that your decision to have lunch was not free? Of course not! In fact, we are inclined to see a person as acting freely to the extent that their choices accord with their desires—that is, when they do what they desire to do. Compatibilism shows that determinism per se does not entail moral nihilism. Psychoanalytic theory is premised on determinism, but not on hard determinism, so its commitment to determinism does not entail a commitment to moral nihilism (Wallwork, 1991).

MORAL JUDGMENTS HAVE UNCONSCIOUS CAUSES; THEREFORE, GOOD AND EVIL ARE UNREAL

The next argument uses an entirely different strategy to claim that psychoanalysis is a morally nihilistic theory. The argument's point of departure is the premise that, according to psychoanalytic theory, moral judgments arise from nonrational, unconscious processes. This is then taken to entail that morality is entirely subjective, and therefore that there are no moral truths other than truths about our moral beliefs (by analogy, there are no truths about unicorns, but there are truths about beliefs about unicorns).

Before explaining what is wrong with this argument, it will be useful to say a few words about what motivates it. One of the long-standing problems in moral philosophy is the seeming futility of attempting to situate moral values in a scientific worldview. The problem turns on the fact that moral concepts pertain to how things *ought* to be, while empirical concepts—the sort of concepts used in science—pertain to how things *are*. Psychology is an empirical science, so anyone offering a psychological account of morality is obliged to find a way to bridge the gap between the empirical "is" and the moral "ought" by incorporating moral properties into a scientific description of the world. Moral *realists* of a naturalistic bent believe that this can be done and have proposed various ways of doing it, none of which have won universal acceptance. Moral *anti-realists* argue that it cannot be done, because moral properties like good and evil do not exist.

The problem that I have just described is a metaphysical problem—that is, a problem concerning the way things *are*. It is easily confused with a related problem about the epistemic grounds for moral judgments. Normally, we make judgments about the properties that things possess by observing them. Observations are mediated by our sense organs, which are responsive only to empirical properties like size, shape, texture, color, and so on. If you touch a stone and judge it to be smooth, your perceptual judgment is explained by a causal connection between the stone's property of smoothness and the tactile receptors in your fingertips (as well, of course, as various processes in your brain occurring further downstream). Moral judgment does not seem to work like this. When you judge the torture of a child to be evil, you do not perceive the evil of the act in the same way as you might perceive the smoothness of a stone. You do not have good and evil receptors analogous to the tactile receptors in your skin, so it looks as though if good and evil exist "out there" in the world, they must be epistemically inaccessible to us.

If this is right, then where do our moral judgments come from?

The 18th century philosopher David Hume offered an influential response to this question. He proposed that moral judgments are affective states rather than cognitive ones. We do not *perceive* moral properties or infer their existence. Instead, we judge things to be bad when they elicit feelings of disapproval in us and judge things to be good when they produce feelings of approbation (Norton & Norton, 2000; Prinz, 2007). Psychoanalysis embraces a broadly Humean approach to moral judgment.

As I indicated earlier, there are people who think that this account of moral judgment implies that good and evil are unreal (e.g., Mackie, 1946). If this is a valid inference, then it follows that psychoanalysis endorses the view that good and evil are unreal. But it is *not* a valid inference, and psychoanalytic theory has no such irrealist implication. Freud explained why this sort of reasoning is fallacious in a paper entitled "On the Claims of Psychoanalysis to Scientific Interest" (1913/1955a). In the section of the paper dealing with why psychoanalysis ought to be of interest to philosophers, Freud underscored the fact that although psychology "can indicate the subjective and individual motives behind philosophical theories which have ostensibly sprung from impartial logical work" this "does not in the least invalidate [their] . . . truth" (p. 179). Freud insisted that one's motives for accepting a proposition as true have no bearing on the truth or falsity of that proposition (to think otherwise is to fall victim to what philosophers call the *genetic fallacy*).

Applying this principle to the sphere of moral philosophy leads to the conclusion that the psychological origin of moral beliefs does not entail that moral beliefs are false. To conclude otherwise would require the additional premise that beliefs caused by unconscious processes cannot be true, but it is difficult to see how this premise can be justified. Freud never endorsed the extra premise, so his account of moral judgment does not entail moral nihilism.

BECAUSE OF REGRESSION, WE ARE NOT AS MORALLY RESPONSIBLE AS WE SUPPOSE

In this section, as well as the next one, I consider interpretations of psychoanalytic theory that are considerably weightier than those that I have canvassed thus far. The first is the argument that psychoanalytic theory suggests that people are less responsible for their actions than is generally assumed.

We can begin by considering what is involved in attributions of moral agency. We think of people as moral agents if they are responsible for their behavior. It is difficult to specify exactly what this notion of responsibility comes down to without lapsing into vacuous circularity, but we can get reasonably close. A person is responsible for his or her behavior only if that behavior is *self-determined*. For a person to be a self-determiner, various psychological capacities must be in place. He or she must be able to choose a course of action over its alternatives, and this requires an ability to conceive of alternative courses of action, anticipate their consequences, and evaluate their pros and cons. Self-determiners must also have enough impulse control to enable them to pause and deliberate rather than act precipitously. In short, to be a moral agent, one must be able to engage in practical reasoning.

People do not enter the world as full-blown moral agents. According to Freudian theory, becoming a moral agent depends on one's making a developmental transition from the dominance of the *pleasure principle* during the earliest years of life to the dominance of the *reality principle* later on (Freud, 1911/1958a). Three features of this process are especially important in the present context. The first is its unevenness. Adults often remain infantile or readily become infantile in some areas of their personality but not in others. The second is its reversibility. We are all vulnerable to *regression* from a more sophisticated psychological organization to a more primitive one. This is because we all retain the potential to revert to infantile modes of functioning.

> The earlier mental state may not have manifested itself for years, but none the less it is so far present that it may at any time again become the mode of expression of the forces in the mind, and indeed the only one, as though all later developments had been annulled or undone. This extraordinary plasticity of mental developments is not unrestricted as regards direction; it may be described as a special capacity for involution —for regression— since it may well happen that a later and higher stage of development, once abandoned, cannot be reached again. But the primitive stages can always be re-established; the primitive mind is, in the fullest meaning of the word, imperishable. (Freud, 1915/1957, pp. 285–286)

The third feature, which is also alluded to in the passage just quoted, concerns the nonanalogical character of regression. Freud did not mean to say that when we regress, our psychological functioning merely resembles that of an infant, in the sense that a forgery of something resembles the original. He meant to say that some feature of the regressed person's psyche becomes infantile. The regressed person does not *behave like* a child. He or she *becomes* partially a child.

Freud believed that dreaming is a transient form of regression. In our dreams, we revert to a psychological mode that recapitulates that of a small infant. The psychoanalytic theory of dreaming is quite complex, and describing it in any detail would exceed the scope of this paper, but I will gesture toward some aspects of it that are important for assessing the moral significance of psychoanalytic theory. The Freudian story has it that dreaming is closely bound up with repression. *Repression* is the unconscious cognitive process that prevents mental representations of certain desires from becoming conscious. Repressed desires find expression in our dreams, but only in disguise, so that we cannot recognize them. They are unconsciously "censored" because they clash with our moral sensibilities.

Lusts which we think of as remote from human nature show themselves strong enough to provoke dreams. Hatred too, rages without restraint. Wishes for revenge and death directed against those who are nearest and dearest in waking life, against the dreamers' parents, brothers and sisters, husband or wife and his own children are nothing unusual. (Freud, 1916–1917/1961c, p. 143)

Freud argued that the "wickedness" of dreams—the fact that dreams give free reign to morally unacceptable desires—stems from their being products of regression to a premoral state of mind. Once we recognize this, Freud (1916–1917/1961c) claimed, we are no longer inclined to hold people responsible for the desires revealed by analysis of their dreams, and "the strange impression of there being so much evil in people begins to diminish" (1916–1917/1961c), for the following reason:

This frightful evil is simply the initial, primitive, infantile part of mental life, which we can find in actual operation in children, but which, in part, we overlook in them on account of their small size, and which in part we do not take seriously since we do not expect any high ethical standard from children. Since dreams regress to this level, they give the appearance of having brought to light the evil in us. But this is a deceptive appearance, by which we have allowed ourselves to be scared. We are not so evil as we are inclined to suppose from the interpretation of dreams. (Freud, 1916–1917/1961c, p. 210)

The change of perspective has this effect because

if the evil impulses of the dream are merely infantilism, a return to the beginnings of our ethical development, since the dream simply makes children of us again in thinking and in feeling, we need not be ashamed of these evil dreams if we are reasonable. (Freud, 1916–1917/1961c, p. 210)

Freud's point was not that once we understand the psychology of dreaming we have an *obligation* to exempt dreamers from moral responsibility for their desires. It was that once we understand that dreamers are in effect infants, we cannot but cease to regard them as moral agents. Of course, if regressed people merely *behaved* like infants, as opposed to being infants, we could reasonably hold them responsible for doing so and therefore reasonably continue to regard them as moral agents. But if Freud was right, there is a sense in which they *are* infants, and this is incompatible with ascribing moral agency to them. Now, recall that dreaming is just one example of regression, which is a much more general phenomenon. Regression in waking life may also activate "evil" impulses, but when this happens the impulses are *enacted* (either directly or in disguise) rather than dreamt. Freud gave many examples of the toll taken by regression on waking human behavior, including the atrocities of war (1915/1957) and acts of mob violence (1921/1955b). War and mob violence are collective manifestations of regression. On the individual level, Freudian theory claims that many forms of psychological disturbance involve regression and that virtually all people suffer from a measure of psychological disturbance. Taken in conjunction with his remarks about the exculpatory character of regression during sleep, the implication is that when ostensibly evil acts are consequences of regression, we should not consider their perpetrators as being morally responsible for them, because the perpetrators are, psychologically, infants.

Consider the following remarks written in 1969 by the distinguished German historian Ernst Nölte about Adolf Hitler:

> The dominant trait in Hitler's personality was infantilism. It explains the most prominent as well as the strangest of his characteristics and actions. The frequently awesome consistency of his thoughts and behavior must be seen in conjunction with the stupendous force of his rage, which reduced field marshals to trembling nonentities. . . . Hitler's rage was the uncontrollable fury of the child who bangs the chair because the chair refuses to do as it is told; his dreaded harshness, which nonchalantly sent millions of people to their death, was much closer to the rambling imaginings of a boy than to the iron grasp of a man. (As cited in Webster, 1995, p. 368)

If Freud was right, taking these remarks seriously has the effect of altering our assessment of Hitler's moral character. Reframing his apparently evil behavior as infantile prevents us from thinking of it as morally evaluable.

This way of thinking has a striking affinity with an analysis of moral attitudes developed over 40 years later by the British philosopher Peter Strawson. Strawson (1962/2008) pointed out that we implicitly demand an attitude of goodwill and consideration from others, and we respond to their meeting or failing to meet our expectation with what he called *reactive attitudes* such as gratitude (when the demand is met) and resentment (when it is not). In responding to people in this way, we hold them responsible for their behavior. There are circumstances in which we are prepared to excuse behavior that violates our expectations. These are situations

> which might give occasion for the employment of such expressions as "He didn't mean to", "He hadn't realized", "He didn't know"; and also all those which might give occasion for the use of the phrase "He couldn't help it", when this is supported by such phrases as "He was pushed", "He had to do it", "It was the only way", "They left him no alternative", etc." (Strawson, 1962/2008, pp. 7–8)

There are other circumstances that exempt a person from responsibility rather than merely excusing them. There are two sorts of exempting conditions. Strawson said of the first that they are captured by statements like "He wasn't himself," "He has been under very great strain recently," and "He was acting under post-hypnotic suggestion" (p. 8). He said of the second that they are captured by statements like, "He's only a child," "He's a hopeless schizophrenic," "His mind has been systematically perverted," and "That's purely compulsive behavior on his part" (p. 8). In both kinds of exempting circumstances, reactive attitudes yield to what Strawson called the objective attitude. When one adopts the objective attitude toward a person, one sees her "perhaps, as an object of social policy; as a subject for what, in a wide range of sense, might be called treatment; as something certainly to be taken account, perhaps precautionary account, of; to be managed or handled or cured or trained; perhaps simply to be avoided" but not as a full member of the moral community (p. 9). Considering Freud's remarks on regression in conjunction with Strawson's theory of reactive attitudes, we can see that regression plausibly counts as an exempting (or, perhaps, excusing) condition. This would explain why thinking of a person as regressed is inconsistent with conceiving of him or her as evil.

Regression introduces a note of uncertainty into our assessments of moral agency because it implies that the distinction between adult and child psychology, and therefore the distinction between moral agents and those absolved from moral responsibility, is neither as absolute nor as obvious as one might otherwise be inclined to assume.

THE SUBPERSONAL PERSPECTIVE IS INCOMPATIBLE WITH A MORAL STANCE

The final topic I discuss is the most substantial and far-reaching, and it is bound up with some of the most profound questions in the philosophy of psychology.

I need to begin with some history. Prior to the 20th century, the predominant view of the relation between mind and body was that bodies are physical things and minds are nonphysical things, a doctrine known as *dualism*. As science progressed, the dualist story became less and less appealing, and by the second half of the 20th century physicalism had overtaken dualism as the prevailing theory of the mind–body relationship. Put very roughly, physicalism posits that mental states are brain states. Freud converted to physicalism early in his career: From 1895 onward, when most of his colleagues were still unrepentant dualists, Freud held that mental phenomena are physical phenomena in the brain, and he built his psychoanalytic theories on this foundational assumption (Smith, 1999, 2003).

There is something deeply intuitive about dualism. Part of its attractiveness stems from the sense that purely physical creatures—fancy flesh-and-blood machines—could not be morally responsible, rational agents. But this is an illusion, for dualism does not do any better at this than physicalism does. This suggests that the problem is more explanatory than metaphysical. It is a problem about bringing two very different sorts of *explanations* into relation with one another, rather than a problem about understanding the relation between two different kinds of *thing*. On the one hand, we have explanations of human behavior that are couched in the language of intentional psychology. These invoke belief and desire, rationality, responsibility, and agency. And on the other hand, we have explanations of human behavior framed in terms of neurons, neural systems, cognitive maps, schemas, modules, and the like, which seem indispensable for a scientific account of human behavior. The former are explanations at the *personal* level, and the latter are explanations at the *subpersonal level*. The problem confronting us is that of establishing the relation between personal and subpersonal levels of explanation (Bermúdez, 2005).

Where does psychoanalysis stand with respect to the personal/subpersonal distinction? Freudian explanations make liberal use of the language of agency. In fact, psychoanalytic case studies are so saturated with this idiom that Freud (1950/1966) once expressed embarrassment that they read more like novellas than scientific reports. However, it is a mistake to think of psychoanalytic explanation as just an extended form of personal-level explanation, as some have done (e.g., Fodor, 1991; Hopkins, 1982). Freud made it clear that psychological explanations must go beyond personal-level processes to the subpersonal mechanisms that underpin them. He called these sorts of explanations *metapsychological,* on the analogy with metaphysics. Metaphysics is that branch of philosophy dealing with the ultimate nature of reality beyond what is merely apparent. Analogically, metapsychology is the branch of psychoanalysis that deals with the ultimate nature of mental reality—namely, the subpersonal mechanisms of the brain (Gomez, 2005).

Freud called his theory *psychoanalysis* because it aimed to analyze mental phenomena into their basic constituents. To understand this aim, we must clarify what sort of mental phenomena psychoanalysts attempt to decompose, what the project of decomposition consists in, and what components result from the analysis. The targets of psychoanalytic explanations are psychological phenomena understood at the personal level, which are *ultimately* analyzed into their subpersonal components. The paradigmatic form of personal-level discourse is called *propositional attitude psychology*. Propositional attitudes are subjects' psychological attitudes toward propositions. The statements in language of propositional attitude psychology typically consist of a subject term (*naming the agent*), a psychological verb (*believes, hopes, fears,* and so on), and a clause giving the proposition that the subject had the attitude toward, presented as an embedded declarative sentence (e.g., "that Harry loves Sally," "that life is short," "that Zadie is adorable"). With a little ingenuity, most personal-level psychological states can be characterized using this simple semantic apparatus. It is important to separate the clinical aims and methods of analysis from their metapsychological underpinnings. Suppose that a person comes to analysis with a phobia. The psychoanalyst's explanatory task in this case is twofold. First of all, he tries to understand the phobia at the personal level. The object of fear unconsciously *means something* to the sufferer: Perhaps it represents the fulfillment of a forbidden desire. Carefully listening to the patient's free-associative discourse, the analyst tries to make sense of the phobia in the context of her desires, fears, resistances, and so on. From time to time, the analyst offers an interpretation to the patient—a hypothesis about what is unconsciously going on—and in doing so addresses her at the personal level. "I noticed just now that when you began to speak about your brother, you quickly fell silent and began to twiddle your fingers in a way that looked nervous," he might say, "I get the sense from that that there's something that makes speaking freely about your brother feel scary." This sort of understanding is supposed to have therapeutic effect. However, privately—and when theorizing about patients—psychoanalysts in the Freudian tradition often try to formulate what is going on in terms of interactions between subpersonal systems, forces, and mechanisms.

Because little is known about how neural processes give rise to mental states, cognitive scientists generally frame subpersonal explanations in *functional* terms. Functional explanations abstract away from the neurological details. They focus on the component *tasks* that the brain (or any other suitably structured system) must perform for a given psychological process to occur. There are several varieties of functionalism. The kind that is most attractive to psychologists is called *psychological functionalism, psycho-functionalism*, or sometimes *homuncular functionalism*. This approach to the mind focuses on functional *systems* in the brain—subpersonal entities that perform information-processing tasks. The tasks performed by these systems can, in turn, be broken down into those performed by subsystems, which can (in principle, if not in practice) be broken down into sub-subsystems, and so on, right down to the level of individual neuron (Cummins, 1983; Dennett, 1971, 1991). As the philosopher William Lycan (1988) described it, this brand of functionalism

> sees a human being or any other sentient creature as a kind of corporate entity—as an integrated system of intercommunicating "departments" that cooperatively go about the business of interpreting the stimuli that impinge upon the corporate organism and of producing appropriate behavioral responses. (p. 5)

Sometimes these subsystems (especially the more complex ones) are personified as miniature agents engaged in intentional activities (as when, for example, one system "alerts" another to an incoming stimulus)—hence the term homuncular.

Although functionalism was first formally set out by the Harvard philosopher Hilary Putnam in the 1960s (Putnam, 1960/1975a, 1967/1975b), the basic idea was articulated by Freud in 1926 in a manner that would do any present-day functionalist proud. Freud represented the mind as a machine, which he called the "mental apparatus" (of course, computers had not yet been invented, so the "apparatus" was not described using the computational trope[1]). "It will soon become clear what the mental apparatus is," he wrote, "but I must beg you not to ask what material it is constructed of" (Freud, 1926/1959, p. 146).

> That is not a subject of psychological interest. Psychology can be as indifferent to it as, for instance, optics can be to the question of whether the walls of a telescope are made of metal or cardboard. We shall leave entirely on one side the material line of approach, but not so the spatial one. For we picture the unknown apparatus which serves the activities of the mind as being really like an instrument constructed of several parts . . . each of which performs a particular function and have a fixed spatial relation to one another: it being understood that by spatial . . . we really mean in the first instance a representation of the regular succession of the functions. (Freud, 1926/1959, p. 146)

Freud proposed several such functionalist models during the course of his lengthy career, and all of them departed from standard functionalist approaches, as described by Lycan, in important respects. Because present-day cognitive scientists are interested almost exclusively in conflict-free mental processing (for example, the processing of language or visual information), Lycan took it for granted that functional systems operate cooperatively and that their interactions produce what he called "appropriate" (i.e., adaptive) behavior. In contrast, Freud was interested in psychological conflict and disorder, and he therefore assumed neither cooperative functioning nor appropriate behavioral outputs. His account of the subpersonal architecture of the mind was inferred from close attention to the phenomenology of conscious experience. Introspection of oneself as well as observation of others shows that most of us are capable of both first- and second-order propositional attitudes. For example, you might believe that it is raining (first-order), as well as that your belief that it is raining is a neurological state (second-order),

---

[1]Nevertheless, his very first functional model, published posthumously as the "Project for a Scientific Psychology," is what is now called a connectionist model of the mind. More remarkable still, the neural learning mechanism that Freud postulated in this model is the basis for the computational learning algorithm known as the backpropagation of error (Werbos, 1994).

or you might love it that today is your birthday (first-order), as well as fear to love it that today is your birthday (second-order). Throughout his writings, Freud placed particular emphasis on the relations that hold between first- and second-order *desires* because he found that they are especially apt for producing psychological conflict. One of the interesting and significant features of human psychology is that we have both first-order and second-order desires: That is, we have both desires and desires about those desires (Frankfurt, 1971). Consider a person who wants to give up smoking. She desires to smoke (a first-order desire), but she also desires to not desire to smoke (a second-order desire). This is an example of conflicting desires. Now, conflict can occur between first-order desires (as when you are torn between two choices on a menu) or between second-order desires (as when you are torn between two moral stances), but the paradigmatic form of conflicting desire is conflict between first- and second-order desires. There are two forms of this sort of conflict. One might want to desire something that one does not actually desire (the dilemma of those who cannot motivate themselves to perform a task that they feel they ought to perform—for instance, a person who would like to desire to exercise, but who does not, in fact, desire to exercise). Alternatively, it is possible to have a desire that one does not want to have (e.g., a person with homosexual desires who is ashamed of having these desires and wishes not to have them). Freud held that all of us are troubled by desires that we would rather not have, and he regarded this as the paradigmatic form of psychological conflict.

What is it that motivates conflicts of the kind to which I have just alluded? Freud believed that if one attends closely to the conflicts between first- and second-order desires, repetitive patterns become evident. One of them concerns the clash between hedonistic (paradigmatically, sexual) desires and the desire for safety. Some hedonistic desires can be dangerous to act upon in some circumstances, either because they put one in physical peril or because they threaten to undermine the fulfillment of other commitments that one holds dear. Freud observed that such conflicts do not make the offending desire disappear, and he reasoned that this implies that hedonistic desires and self-protective desires must be products of two distinct and relatively autonomous functional systems. He also noticed that the desire for safety has the felt quality of being "one's own," whereas the desire for pleasure can be experienced as intrusive, alien, and even persecutory. He thus named the functional system producing the latter the *id* (in German, *das Es*, meaning "the it") and that responsible for the former the *ego* (in German, *das Ich*, meaning "the I"). Another reason why one might not want to have a particular hedonistic desire is because it makes one feel guilty or ashamed— as morally culpable, or even evil. One has the sense of an oppressive power bearing down on one, an imperative rather than a desire, from which one cannot escape. Freud reasoned that this must reflect the operation of a third functional system, which he called the *superego* (in German, *das Überich*, meaning "the over-I"). The ego is thus a "poor creature" that is "driven by the id, confined by the superego, repulsed by reality, struggles to master itstask of bringing about harmony among the forces and influences working in and upon it" (Freud, 1923/1961b, p. 55; 1933/1964, p. 78).

Freud referred to ego, id, and superego as subpersonal *agencies* (*Instanzen*) within the subject, which, however, he often figuratively endowed with intentional states. As I have noted, this is a rhetorical strategy that is often adopted by homuncular functionalists. Picturing the superego as punitive person with the ego as his long-suffering victim is much more engaging than speculations about the functional roles occupied by certain sorts of neural activation vectors, but it is a mistake to seriously attribute personal-level characteristics to parts of persons. A person's ego, id, and superego are neither states *of* the person nor little agents inside of the person. They are subintentional systems that are constitutive of that person. It is a mistake to literally attribute propositional attitudes to them, and it is therefore a mistake to conceive of them as moral agents. People *are* moral agents; but they are *not made out of* moral agents.

We are accustomed to thinking of intentional states as providing causal explanations of behavior. But if behavior can be fully explained at the subpersonal level, then it looks as if intentional states do not have any explanatory work to do. If a piece of behavior (say, the decision to initiate genocide) is fully explicable in terms of events going on inside that person's brain, or interactions between his ego, id, and superego, or some other subpersonal story, then there is no need to invoke personal-level explanations for his behavior. Intentional explanation becomes otiose, and given that behavior is apt for moral judgment only when given a *personal-level* description, it follows that a *fully* metapsychological account of human behavior cannot address the moral significance of human behavior. So, because good and evil, right and wrong, cannot be predicated of aggregates of subpersonal mechanisms, the metapsychological picture of human nature upon which Freud pinned his theoretical hopes must exclude moral considerations entirely. This need not suggest irrealism about morality. However, it does imply that psychoanalysis—or any other psychological theory that seeks to explain human behavior by recourse to subpersonal mechanisms—cannot coherently address moral issues. For, as another Viennese seeker after truth once said, "What we cannot speak about we must pass over in silence" (Wittgenstein, 1922/2001, p. 89).

As one might imagine, these theoretical considerations have significant implications for the dimension of clinical practice. All forms of psychotherapy involve a certain kind of attitude on the part of the therapist. By *attitude*, I mean a general stance or orientation that determines how the therapist is to interact with her clients. The psychoanalytic attitude is best captured by the attitude *of neutrality* (sometimes misleadingly called the "rule" of neutrality). The rule of neutrality enjoins the analyst to refrain from taking a judgmental attitude toward her clients. Roy Schafer (1983) described this very nicely in his book *The Analytic Attitude*:

> In his or her neutrality, the analyst does not crusade for or against the so-called id, superego, or defensive ego. The analyst has no favorites and so is not judgmental. The analyst's position is, as Anna Freud (1936) put it, "equidistant" from the various forces at war with one another. The simplistic, partisan analyst, working in terms of saints and sinners, victims and victimizers, or good and bad ways to live, is failing to maintain the analytic attitude. (p. 5)

The attitude of neutrality is sometimes justified pragmatically (e.g., Freud, 1912/1958b) or on ethical grounds (e.g., Schafer, 1983). Whatever the virtues of these interpretations of neutrality, there is something more and, I think, deeper involved. As I have already shown, thinking of a person as having regressed to an infantile psychological mode, or conceiving of that person in terms of the subpersonal psychological mechanisms that constitutes his or her mind, is inconsistent with viewing the person through a moral prism. So, refraining from moral judgment in psychoanalysis should not be considered a matter of following a *rule*. If this were the case, it would enjoin psychotherapists merely to conceal their judgments and thus to function as hypocrites in the consulting room. The notion of neutrality, correctly understood, is far more radical. It embodies the principle that conceiving of one's clients as having regressed to infancy or as aggregates of subpersonal mechanisms is incompatible with conceiving of them as moral agents and making moral judgments about them. If a psychotherapist finds herself thinking of her clients as virtuous, or bad, or even evil, then this indicates that she has ceased thinking about her clients in a psychoanalytic way. *She has in effect ceased being a psychoanalyst,* for the analytic attitude is—in a very profound sense—beyond good and evil.

REFERENCES

Bermúdez, J. L. (2005). *Philosophy of psychology: A contemporary introduction*. New York, NY: Routledge.

Cummins, R. (1983). *The nature of psychological explanation*. Cambridge, MA: MIT Press.

Dennett, D. C. (1971). Intentional systems. *The Journal of Philosophy, 68*, 87–106. doi:10.2307/2025382

Dennett, D. C. (1991). *Consciousness explained*. Harmondsworth, England: Penguin.

Fodor, J. (1991). Replies. In B. Lower & G. Rey (Eds.), *Meaning in mind: Fodor and his critics* (pp. 255–320). Oxford, England: Basil Blackwell.

Frankfurt, H. G. (1971). Freedom of the will and the concept of a person. *The Journal of Philosophy, 68,* 5–20. doi:10.2307/2024717

Freud, A. (1936). *The ego and the mechanisms of defense*. New York, NY: International Universities Press.

Freud, S. (1955a). The claims of psycho-analysis to scientific interest. In J. Strachey (Ed.), *The standard edition of the complete psychological works of Sigmund Freud* (Vol. 13, pp. 165–175). London, England: Hogarth Press. (Original work published 1913)

Freud, S. (1955b). Group psychology and the analysis of the ego. In J. Strachey (Ed.), *The standard edition of the complete psychological works of Sigmund Freud* (Vol. 18, pp. 67–145). London, England: Hogarth Press. (Original work published 1921)

Freud, S. (1955c). A note on the prehistory of the technique of analysis. In J. Strachey (Ed. & Trans.), *The standard edition of the complete psychological works of Sigmund Freud* (Vol. 18, pp. 263–265). London, England: Hogarth Press. (Original work published 1920)

Freud, S. (1957). Thoughts for the times on war and death. In J. Strachey (Ed.), *The standard edition of the complete psychological works of Sigmund Freud* (Vol. 14, pp. 275–288). London, England: Hogarth Press. (Original work published 1915)

Freud, S. (1958a). Formulations on the two principles of mental functioning. In J. Strachey (Ed.), *The standard edition of the complete psychological works of Sigmund Freud* (Vol. 12, pp. 213–226). London, England: Hogarth Press. (Original work published 1911)

Freud, S. (1958b). Recommendations to physicians practising psycho-analysis. In J. Strachey (Ed.), *The standard edition of the complete psychological works of Sigmund Freud* (Vol. 12, pp. 109–120). London, England: Hogarth Press. (Original work published 1912)

Freud, S. (1959). The question of lay analysis. In J. Strachey (Ed.), *The standard edition of the complete psychological works of Sigmund Freud* (Vol. 20, pp. 179–260). London, England: Hogarth Press. (Original work published 1926)

Freud, S. (1961a). Civilization and its discontents. In J. Strachey (Ed.), *The standard edition of the complete psychological works of Sigmund Freud* (Vol. 21, pp. 59–148). London, England: Hogarth Press. (Original work published 1930)

Freud, S. (1961b). The ego and the id. In J. Strachey (Ed.), *The standard edition of the complete psychological works of Sigmund Freud* (Vol. 19, pp. 12–68). London, England: Hogarth Press. (Original work published 1923)

Freud, S. (1961c). Introductory lectures on psycho-analysis. In J. Strachey (Ed. & Trans.), *The standard edition of the complete psychological works of Sigmund Freud* (Vol. 15, pp. 15–463). London, England: Hogarth Press. (Original work published 1916–1917)

Freud, S. (1964). New introductory lectures on psycho-analysis. In J. Strachey (Ed.), *The standard edition of the complete psychological works of Sigmund Freud* (Vol. 22, pp. 7–184). London, England: Hogarth Press. (Original work published 1933)

Freud, S. (1966). Project for a scientific psychology. In J. Strachey (Ed.), *The standard edition of the complete psychological works of Sigmund Freud* (Vol. 1, pp. 283–398). London, England: Hogarth Press. (Original work published 1950)

Gomez, L. (2005). *The Freud wars: An introduction to the philosophy of psychoanalysis.* New York, NY: Routledge.

Grünbaum, A. (2010). Psychoanalysis and theism. In B. Beit-Hallahmi (Ed.), *Psychoanalysis and theism: Critical reflections on the Grünbaum thesis* (pp. 43–58). Lanham, MD: Jason Aronson (Reprinted from *The Monist, 70,* 152–192)

Hopkins, J. (1982). Introduction: Philosophy and psychoanalysis. In R. Wollheim & J. Hopkins, (Eds.), *Philosophical essays on Freud* (pp. vii–xiv). Cambridge, England: Cambridge University Press.

Lear, J. (1990). *Love and its place in nature: A philosophical interpretation of Freudian psychoanalysis.* New Haven, CT: Yale University Press.

Lycan, W. (1988). *Judgment and justification.* New York, NY: Cambridge University Press.

Mackie, J. L. (1946). A refutation of morals. *Australasian Journal of Psychology and Philosophy, 24,* 77–90. doi:10.1080/00048404608541486

Norton, D. F., & Norton, M. J. (Eds.). (2000). *David Hume: A treatise of human nature.* New York, NY: Oxford University Press.

Prinz, J. J. (2007). *The emotional construction of morals.* New York, NY: Oxford University Press.

Putnam, H. (1975a). Minds and machines. In H. Putnam (Ed.), *Mind, language, and reality* (pp. 352–385). Cambridge, England: Cambridge University Press. (Original work published 1960)

Putnam, H. (1975b). The nature of mental states. In H. Putnam (Ed.), *Mind, language, and reality* (pp. 421–440). Cambridge, England: Cambridge University Press. (Original work published 1967)

Reiff, P. (1961). *Freud: The mind of the moralist.* Garden City, NY: Doubleday.

Schafer, R. (1983). *The analytic attitude.* New York, NY: Basic Books.

Seligman, M. E. P. (2002). *Authentic happiness: Using the new positive psychology to realize your potential for lasting fulfillment.* New York, NY: Free Press.

Smith, D. L. (1999). *Freud's philosophy of the unconscious.* Dordrecht, Netherlands: Kluwer Academic Publishers.

Smith, D. L. (2003). "Some unimaginable substratum": A contemporary introduction to Freud's philosophy of mind. In M. C. Chung & C. Feltham (Eds.), *Psychoanalytic knowledge* (pp. 54–75). London, England: Palgrave.

Strawson, P. (2008). *Freedom and resentment and other essays.* New York, NY: Routledge. (Original work published 1962) van Inwagen, P. (1986). *An essay on free will*. New York, NY: Oxford University Press.

Wallwork, E. (1991). *Psychoanalysis and ethics*. New Haven, CT: Yale University Press.

Webster, R. (1995). *Why Freud was wrong: Sin, science and psychoanalysis*. New York, NY: Basic Books.

Werbos, P. (1994). *The roots of backpropagation: From ordered derivatives to neural networks and political forecasting*. New York, NY: Wiley-Interscience.

Wittgenstein, L. (2001). *Tractatus logico-philosophicus*. D. Pears & B. McGuiness (Eds. & Trans.). New York, NY: Routledge. (Original work published 1922)

11

DENY NO EVIL, IGNORE NO EVIL, REFRAME NO EVIL: PSYCHOLOGY'S MORAL AGENDA

RONALD B. MILLER

The exchange of letters between Rollo May and Carl Rogers on "The Problem of Evil" (May, 1992; Rogers, 1992) addresses critical questions concerning both human nature (or personality) and psychotherapeutic technique. First, May asked us to consider whether human destructiveness might be the result of the human drive toward creativity and power (the *daimonic*) derailed by adverse environmental circumstances (e.g., disrespect, neglect, abuse, traumatic loss through natural causes). Second, given that May believed that was indeed the case, he asserted that a psychotherapist must be alert to indications that the client might well be acting out such impulses in various direct and indirect ways. He argued further that psychotherapists must find effective ways to confront aggression and anger within the therapeutic relationship.

As crucial as these substantive questions and recommendations are for contemporary psychology and psychotherapy, I maintain that the May–Rogers

DOI: 10.1037/13941-011
Humanity's Dark Side: Evil, Destructive Experience, and Psychotherapy, A. C. Bohart, B. S. Held, E. Mendelowitz, and K. J. Schneider (Editors)

dialogue on the problem of evil is just as important, or more so, for its impact on metapsychology. By *metapsychology* I mean our own attempts at self-definition as a discipline, the exploration of the philosophical assumptions we bring to that task, and our own self-understanding of what it means to be a psychologist or psychotherapist. What May and Rogers have preserved for us in their dialogue is our ability to recognize for psychology and psychotherapy the importance of the pervasive capacity of humans to do evil and the typically masked, but intrinsic, capacity of psychology and psychotherapy to openly contribute to the moral conversation of the West.

In so doing, this dialogue challenges one of the most fundamental assumptions of both scientific and professional psychology: the proposition that psychological theory and practice must be undertaken from a position of complete moral neutrality vis-à-vis the actions of those whom we study or attempt to influence. On this mainstream view it is not only logically possible but absolutely necessary to offer a complete theoretical account of human actions, and interventions to influence or alter human actions, without employing moral concepts or judgments (see Miller, 2001, 2004, for further discussion of this common assumption in both scientific and professional psychology). This chapter explores the sense in which clinical theory, research, and practice are, whether explicitly or implicitly, exercises in moral and ethical reasoning and judgment, and how in making these judgments explicit and open to dialogue within psychology we can work far more effectively for the greater good.

Discussion of a topic that, however important, has been largely ignored within a discipline is difficult. The topic will be approached in three steps. First, it is necessary to clear away the resistance and objections typically encountered in such attempts. These are identified in what follows as (a) "terminal philosophical ambivalence," or being deterred by the resistance of colleagues who find moral dialogue foreign or distasteful while using moral arguments in their own favor when convenient; (b) naïvely falling into the repeating of the well-worn moral arguments of the "culture wars" while ignoring the considerable scholarly work in philosophy that has promoted a more thoughtful approach to these problems; (c) ignoring the historical development of institutional forces that present social and ideological resistance to the inclusion of moral dialogue within scientific psychology; (d) fear and trembling in the face of the uncanny; (e) de-moralizing evil with psychological constructs; and (f) naturalizing evil as a biological construct.

Once these impediments to moral dialogue have been addressed, the second section of the chapter identifies the moral component in clinical psychology, what I refer to as "morally infused clinical judgments," and their link to the broader theory of moralized emotions in contemporary moral philosophy and psychological research on emotion. Finally, building on this conceptual innovation, the third and concluding section addresses how genuine moral dialogue within the discipline and profession of psychology might yield a broad consensus on the fundamental human moral values that ought to guide psychological theory, research, and practice.

IMPEDIMENTS TO DIALOGUE

Terminal Philosophical Ambivalence

I regularly discuss metapsychological issues in my graduate course on theories of psychotherapy, and a reader I put together for that purpose (Miller, 1992) includes the May–Rogers exchange of letters on the problem of evil. I have found that for many, if not most, students, the topics introduced in the May–Rogers exchange are difficult to engage without first dealing with the intellectual and emotional discomfort of being assigned a reading on the topic of evil in a psychology course. The topic of evil connotes issues having to do with religious faith or theological and philosophical arguments about human nature and morality. May's subject matter seems to these readers antithetical to scientific discourse, and psychology as a natural or proto-natural science has become the almost unquestioned conceptual scaffolding of psychology, psychotherapy, and other mental health professions. May took one step in addressing this discomfort by referring to the *daimonic* rather than the demonic force in human personality development, a clear attempt to put the discussion into the secular rather than the religious realm.

Even so, May still titled the paper "The Problem With Evil," and not "The Problem With Aggression" or even "The Problem With Human Destructiveness." In doing so, he invited us to consider what many humanistic psychoanalysts of his day (e.g., Karen Horney, Erich Fromm, Erik Erikson, Thomas Szasz) viewed as of central concern: the moral impact of psychology on Western culture. These mid-20th century psychotherapists realized that psychotherapy was a moral enterprise and that the specific moral direction that psychotherapy was taking was not well agreed upon, and various kinds of moral advocacy would be required of them. Rogers's separate series of debates with B. F. Skinner on the social impact of applied behaviorism (see Kirschenbaum & Henderson, 1989) was another excellent example of this kind of moral dialogue. A morally engaged academic psychology was, of course, a minority position as psychology increasingly wrapped itself in the mantle of the natural sciences and in so doing claimed proudly for itself "amoral" status (see Kendler, 2008, for a clear contemporary statement of this position). Granted, when considering much of the work of experimental psychologists on neuroscience, cognition, memory, and learning, unpacking the connection to a moral agenda is quite complex and typically involves a fairly intricate logical and social analysis (see Adams & Miller, 2008). Nonetheless, on occasion the connection of the descriptive/explanatory propositions with moral judgments appears briefly in clear view for all (who wish) to see. One need only examine research funding proposals in experimental psychology and the funding agencies to which these experiments in "pure" science are submitted. Such proposals typically justify the expenditure of research funds by arguing the likelihood of the direct benefit to the common good or advancement of a particular national policy goal that will accrue to the Department of Defense, the National Institutes of Health, the Department of Education, the Federal Bureau of Prisons, and so forth.

As Herman (1995) ably documented, much of the success of psychology as an academic and applied profession has been the result of championing its contribution to furthering the social, political, and military agendas of the political elites in Washington. Research funds, jobs, and status were the rewards that followed to a profession that had been seen as useful to the national war efforts and the postwar recovery of veterans.

In much of applied social, developmental, and clinical psychology, the moral agenda grounding the research is often in areas of such broad cultural moral agreement that the moral values remain implicit in the research agenda. Widely shared moral values that are never debated become assumptions we take for granted in our decision making, and we hardly notice the impact of the moral values on the framing of a research or clinical hypothesis, data observations, or interpretation of an empirical study (see Miller, 2004, Chapter 3). We only tend to notice the implicit values in a study, diagnosis, treatment, or community program when the values clash with our own.

May sagaciously brought a major exception to this pattern to our attention: the problem of evil. As psychologists approach the ultimate moral wrongs and the greatest of social injustices, the pretense of moral neutrality seems to drop away. When the social psychologists Milgram (1972/2004), Baumeister (1999), Staub (2001), and Zimbardo (2007) attempted to understand the psychological forces behind genocidal actions by soldiers or the brutality of prison guards, and the psychiatrist Peck (1998) explored the nature of antisocial personality, the gruesomeness and horror of the phenomena are a constant reminder that these are behaviors that are of interest because they "must be stopped." The pretense of doing research or developing social interventions that might be used for good or evil (a typical claim of those who would deny moral agendas in psychological research), but that are claimed to be in themselves "amoral," is nowhere to be found. It is clear that what is being studied is evil behavior, and the authors want to find ways to change it. How are we to understand this lapse in scientific neutrality occurring in research that includes some of the best-known psychological research programs of the 20th century? The explanation is quite clear. Milgrim and Zimbardo chose topics to study that addressed what every schoolchild in the United States had been taught were the defining moral evils of the 20th century, the Holocaust and Stalinist purges of the World War II era. Moral judgments that are never disputed are safe to explore and promote with psychological research and practice. However, should one venture in one's research or practice into moral judgments about which the culture is divided (e.g., the widespread prescribing of antidepressants and psychostimulants by primary care physicians, the use of time-out rooms in public schools, the reliance of the public mental health system on antipsychotic medication as the primary treatment intervention for patients with severe problems), then one must present one's moral arguments in the amoral language of technical expertise and science or be marginalized as a radical advocate of the antipsychiatry movement.

Philosophical Context

Although religion and theology are the historical sources, the concept of evil is also a part of the moral, social, and political discourse of Western culture (Neiman, 2004). The concept of evil conveys the everyday meaning that the phenomena under scrutiny are completely and utterly intolerable, horrifying, and so outside the bounds of human decency that our inner being screams "How can you do this? Stop!" Bernstein (2002) noted that in the philosophical literature of the West, modern and postmodern thinkers are in general agreement that evil is both real and either the most or one of the most central issues in philosophy. Though the concept of evil resists precise definition, the topic is central to how we are to understand what it means to be person, how we organize human societies, whether we can find living in this world bearable, and what role we assign to the human sciences.

At the dawn of the modern era (ca. 1600), Judeo–Christian theology bequeathed to the emerging discipline of modern philosophy the task of explaining how human beings could be both rational agents created by an all-powerful and merciful deity and yet be capable of choosing to do evil in the world (Neiman, 2004). As modern philosophy and the physical and social sciences matured, many scholars and scientists found the concept of free will that was implicit in this question to be naïve and anachronistic, and instead they sought to explain evil not as the result of human choice but rather as the result of subtle biological, cultural, historical, social/economic, or political forces and pressures that are beyond the perpetrators' personal control. Both options for the human sciences assume that even if evil actions are not in themselves the result of rational processes, a rational approach to the problem of evil is warranted, since both the free will and deterministic accounts are presented as rational theories (i.e., attempts to explain what might be irrational phenomena).

Always lurking in the wings is the scientist's worst fear: that such problems cannot be solved through rational inquiry at all and by their very nature must lead us back to religious faith or leave us teetering on the edge of nihilism. These options are beyond the scope of this chapter, though it should be noted that theological explanations generally accounted for the evil experienced by human beings in the world in one of three ways: (a) human agency—the deity did not create evil, humans did by abusing their free will; (b) the failure of humans to properly judge the import of the suffering they experience—it is meaningless when compared with the glory of the next life or the much worse suffering that awaits a world devoid of faith in the deity; or (c) Manichaeism—the existence of the forces of the devil opposing the deity (Neiman, 2004). It might fairly be said that the road back to a theological understanding of evil also is not an easy one.

Historical Factors in Psychology's Denial of Evil

For psychology as a profession and discipline to enter into the moral conversation of our time means that we must directly encounter a variety of moral, political, and religious traditions that have a seat at the table. These moral traditions do not exist in a vacuum, for those who use the terms of ultimate moral judgment (good and evil) are embedded within national and international networks of religious and educational organizations and are linked to political power centers and ideologies even in countries, like our own, that espouse the separation of church and state. Witness how often in countries of the world, including our own, it seems almost required political rhetoric to categorize another nation or political group as "evil" before launching a first-strike military attack.

It was a long history of sectarian religious conflict and bloodshed that the Enlightenment sought to amend with the development of secular learning, philosophy, and ultimately, natural science. As Toulmin (1990) showed, this growth in secular learning and the rise of natural science coincided exactly with the rise of secular political power (nation states), and the natural sciences were valued for the power over nature and enhanced military weaponry provided to secular authority. Scientific theory rivaled theology in explaining the origins of life and the universe and seemed a worthy rival for the power of theology to explain our existence and control our fate.

Consequently, to introduce into presumably scientific discussions theological concepts such as evil would seem to undermine the entire scientific enterprise of the last 500 years. Indeed, if it were in fact the case that the rise of natural science had made moral discourse in our culture superfluous, irrelevant, or moot, this danger to the scientific enterprise would be a compelling argument for ending the discussion here.

Toulmin's (1990) ultimate conclusion from the study of the history and philosophy of the natural and social sciences is, however, a very different one. He concluded that natural sciences have always been founded upon various moral and even cosmological beliefs and assumptions, that is to say, various articles of moral and metaphysical faith. Science only appears to have replaced the need for moral discourse because it is at its deepest level a form of moral and metaphysical discourse. Though an oversimplification, the well-worn observations that empirical science is based upon the epistemological theory of empiricism and the metaphysical theory of materialism provide an entrée into Toulmin's argument. For both empiricism and materialism are (even today) controversial philosophical positions that are nevertheless taken for granted as self-evident truths by most bench scientists. Yet, as one moves to the more theoretical domains of the natural sciences one encounters less objective, social, and even intuitive or mystical accounts of knowledge, and a more ethereal sense of reality.

What Toulmin (1990) added to this familiar account of the limits of an empiricist and materialist vision of science is the notion that moral and political interests and beliefs have also infiltrated our sense of what can count as a "fact" or a "rational" theory about how the world works. Perhaps this is one of the reasons why so many seemingly empirical scientific controversies stir such passions and interpersonal animosities more typically associated with frankly moral or ethical arguments. Toulmin noted, for example, that many of the foundational ideas of physics were heavily influenced both by the religious beliefs of Newton and the political allegiances of the various religious sects in England at the time Newton was writing. He pointed out that Newton's theory was received more favorably than might otherwise have been the case because Newton proposed a theory in which mass was inert, without energy or force. The restive masses of the populace that would in the next century overthrow kings were thus defined as requiring forceful treatment (from above) in order to overcome their own inertia. In other words, they need direction (vectors of force) applied to them.

There are in addition more immediate practical objections to a psychology of evil qua evil that parallel Toulmin's (1990) point concerning the influence of political ideas on scientific ones. In the emotionally charged linguistic climate of our current "culture wars," it would at first seem prudent to avoid terms like *good* and *evil* when undertaking scholarly research. Otherwise one risks becoming embroiled at every turn in the political and social conflicts of the day. Scholars, researchers, editors, and especially administrators of universities, foundations, and government agencies are still citizens bound to be caught up in the critical national and international events and debates affecting their institutions and daily lives. Whether as public intellectuals or private citizens, psychologists and other mental health professionals must navigate a climate of opinion in which the concepts of good and evil are still much in use and often employed as justifications for important decisions in the public and private realms. In applying for a research grant, or in one's capacity as a program consultant, it is much better to appear to be above the fray and studying "scientific" topics, such as anti- or prosocial behavior, delayed gratification, posttraumatic stress disorder, conflict resolution, and other sanitized, de-moralized issues. While such strategic forms of self-presentation in the scientific community might be essential to self-preservation in a highly charged political environment, they also belie the claim that science is itself amoral and apolitical.

Fear, Trembling, and the Moral Imperative

There are more personal reasons to avoid the concept of evil. There is a terror at confronting the human capacity for cruelty and mayhem as it exists in the real world, rather than observing the analogue situations carefully constructed and controlled in the world of a scientific study. In contemplating real-world evil, one has to consider the slaughter of innocents by the tens and hundreds of thousands (and millions, if one considers the horrors of Hitler and Stalin); blood flowing in the streets, disfigured bodies, and the agony of the dying of those who cannot be saved; the orphaned children wandering the fields or streets screaming for their mothers, or exhausted at not finding them, and withdrawing into lifeless states of detachment. One encounters this in writing about suffering as well. Such suffering is painful to contemplate and deeply depressing. However, writing about the states of mind and social conditions in which individuals deliberately and systematically create this suffering in the lives of nameless others, with whom they have no individual grievance or even familiarity, is to contemplate our own vulnerability to social forces that might destroy the social and material fabric of our own lives. It is not just painful but bloodcurdling, bone chilling, and terrifying, as if one has entered a waking nightmare. There is a sense of violating a fundamental taboo by uttering words on topics about which one should remain silent and a fear (however irrational or superstitious) that to address such a topic might bring oneself into the orbit of such heinous forces.

Despite these trepidations, one must proceed. Not to proceed would imply resignation and defeat, a prospect even more terrifying and uncanny. Worse yet, in avoidance there is a sense of complicity, for there is a very heavy, perhaps devastating, price to be paid for psychologizing evil and sanitizing the language we use to explore the phenomena before us. The concept of evil, though moral and theological in origin, conveys a sense of urgency, force, and threat that cannot be captured in terms like *inappropriate*, *dysfunctional*, *destructive*, *violent*, *antisocial*, or *predatory* behavior. Equally, to speak of actions as *good*, *noble*, or *virtuous* is to say something more powerful than that an action was appropriate, adaptive, healthy, or functional. The terms *good* and *evil* convey an urgency about events and actions that will have a pervasive and lasting impact on the individuals involved and, perhaps, the entire community or culture. I would submit that even if one does not subscribe to the religious beliefs from which these terms evolved, our world requires language terms that convey the urgency, extremity, and pervasive cultural impact found in the moral concepts of good and evil.

De-Moralizing Evil

As noted above, psychology and other mental health professions typically respond to the dilemma of evil in a manner consistent with how moral issues in general are approached in the context of clinical practice or research on clinical practice, namely, by relegating the concerns to the private realm. An individual psychologist's moral values are viewed as a private matter to which psychology as a science has nothing to contribute; it remains above the fray, "amoral." One need not practice in arenas that one finds evil or even morally objectionable, and others with different moral ideals will fill the gap in professional services. So, for example, if one is opposed to abortion, one need not be the mental health consultant to Planned Parenthood, or if one is morally opposed to the use of enhanced interrogation methods (i.e., torture), one need not be a military psychologist consulting at Guantanamo Bay or CIA black sites.

On this view, it is believed that psychological case formulations and diagnoses contain objective problem descriptions and that psychological interventions are empirically validated or supported in such a manner that diagnosis and treatment can be applied to a given clinical situation regardless of the moral beliefs of the practitioner. This entails the belief that one could approach consulting at Planned Parenthood or Guantanamo Bay as a purely technical matter, without being morally in favor or opposed to the process itself. In this context, the words *good* and *bad*, when applied to professional practice, carry the notion of technical proficiency or malfeasance and presumably are not burdened by moral content. In this framework of privatized moral judgment, the professional psychologist's only ethical concern as a psychologist is to conform her or his conduct to the "Ethical Principles of Psychologists and Code of Conduct" (American Psychological Association, 2010). If an act is not specifically prohibited by the code, then there is no need for ethical or moral concern.

It has long been my view (Miller, 1983, 1992, 2004) that privatizing the moral dimension of clinical work produces an anemic caricature of how the everyday clinician practices and is based upon a fundamental neglect of the implicit (and sometimes explicit) moral judgments in psychological theory, research, and practice. It confuses moralizing at clients (which does need to be generally avoided) with practicing from within a moral framework and tradition, which far from being unwise is logically necessary in any helping profession. At critical junctures clinical judgments about client problems and therapist effectiveness contain implicit or explicit moral judgments. Since moral judgments are ostensibly about how people *should* behave (or as I prefer to say, "act"), rather than how they *actually do* act in a given situation, the existence of moral judgments interwoven or implicit in clinical observations and clinical inferences constitutes a theoretical and practical barrier to the development of the mental health profession as simply extensions of natural science.

This same mainstream view of the natural sciences that asserts the amoral quality of scientific theories requires that scientific propositions be restricted to descriptive and explanatory statements (how the world is and what causes it to be that way). Prescriptive claims about how the world should or ought to be (in terms of making this a better world for us to live in) are prohibited from science itself. The development and implementation of technology is prescriptive and guided by human choices concerning the fashioning of the "good life." Technology may use scientific concepts and theories, but it does so in the service of some desired "social good."

The value of this insight (that psychology, especially clinical psychology, is an intrinsically moral enterprise) has been maintained by a long line of distinguished psychotherapists, philosophers, psychiatrists, and psychologists who have come to this position despite widely different professional and theoretical backgrounds. Beginning with a member of Freud's original inner circle, Alfred Adler, and continuing through the psychiatrist Thomas Szasz, learning theorist O. H. Mower, the godfather to this generation of philosophical psychologists, Joseph Rychlak, and Wittgenstein's student, the philosopher of science Stephen Toulmin, the position has been well developed and supported; see Miller (1992, 2004) for extensive historical references.

In nearly every decade of the 20th century, the view that moral judgment is implicit in, and central to, clinical judgment was both strongly argued by respected scholars and practitioners and largely ignored by psychology, psychiatry, and the other mental health professions. The literature of clinical practice (particularly case studies) is replete with the moral dilemmas that bring clients/patients into treatment, the moral judgments that infuse clinical assessments, and the moral dialogues that are woven into clinical interventions (see Miller, 2004, Chapter 5). The exclusion of the concept of evil from clinical discourse is the most dramatic example of how clinical practice has become de-moralized, but it is far from the only important example.

Naturalizing Evil

Within the mainstream of scientific psychology and the clinical science approach to clinical training and practice, the moral connotations of evil are first privatized and then naturalized. The psychological scientist identifies the observable phenomena that give rise to the linguistic label *evil* and approaches them as natural phenomena. Johnson (2005) carefully analyzed how the scientific approach to emotionally disturbed, exceptionally violent, and dangerous offenders in the United Kingdom prison system precludes the possibility of any real help being obtained by these prisoners. He found that hardened, violent, sadistic, repeat offenders respond remarkably well to intensive psychotherapy in a maximum security prison psychiatric unit when the treatment is based on three moral principles: client and therapist must tell the truth, treatment must be based on the free consent of the patient without coercion from penal authorities, and patient and therapist must earn each other's trust through mutual respect. His successful treatment program was shut down by a Conservative government committed to the view that such offenders were incorrigible.

Johnson (2005) contrasted this treatment with the mainstream research and treatment approach to such offenders in the correctional system of the United Kingdom. Armed with operational definitions of observable behaviors (or hypothetical constructs), reliable and valid measures, population sampling strategies, and controls for confounding explanatory factors, one can isolate extremely deviant or dysfunctional behaviors and attempt to link them to various environmental, developmental, social, or physiological correlates. Over time and with sufficient funding, causal claims emerge of this genetic predisposing factor, that brain abnormality, or a variety of social predictors such as early violent abuse, chaotic family circumstances, abandonment, and so forth. However, these social factors are beyond the control of anyone working in the psychiatric treatment programs and are quickly lost from view.

What is exceptionally easy to control is the dispensing of pharmaceutical agents to a captive population, who in turn become more compliant and docile, at least in the short term. This is justified as treatment by the tortured scientific reasoning that since drugs change behaviors and the brain abnormalities cause violent behavior, then the drug must be correcting whatever brain abnormalities are hypothesized to cause the behavior. As Valenstein (1998) observed, based on this logic, headaches are caused by a depletion of aspirin in the brain. Unfortunately, there is no cure per se, and so the patients will need to remain on the medications for life. Although life-threatening or life-shortening side effects occur in almost all patients who remain on these drugs for life, the benefits are claimed to far outweigh the risks. After all, it is argued, without treatment and incarceration the symptoms are likely to remain or worsen and in some instances result in suicide or further homicide.

Case descriptions of treated patients include descriptions of heinous acts of brutality and mayhem: serial murders, home invasion, gang violence, drive-by shootings, hate crimes, and other random actions perpetrated on strangers, ultimately terrorizing entire communities. This is not a patient population that is often seen on a voluntary basis outside of an institutional setting, and so treatment is often associated with the punishment and retribution meted out by the criminal justice system. In this context, it is clear that the needs of the community for control and personal safety take precedence over the hopes for fundamental personality change through psychological interventions.

Notice in the above description of the clinical population being treated how difficult it was to avoid the language of evil ("heinous acts," "murder," "hate," "terror"). The legal system, as an extension of the community's sense of right and wrong, guilt and innocence, and good and evil, does not avoid moral language, thoughts, or concepts. Western legal systems require the concept of personal responsibility for individual actions and codify notions of the degree of severity of wrongdoing, linking the extent of punishment with the severity of the crime (i.e., evil). This is one of the most visible difficulties for psychology (and other mental health professions) in privatizing and naturalizing evil. As with the "pure science" research funding proposals submitted to government agencies with political and social engineering agendas and goals that belie the claims to an amoral academic discipline, those institutions that most require our clinical and applied services (governmental departments and agencies involved in programs of social influence, control, and punishment) live in the world of good and evil. The best illustration of this in the past decade has been the debacle within the American Psychological Association over the application of the Ethics Code to psychologists advising the military on the effects of enhanced methods of interrogation (Costanzo, Gerrity, & Lykes, 2007; Hubbard, 2007). Reports of psychologists witnessing waterboarding, sleep deprivation, techniques of sexual humiliation, and so forth brought cries of shame, horror, and moral outrage from critics. Advocates of this role for psychologists in the "War on Terror" cited the dangers to the United States from the forces President George W. Bush referred to as the "Axis of Evil" and the necessity of preventing further terrorist attacks on the United States, including the possibility of the use of weapons of mass destruction on civilian population centers. Regardless of one's position on this life-

and-death matter, it is impossible to imagine such a debate proceeding within psychology as an academic discipline in the absence of the concept of evil as a moral (i.e., as a moral imperative, "this must be stopped") rather than simply descriptive concept. Were this discussion to have been framed instead as one concerning the investigation of the "socially maladaptive" activities of the accused terrorists, and the "unhealthy conditions" produced during the interrogations due to inadequate supervision by the psychologists, it is unlikely to have raised much concern, nor led to any of the important revelations with which we are now familiar.

Words are powerful because of the meaning conveyed. A change in words is often a change in meaning, and politicians, public relations, and advertising experts know this well. Many of these professions have learned this lesson from the fields of rhetoric and psychology (Lakoff, 2005). The shift from "torture" to "enhanced methods of interrogation" is not unlike the shift from "evil" to "destructive behavior" or "antisocial personality disorder." In both cases, what are widespread moral judgments concerning critical social phenomena become within psychology privatized and naturalized, creating an amoral arena for the ensuing discussion within the discipline.

Anyone familiar at all with the newer histories of academic psychology (Herman, 1995; Jansz & van Drunen, 2004) understands that almost from its inception as a laboratory science, experimental psychologists have sought recognition for their work in its application to forensic, educational, medical, industrial, and military problems. The same discipline that claimed moral neutrality systematically and methodically injected itself into the morally charged issues of determining the veracity of forensic evidence, correcting the misbehavior of schoolchildren, managing unproductive employees, improving dangerous industrial machinery, altering the military draft selection process and troop morale, creating propaganda to psychologically destabilize enemy civilian and military populations, and so forth. This blurring of basic research and applied psychology is so pervasive as to leave the general public with the belief that all psychologists are really practitioners. (Ironically, this belief is then decried by the experimentalists as a great disservice—perpetrated by practitioners—to the noble practitioners of pure science.)

Historians and philosophers of science are divided on the extent to which the social, economic, and political institutions that support the growth of the natural sciences also limit the objectivity of scientific research. Toulmin (1990), Gergen (2009), and Martin and Sugarman (2000) are quite doubtful as to whether objective truth is possible, whereas others (e.g., Held, 2007; Meehl, 1997) have been more sanguine. Toulmin was persuasive in describing the claims of pure science to objectivity as a form of intellectual puffing and self-promotion intended to disarm detractors and critics. He showed how this began 500 years ago in the attempts of science to free itself from ecclesiastical control. Ultimately, the claim to scientific objectivity replaced the claim to divine authority as a means of ending contentious disagreements. Only those who followed the scientific method were permitted to challenge a scientific statement, just as only those trained in theological hermeneutics were permitted to challenge interpretations of the holy scriptures. Thus, criticism is limited to those who have already accepted the important assumptions and presuppositions of the point in question. Whatever conclusions can be drawn for the objectivity of the natural sciences in general or for the limited number of pure research endeavors in experimental psychology, it seems beyond the bounds of logic to maintain that we can ever have an applied/professional psychology that is not centrally involved in attempting to contribute to the resolution of the moral, social, political, and economic crises of the day. At the very least, we must stay relevant to the concerns of consumers and funding agencies that grapple with these issues. The moral, social, and political values that are implicit in the way we conceptualize psychological problems, form clinical judgments, and carry out clinical and community interventions, far from being inherently problematic, are actually what make it possible for us to enter into these discussions and contribute to the possible solutions. How else can one participate fully in a discussion of moral or political values than by offering a moral argument?

MORALLY INFUSED CLINICAL JUDGMENTS AND MORALIZED EMOTIONS

Typically clinicians who encounter the claim that moral judgments are implicit in clinical judgments will reply, "Well, that may be so in some abstract sense, but when I see a patient having a psychotic reaction and I note that in his record, I am making a clinical judgment, pure and simple. I am just describing what I see and judging how that behavior matches various categories." I have come to describe this as a problem where clinical observations and judgments are "infused" with moral judgments. I say this to acknowledge that, upon cursory examination, many such clinical observations and judgments appear to be based on straightforward empirical observations that establish the existence of patterns of empirical regularities in human behavior. Indeed, most human actions involve an observable as well as an interpretable component. When does physical roughhousing among grade school boys become aggressive or sadistic? At what point does social networking stop being just socially skillful and adaptive and, instead, become narcissistic or manipulative? Our interpretations involve (a) judgments about a person's intentions or motivation and (b) judgments of approval or disapproval in the moral realm. "Inappropriate," "unhealthy," "dysfunctional," and "antisocial" are simply glosses for behavioral descriptions to which we wish to add a connotation of wrong, bad, or evil.

I have not paid sufficient attention to another element in these judgments in my account of suffering and the moral engagement of clinical practice, namely, the role of *moralized emotions*. Moralized emotions have come under intense scrutiny in recent years in moral philosophy and in basic research on the psychology of emotion (e.g., Haidt, 2004; Prinz, 2007). Emotions such as feelings of disappointment or betrayal, shame, guilt, righteous anger, jealousy, disgust, terror, and pride are moralized emotions in that one feels the emotion in conjunction with certain cognitions that are of a moral nature. Moralized emotions also involve physiological sensations, urges, and impulses to act. When we find the actions of someone evil, we are horrified. We cringe, feel a chill up and down the spine, become frightened or anxious as to what might happen next, or feel the urge to retaliate or escape. These are not simple cognitive judgments, as would be concluding that a client has red–green color blindness, has lost 10 pounds in a month, or now possesses a new laptop computer. The cognitions that accompany these moralized emotions are actually ethical and moral judgments. John stole my laptop. I am angry, hurt, betrayed, in part because *he has no right to it, and I hope the police catch him*. My heart is pounding, I am trembling with rage, my thoughts are morally judgmental, and I want to chase after him and see that he is caught. Affect, physiological arousal, moral judgment, and impulse to action are integrated into one complex phenomenon. Emotions have a checkered history within the discipline of psychology, sometimes seen as primarily physiological phenomena, other times claimed as the province of the psychoanalytic unconscious, and more recently of interest to cognitive and social psychologists. As William James noted, there is a strong physiological reaction in emotion that is either very pleasurable or very unpleasant, if not painful. As such, emotions invite objectification and physiological measurement (e.g., heart rate, blood pressure, galvanic skin response, functional magnetic resonance imaging). To some extent, other mammals and primates demonstrate emotional displays not unlike our own that can be studied as well (Panksepp, 2008). Often when intense emotions are present, we find ourselves not thinking clearly and tend to see ourselves as overcome with emotion and unable to bring our rational or cognitive powers to bear upon the situation. Nevertheless, as both psychological theorists and moral philosophers have noted in recent years, the emotions experienced as irrational or noncognitive are altered by the social, cognitive, and moral context in which they are experienced. We are not nearly so enraged at the theft of our laptop computer if we know that we had lost one belonging to this same friend who took it and that we had promised that we would replace it immediately, but had not. If that were the case, then the disappearance of our laptop becomes a social irritant ("He could have asked, I was about to give it to him") rather than an enraging betrayal.

Many of the intense emotions experienced by our clinical clients are moralized emotions. In other words, the clinical phenomena that we are observing include emotional displays that have already blended a physiological response with the client's own moral judgment. Shame and guilt are emotional phenomena *and* forms of moral self-condemnation. No matter how a clinician responds, she or he has entered the moral realm, the moral realm of the client. If a therapist decides to offer assistance to lessen shame and guilt, then she or he is taking a moral position that the shame and guilt was not warranted, that the client does not deserve to feel self-loathing for what was done.

Many of the emotional aspects of personality disorders (the self-absorption of the narcissistic personality, the absence of empathy in the hurt and harm caused others in the antisocial personality, the intense and erratic anger of the borderline personality) are expressed by the client in the moral language of worth, just deserts, and betrayal. The client feels morally justified in her or his emotional response, and we judge the emotions as clinically significant because we do not find those moralized emotions justified or proportionate to the social circumstances. If we did find the emotions morally justified, we would no longer find the application of the personality disorder terminology fitting. To do so does not require making an overt moral judgment. In effect, when we challenge the client's irrational cognitions or interpret the influence of past relationships on current perceptions, we do so based on our own moral judgment that the current circumstance does not warrant the judgment the client is making, and if the judgment is altered, then so will be the emotion.

Many of the irrational cognitions being modified by cognitive–behavior therapy (CBT) are moral judgments, "the tyranny of the shoulds," as Ellis phrased it. "If anyone doesn't like me, then I am a terrible person." "If people take advantage of me, I must deserve it." "If I am not perfect, I am worthless." These are not just depressing thoughts, these are the *moral judgments* that are a component of the self-condemnatory aspects of depression. When the therapist responds, "No, you aren't worthless when you aren't perfect, you are just simply human," that is a contrary moral judgment, and unless that judgment prevails, the chances of success in the therapy are limited. True, these are not the moral judgments we were warned against making in our training—for example, telling a client that her or his behavior is wonderful or deplorable—but these are moral judgments nonetheless.

Renaming the distorted moral judgment as irrational (as in CBT) or as displacement or splitting (as in psychoanalysis) does not change the essence of the practice. However, it does help us to see how we have so easily failed to notice the role of moral judgment in clinical observation and judgment.

First, we are diverted from the moralized emotion to the purely physiological aspects of emotion wherein thought of any kind has been largely lost from the immediate phenomenological experience. Second, the moral judgments are presented in a folksy way as mere irrational thoughts or cognitive errors because these are moral judgments about abstract moral principles and not specific judgmental responses to a client's daily activities. In so doing, we appear to maintain the moral neutrality of psychotherapy techniques and protect psychology from appearing to have a moral agenda. We sidestep some of the culture wars about moral values. We can say we simply are working with emotional disturbances, irrational thinking, or dysfunctional behaviors. Perhaps in a world where all of the lies were little white ones, all of the thefts petty, and all of the assaults simple, this might not be such a bad strategy. Unfortunately, that is not the world we live in, and our strategy leaves us conceptually and theoretically ill equipped to address the problem of evil when we encounter it in our professional lives.

FOUNDATION OF A CLINICAL ETHIC:
A NONRELATIVIST PROPOSAL

In facing evil, we need a strong moral position that reduces divisiveness among clinicians and promotes consensus in the field. The theory of moralized emotions points toward such a solution. It helps to explain those aspects of our moral intuitions or sentiments that seem widely shared if not universal. The sight of innocent children and their mothers in great pain and suffering will generate in observers intense emotions that within a wide variety of moral beliefs will yield a moral judgment of condemnation: "That just shouldn't be, something is terribly wrong here, it must be stopped." I have argued elsewhere that moral claims are never determined solely by the brute data of the facts on the ground but also by the social constructions we bring to an understanding of the meaning of those facts (Miller, 2009). Contemplating the problem of evil in the context of the moralized emotions of disgust, horror, and revulsion at the sight of the carnage brought about by human evil brings me to amend my previous account. Such moralized emotions, although perhaps not universal, strike me as far less culturally or even personally constructed than are the abstract moral principles related to matters of social policy, which had been the focus of my previous position. Those who can look firsthand at the genocidal mass graves of the American Indian wars, Bosnia, Rwanda, and Armenia, or at the death camps of Hitler or Stalin, and not be overcome with horror, nausea, disgust, and terror, must be few and far between. We are so emotionally upset by witnessing human carnage, nauseated by the scenes before our eyes and by the smell of burning or rotting flesh in our nostrils, that the thought "this is vile and evil" forms a bedrock moral judgment that is unassailable by cognitive argument. At a later time, such a moral judgment may be defended or critiqued using more abstract moral principles with sophisticated cognitive content. Perhaps this is one reason why it is so difficult to persuade someone to move away from her or his core moral judgments with such abstract moral arguments and why such shifts only seem to happen after one has been exposed to intensely emotional, life-shattering events inconsistent with one's prevailing understanding of the world. Polemicists know this and search for ways to present information about events in the world that tap into deeply felt emotions: "This is wrong and terrible and something *must be done* to change it."

Moralized emotions are emotions that move us to action so that we never have to feel that terror or revulsion again. No doubt not all human beings, regardless of their prior experience, moral education, and emotional reactivity, will necessarily experience the intense emotions described above in the face of human carnage. Nonetheless, it seems evident that the response will be pervasive and not limited to one cultural group, nationality, or social class. So although the self-justifying perpetrators of genocide may always be among us, they will have to conceal or camouflage their intentions and actions from public view because the great majority of witnesses will be horrified and outraged.

Ethical or moral theory often stumbles on the problem known since the ancient Greeks as *akrasia* or weakness of the will. How do we move from a cognitive judgment ("This is right [or wrong])" to an action ("I must do something about it now")? The theory of moralized emotions also solves this problem in ethical theory since emotions are already viewed as one critical type of motivating force in human behavior. Interestingly, this is consistent with both psychoanalytic theory, which has come to view unconscious drives as constellations of hidden feelings and emotions (Malan, 1995), and emotion-focused therapy (Greenberg, 2004), which asserts that behavior change and symptom relief are best sought through a process of self-discovery that identifies and then releases previously dissociated intense emotions tied to earlier critical interpersonal relationships.

Building a Clinical Ethic on the Foundation of Moralized Emotions

To intervene effectively in a situation that triggers emotional revulsion and disgust, a "this must be stopped" reaction, we must come to an understanding of how this carnage came to be in the first place and the consequences for perpetrator and victim. Here there seems to be a tendency to either blame the perpetrators for their cruelty, to blame the victims' stupidity or weakness in having left themselves open to such attack, or to refuse to blame anyone. In the first case, blaming the perpetrators, one begins to build an ethic of compassion for the weak and the poor and a skepticism about the motivation of those in power (as in democratic socialism and liberation theology). In the second, one resolves to strengthen future potential victims through education; physical self-defense training; and provision of equipment, technology, and infrastructure for self-defense so that they will no longer be vulnerable to abuse or attack. In the third strategy, no one is to blame, an ethic of compromise and negotiation seeks to remove mistrust between those in power and the powerless. An emphasis is placed upon misperceptions and misunderstandings, attribution errors, self-fulfilling prophesies, and the like (as in various schools of mediation and Gandhi-inspired nonviolent conflict resolution). In each approach, the initial perception of a moral evil leads to the development of more specific moral principles or positions on what steps must be taken to promote good in the world and reduce the likelihood of evil.

In addition to the initial cognitive response to the intense emotional side of moralized emotions, moral judgments are made about the social contexts that may precipitate or follow from such intense experiences. We search for ways to generalize from these watershed moments. Perhaps we see endorsing the sanctity of all human life or the golden rule of "do unto others . . . " as a bulwark against the slippery slope leading to slaughter. Seeing the role that group prejudices play in ethnic cleansing, we heighten our moral condemnation of ethnic stereotyping or hate speech. Numerous moral principles, some specific and some very broad, emerge out of our horror at such carnage. All of them are justified in moral reasoning by their ability to prevent a future slaughter of innocent human life and to prevent witnesses and participants from experiencing the moralized emotion of abject horror.

Once we have developed moral principles from our experiences of moralized emotions, we can make inferences from known to new and unforeseen contexts. Our first principles might start with emotional revulsion as discussed or from the other side of moral experience—that which is good, noble, holy, sublime, or enrapturing. These may be religious or secular goods. From those experiences of the sublime, we may deduce principles of action that lead to or follow from such wondrous experiences, and these are all now painted with the brush of the good life. Our moral principles tell us what to regard as good and evil, right and wrong, rights and responsibilities. The moral principles of psychology will guide us as we attempt to integrate our services with those of the legal, social service, educational, or religious institutions that are more unabashedly concerned with the public good and building the moral fabric of society.

A more self-consciously moral psychology can enter into this societal dialogue without fear of charges of hidden political or social agendas from critics who see through the mask of the claim to being an amoral science. It will also assist us greatly in understanding what parts of those divisions within our own discipline are due to moral beliefs rather than theoretical assumptions or empirical methods. It would be far simpler if we were an amoral science and had only theoretical and empirical differences, but psychology would also be a lot less interesting, socially relevant, and well-funded a profession, and we would have far fewer students in our college and university classes.

The Evil Before Us

Through their dialogue 30 years ago, May and Rogers invited psychologists to consider the moral dimensions of human personality and psychotherapeutic practice. In his debates with B. F. Skinner about free will and behavioral engineering, Rogers also slowed the march to an amoral psychology. Today, with the history of clinical psychology and the profession of psychotherapy spanning more than 100 years, we have much to reflect upon. We have seen the mental health professions increasingly deny the moral import of their work while increasingly participating in a system of care riddled with moral failings. As we try to reduce the suffering in the lives of our clients, we are hard-pressed not to be complicit in providing woefully inadequate services in both managed care and publicly funded programs, while at the same time claiming to provide outcome-based and "empirically validated" treatments. As a result, while the number of mental health professionals continues to grow steadily, the percentage of the population officially disabled and eligible for Supplemental Security Income or Social Security Disability Income for psychological reasons has increased sixfold since 1955 and doubled since 1987 (Whitaker, 2010).

To simply characterize human activities as wrong, stupid, destructive, or hurtful is insufficient in some circumstances. Though *criminal* is sometimes synonymous with evil, in contemporary society it is mostly used to refer to actions that are illegal and punishable by the law. However, some human actions are so vile and destructive that they undermine the very basis of human existence. These actions destroy the fabric of meaning and community that make it possible to lead productive and fulfilling lives and reduce humans to physical shells that are empty, cold, and dead inside. There is evil in the world that psychology must address, and it consists simply of this: Any act that destroys our trust in the reciprocity of human relationships and creates the belief that individuals need only look out for themselves and not one another is human evil. The more subtle, convoluted, devious, dishonest, and deceptive an act of utter self-interest is, the more evil (see Scarry's, 1985, discussion of torture as a paradigm case of intentional harm for the purpose of destroying the sense of personal identity through denial and deception). Blatant self-interest is destructive, but by being transparent it helps to delineate those whom we can trust from those we cannot. Duplicitous self-interest that masquerades as kindness and concern for others is what most thoroughly erodes trust and faith in humanity. It seems that the greatest evils are perpetrated with the most deception and generally result in the greatest immediate advantage to the perpetrator.

Much of what we call mental illness or emotional or behavioral disturbance is simply the human suffering that is produced by this kind of interpersonal betrayal. The harm that is produced by the actions of others is central to the definition of suffering (Miller, 2004). Unless we are able to provide services in a manner that restores trust in human relationship, we cannot be truly helpful. If we should instead further undermine that trust or make it less likely to be attempted in future relationships, we have not lessened but increased human suffering. Consider how often we as practitioners witness clients who have been provided harmful psychiatric medications promoted as "beneficial" or "effective and well tolerated." These legitimized frauds are conducted with impunity and protected by carefully drawn legal instruments such as informed consent to treatment, forgiving standards of malpractice, corporate liability shields, and corrupted research and publishing practices.

The evil we must guard against in our clinical work comes as much from our own professions and institutions as from the nature of the personality of our clients. In seeking to be powerful players in the national political economy, we have succumbed to the same corporate mentality that pervades our society. Poverty is perceived as the only evil and wealth as the only real good. If the agency, clinic, social service program, or private practice is prospering, then it must be doing good in the world. Programs (including graduate programs) that are losing money or funding are failures and deserve to be closed down. Even in the intense atmosphere that pervades entrance to our profession through highly competitive graduate programs, highly competitive job openings, research funds, and tenure and promotion opportunities, we most heavily reward self-interested actions (so long as they are wrapped in the mantle of the noble pursuit of truth and service to others).

Those doubtful that psychiatry (and those in the other mental health professions that align with psychiatry) could be as self-serving and politically complicit as suggested by these remarks would do well to read Lifton's (1986/2000) *The Nazi Doctors.* Lifton's account of the Nazi government's use of the medical profession as a vehicle for justifying and concealing euthanasia and genocide is one of the most chilling accounts of the Holocaust on record. Faculty members at German medical schools were the first nonpolitical recruits to what became known as the "Final Solution." This took the form of an increased emphasis on the teaching of eugenics as a form of revolutionary public health that would save the nation from further decline in the aftermath of World War I. Next came similar changes in the curriculum taught to medical students who were encouraged to step forward and be heroes prepared to engage in practices of euthanasia that weaker, less patriotic students would refuse. Then after the gas chambers were developed (in response to the demoralizing effect on infantry troops who had begun the genocidal programs of the Third Reich with shooting civilians in mass graves), the medical profession was ready to take charge of the "selection" process at the extermination camps. The doctors greeted the patients as they disembarked from the cattle trains and separated those who would perform slave labor first from those who would be put to death immediately.

By using the image of the trusted family doctor to conceal the work of an executioner, the Nazis and the Nazi doctors perpetrated an unspeakable crime, a form of what Kant called "radical evil"—knowingly choosing to harm other human beings—while concealing from the victims until it was too late to escape the nature of the harm awaiting them. Although we might excuse some of the participants in the Holocaust as not fully understanding what they were doing, it is hard to imagine that individuals teaching or learning at the best medical schools in Europe lacked the ability to discern what they were being asked to do. Lifton notes that, contrary to what most people assume, the penalty for doctors refusing to participate was never worse than a less speedy climb in social status within the medical profession (provided one did not publicly object to the entire programs of euthanasia or genocide).

At the time of this collaboration with genocide, German universities were universally regarded as the most scientifically advanced institutions of higher education in the Western world. Rather than being a bastion against the moral depravity of such a great evil as genocide, the proponents of objective scientific rationality and medical "science" proved remarkably easy targets for political control and manipulation. Those of us who live in the world of academic psychology, where moral questions and discussions are outsourced to the philosophy or religion departments, and who frequently hear our colleagues claim that the scientific principles of psychology are experimentally validated, objective, amoral, and therefore lacking the biases of all other contributors to discussions of social policy, are not surprised. We have a moral responsibility to question this dogma of scientific purity that serves as it has before in history to produce research findings that justify the social and political policies of those who finance the research laboratories, regardless of the evil those policies produce.

REFERENCES

Adams, J., & Miller, R. B. (2008). Bridging psychology's scientist vs. practitioner divide: Fruits of a 25-year dialogue. *Journal of Theoretical and Philosophical Psychology, 28,* 375–394. doi:10.1037/h0092064

American Psychological Association. (2010). *Ethical principles of psychologists and code of conduct* (2002, Amended June 1, 2010). Retrieved from http://www.apa.org/ethics/code/index.aspx

Baumeister, R. (1999). *Evil: Inside human violence and cruelty.* New York, NY: Holt.

Bernstein, R. (2002). *Radical evil: A philosophical interrogation.* Cambridge, England: Polity.

Costanzo, M., Gerrity, E., & Lykes, M. (2007). Psychologists and the use of torture in interrogations. *Analyses of Social Issues and Public Policy, 7*(1), 7–20. doi:10.1111/j.1530-2415.2007.00118.x

Gergen, K. (2009). *An invitation to social construction* (2nd ed.). Thousand Oaks, CA: Sage.

Greenberg, L. (2004). Emotion-focused psychotherapy. *Clinical Psychology & Psychotherapy, 11*(1), 3–16. doi:10.1002/cpp.388

Haidt, J. (2004). Intuitive ethics: How innately prepared intuitions generate culturally variable virtues. *Daedalus, 133,* 55–66. doi:10.1162/0011526042365555

Held, B. (2007). *Psychology's interpretive turn: The search for truth and agency in theoretical and philosophical psychology.* Washington, DC: American Psychological Association. doi:10.1037/11588-000

Herman, E. (1995). *Romance of American psychology: Political culture in the age of experts.* Berkeley, CA: University of California Press.

Hubbard, K. (2007). Psychologists and interrogations: What has torture got to do with it? *Analyses of Social Issues and Public Policy, 7*(1), 29–33.

Kendler, H. (2008). *Amoral thoughts about psychology: The intersection of science, psychology and ethics* (2nd ed.). Springfield, IL: Charles C Thomas.

Kirschenbaum, H., & Henderson, V. (1989). *The Carl Rogers reader.* New York, NY: Mariner Books.

Jansz, J. & van Drunen, P. (Eds.). (2004). *A social history of psychology.* Oxford, England: Blackwell.

Johnson, B. (2005). *Emotional health: What emotions are and how they cause social and mental diseases* (2nd rev. ed.). Isle of Wight, England: Trust Consent.

Lakoff, G. (2005). *Don't think of an elephant: Know your values and frame the debate— The essential guide for progressives.* White River Junction, VT: Chelsea Green.

Lifton, R. (2000). *The Nazi doctors: Medical killing and the psychology of genocide.* New York, NY: Basic Books. (Original work published 1986)

Malan, D. (1995). *Individual psychotherapy and the science of psychodynamics* (2nd ed.) Oxford, England: Butterworth-Heinemann.

Martin, J., & Sugarman, J. (2000). Between the modern and the postmodern: The possibility of self and progressive understanding in psychology. *American Psychologist, 55,* 397–406. doi:10.1037/0003-066X.55.4.397

May, R. (1992). The problem of evil: An open letter to Carl Rogers. In R. Miller (Ed.), *The restoration of dialogue: Readings in the philosophy of clinical psychology* (pp. 306–313). Washington, DC: American Psychological Association.

Meehl, P. (1997). Credentialed persons, credentialed knowledge. *Clinical Psychology: Science and Practice, 4*, 91–98. doi:10.1111/j.1468-2850.1997.tb00103.x

Milgram, S. (2004). *Obedience to authority.* London, England: Pinter & Martin. (Original work published 1972)

Miller, R. B. (1983). A call to armchairs. *Psychotherapy: Theory, Research & Practice, 20*, 208–219. doi:10.1037/h0088492

Miller, R. B. (Ed.). (1992). *The restoration of dialogue: Readings in the philosophy of clinical psychology.* Washington, DC: American Psychological Association. doi:10.1037/10112-000

Miller, R. B. (2001). Scientific vs. clinical-based knowledge in psychology: A concealed moral conflict. *American Journal of Psychotherapy, 55*, 344–356.

Miller, R. B. (2004). *Facing human suffering: Psychology and psychotherapy as moral engagement.* Washington, DC: American Psychological Association. doi:10.1037/10691-000

Miller, R. B. (2009, August). The moral context of psychological concepts: Essential dissension. In F. Wertz (Chair), *Do human kinds have essential qualities?* Symposium conducted at the 117th Annual Convention of the American Psychological Association, Toronto, Canada.

Neiman, S. (2004). *Evil in modern thought: An alternative history of philosophy.* Princeton, NJ: Princeton University Press.

Panksepp, J. (2008). Carving natural emotions kindly from bottom up but not top down. *Journal of Theoretical and Philosophical Psychology, 28*, 395–422. doi:10.1037/h0092065

Peck, M. S. (1998). *People of the lie: The hope for healing human evil* (2nd ed.). New York, NY: Touchstone.

Prinz, J. (2007). *The emotional construction of morals.* New York, NY: Oxford University Press.

Rogers, C. (1992). Reply to Rollo May. In B. Miller (Ed.), *The restoration of dialogue: Readings in the philosophy of clinical psychology* (pp. 314–316). Washington, DC: American Psychological Association.

Scarry, E. (1985). *The body in pain.* New York, NY: Oxford University Press.

Staub, I. (2001). Genocide and mass killing: Their roots and prevention. In D. Christie, R. Wagner, & D. D. Winter (Eds.), *Peace, conflict and violence: Peace psychology for the 20th century.* Upper Saddle River, NJ: Prentice Hall.

Toulmin, S. E. (1990). *Cosmopolis.* Chicago, IL: University of Chicago Press.

Valenstein, E. (1998). *Blaming the brain.* New York, NY: Free Press.

Whitaker, R. (2010). *Anatomy of an epidemic: Magic bullets, psychiatric drugs and the astonishing rise of mental illness in America.* New York, NY: Crown.

Zimbardo, P. (2007). *The Lucifer effect: Understanding how good people turn evil.* New York, NY: Random House.

12

FEELING BAD, BEING BAD, AND THE PERILS OF PERSONHOOD

BARBARA S. HELD

When did feeling bad turn into being bad? By *feeling bad*, I mean feeling unhappy. And by *being bad*, I mean being a bad person, one who lacks virtue or goodness of character. Surely this equation did not begin with the positive psychology movement—although in my view no psychologist has done more to promote the equation of positive thoughts and feelings (or happiness) with virtue than has positive psychology's founding leader Martin Seligman, especially in *Authentic Happiness* (Seligman, 2002) and *Character Strengths and Virtues* (Peterson & Seligman, 2004).[1] In both books Seligman relied on Aristotle's ethics—especially Aristotle's notion of *eudaimonia* (often translated as "happiness, fulfillment, or flourishing"; see Fowers, 2008, p. 631)—to

---

[1]Interestingly, in contrast to these two books, the word "virtue" does not even appear in the index of Seligman's (2011) most recent book, *Flourish*.

DOI: 10.1037/13941-012
Humanity's Dark Side: Evil, Destructive Experience, and Psychotherapy, A. C. Bohart, B. S. Held, E. Mendelowitz, and K. J. Schneider (Editors)

237

develop his own tripartite notion of "authentic happiness," which, he said, transcends merely feeling good:

> The pleasant life . . . is wrapped up in the successful pursuit of the positive feelings, supplemented by the skills of amplifying these emotions. The good life . . . is a life wrapped up in successfully using your signature strengths to obtain abundant and authentic gratification. The meaningful life [entails] using your signature strengths in the service of something larger than you are. To live all three lives is to lead a *full* life. (Seligman, 2002, p. 249)

In *Aristotle's Psychology*, Daniel Robinson (1989) reproduced the "tabular form" in which "Aristotle actually summarizes the vices and virtues" in his *Eudemian Ethics* (p. 113). Robinson stated that "a *eudaimonic* life is the life lived by a certain kind of person" (p. 112), or, as Blaine Fowers (2008) put it, "Virtues are the character strengths that are necessary to pursue what is good" (p. 631). Alternatively, "'The original Greek term for virtue was *arête*, best translated as excellence. Virtues are, simply put, human excellences or character strengths that make it possible for individuals to flourish as human beings' (Fowers, 2005, p. 4)" (Fowers, 2009, p. 1012).

The (Aristotelian) "Table of Virtues"[2] reproduced in Robinson (1989, p. 114) is noteworthy for two reasons:

1. First, each virtue defines a "golden mean" between two forms of vice—excess and deficiency (e.g., the virtue "bravery" is the mean between "foolhardiness" and "cowardice"). This is important because a professed overarching mission of positive psychology is to make happy people even happier, a mission justified by psychology's alleged overemphasis on negativity or pathology. As Seligman (2002) said in the first sentence of *Authentic Happiness*, "For the last half century psychology has been consumed with a single topic only—mental illness—and has done fairly well with it" (p. xi). Whether we have done fairly well with treating mental illness is open to debate, as is the assertion that psychology has "been consumed with" mental illness. In any case, Gable and Haidt (2005), who conceded that "the large majority of the gross academic product of psychology is neutral" (p. 104), nonetheless echoed Seligman's sentiment:

> The past half century has seen the study of the psychological aspects of what makes life worth living recede to the background, whereas studies on disorder and damage have taken center stage. The recent positive psychology movement grew out of recognition of this imbalance. (p. 104)

---

[2]As listed by Robinson (1989, p. 114), Aristotle's virtues are: Gentleness, Bravery, Modesty, Temperance, Righteous indignation, The Just, Liberality, Sincerity, Friendliness, Dignity, Endurance, Greatness of spirit, Magnificence, Wisdom.

Seligman (2002) took his own claim one step further:

> But this progress [in treating mental illness] has come at a high cost. Relieving the states that make life miserable, it seems, has made building the states that make life worth living less of a priority. But people want more than just to correct their weaknesses. . . . Lying awake at night, you probably wonder, as I have, how to go from plus two to plus seven in your life, not just how to go from minus five to minus three and feel a little less miserable day by day. . . . The time has finally arrived for a science that seeks to understand positive emotion, build strength and virtue, and provide guideposts for finding what Aristotle called the "good life." (p. xi)

Seligman (2004) delivered his message even more succinctly: "The mission of Positive Psychology, put simply, is to increase the total tonnage of happiness in the world."

The fruits of the seeds sown by Seligman are growing at a rapid rate (see Coyne, Tennen, & Ranchor, 2010, p. 36, for ways to access positive psychology website coaching and "web-based exercise" enterprises). On July 14, 2010, I myself received an e-mail from Jeffrey Levy, MD, with this subject line: "New Positive Psychology Program to Advance Your Teaching, Research and Practice." The body of the e-mail stated the following:

> A new online POSITIVE PSYCHOLOGY TRAINING PROGRAM was developed by the world's leading experts in the field. . . . [It] will help you prepare the next generation with the knowledge and skills to effectively deal with the most pressing emotional health problems, while improving life satisfaction, performance and persistence. . . . Sign up now for the program at www.positivepsychologytraining.com.

What a fitting message for Bastille Day! Moreover, there are now self-help books by Templeton prize-winning positive psychologists with such tantalizing titles as these: *Positivity: Top-Notch Research Reveals the 3-to-1 Ratio That Will Change Your Life*, by Barbara Frederickson (2009), and *The How of Happiness: A Scientific Approach to Getting the Life You Want*, by Sonja Lyubomirsky (2008). The cover art depicts a sliced cherry pie with the caption "*This much happiness—up to 40%* [of the depicted cherry pie]—*is within your power to change.*" Apropos of Seligman's (2004) aforementioned "mission of Positive Psychology," the entry on Lyubomirsky in the *Encyclopedia of Positive Psychology* includes a subsection titled "How Can We Make People Happier Still?" (Howell, 2009, p. 593). Not much golden mean talk here. What would Aristotle say?

2. My second point about the Table of Virtues is that not one of the 14 virtues listed by Robinson seems readily translatable into feeling good, thinking positive thoughts, or optimism, at least not in any ordinary sense of those terms. In fact, a recent article by

positive psychology movement leader Ed Diener is (realistically) titled "Feeling Bad? The 'Power' of Positive Thinking May Not Apply to Everyone" (Ng & Diener, 2009). According to Ng and Diener (2009), those to whom positive thinking may not apply are high in neuroticism. This is hardly news. In her 20-plus years of scientific research on this topic, Julie Norem (2001) repeatedly found much positive value in the use of what she named "defensive pessimism" as a coping strategy for those who have high trait/dispositional anxiety. Defensive pessimists consider how to cope with potential problems *in advance* of anxiety-provoking situations, a strategy that reduces their anxiety and so enhances their performance. Making them think positively diminishes their performance, because it does not reduce their debilitating anxiety. Yet Diener (Ng & Diener, 2009) made no mention of Norem's research here or in his chapter in the second edition of the *Oxford Handbook of Positive Psychology,* where he rightly said that ignoring "scholars who are not in the 'fold' . . . is, of course, a mistake that we should always avoid" (Diener, 2009, p. 10).

In this chapter, I seek not to explore the validity of Seligman's interpretation of Aristotle's theory of virtue/*eudaimonia* (see Fowers, 2008, for problems therein) or his view of disciplinary psychology. Instead, I seek (a) to demonstrate that by sheer virtue of its existence, the positive psychology movement, like prior positive thought movements (see Held, 2004, 2005), has enabled, however unintentionally, the ubiquitous (American) belief that to feel bad is to be unvirtuous; (b) to explore the (historical) basis and detrimental ramifications of this belief; and (c) to link this belief to harm, if not outright evil, in terms of its ironically postmodernlike dismissal or denial of the daunting, and sometimes horrific, realities of human existence, or what I here call the "perils of personhood"—this, despite forthright acknowledgment of those realities by many positive psychologists (e.g., Aspinwall & Tedeschi, 2010b; Diener, 2009; Gable & Haidt, 2005; Seligman, 2011; see Held, 2004, pp. 12–20, for quotations of others).

THE FEELING BAD = BEING BAD, HAPPINESS = VIRTUE EQUATION: WESTERN HISTORICAL/RELIGIOUS ROOTS AND A CONTEMPORARY IMPLICIT ARGUMENT

A quick glance at a subsection of *The Book of Positive Quotations* (Cook, 1993, p. 9) titled "We Have a Duty to Be Happy" reveals that the happiness = virtue equation predated the positive psychology movement by decades, if not centuries. Consider these famous statements:

... So much sadness exists in the world that we are all under obligation to contribute as much joy as lies within our powers.—John Sutherland Bonnell [20th century]

There is no duty so much underrated as the duty of being happy.—Robert Louis Stevenson [19th century]

Pleasure is the object, duty and the goal of all rational creatures.—Voltaire [18th century]

The first quotation (above) of a famous Presbyterian minister should call to mind another even more famous Protestant minister, namely, Norman Vincent Peale, who in his best-selling book *The Power of Positive Thinking* (1952) advanced the virtues of positive thinking in the 20th century to unparalleled effect. In Chapter 3 of *Bright-Sided: How the Relentless Promotion of Positive Thinking Has Undermined America*, Barbara Ehrenreich (2009) gave a clear overview of the religious origins of positive thinking movements in America, beginning with the post-Calvinist "New Thought Movement" (p. 79) launched by Mary Baker Eddy and Phineas Parkhurst Quimby in the 19th century (pp. 74–96). The recent "Complaint-Free World Movement," headed by the Reverend Will Bowen, continues on in this religious tradition of linking positivity to virtue (see S. Simon, "Quit Your Whining, If You Can," *Los Angeles Times*, January 27, 2007).

To be fair, Seligman did not plant his positive psychology movement in religious soil, as he distances his from prior positive thought movements by standing it on the rock of scientific objectivity and evidence rather than on (any form of) religious faith. Still, religious tradition gave Seligman a historical basis for his own brand of positivity, as does this secular chapter title written by Tocqueville (1840/1988) in his second volume of *Democracy in America*: "How Equality Suggests to the Americans the Idea of the Indefinite Perfectibility of Man" (p. 452; see Held, 2002, p. 966, for fuller quotation).

In distinction to Tocqueville, Seligman (2002) and many of his followers adhere more or less to a set-point theory (also discussed as a "hedonic treadmill" or "hedonic adaptation theory"; see Dunn, Uswatte, & Elliott, 2009, pp. 653–654), that is, a theory that limits the outer reaches of a person's quest for greater happiness to genetic dispositions. Ironically, this does not stop some positive psychologists from promoting the pursuit of ever more happiness. As Lyubomirsky (2008) put it in a section of *The How of Happiness* titled "The 40 Percent Solution":

> An astounding 50 percent of the differences among people's happiness levels can be accounted for by their genetically determined *set points*.[3]

---

[3]Regarding set points and her "40 percent solution" to "What determines happiness?," Lyubomirsky (2008, p. 20, notes 10, 13) cited, among several others, Diener, Suh, Lucas, and Smith (1999) and Lucas and Donnellan (2007). Also see Diener, Lucas, and Scollon (2006) and Diener, Oishi, and Lucas (2009) on revisions to set-point/hedonic adaptation theory.

This discovery comes from the growing research done with identical and fraternal twins that suggests that each of us is born with a particular happiness set point that originates from our biological mother or father or both, a baseline or potential for happiness to which we are bound to return, even after major setbacks or triumphs. (pp. 20–21)

Lyubomirsky then continued with the setup to her trans-set-point conclusion:

Perhaps the most counterintuitive finding is that . . . only about 10 percent of the variance in our happiness levels is explained by differences in life circumstances or situations—that is, whether we are rich or poor, healthy or unhealthy, beautiful or plain. . . . A great deal of science backs up this conclusion. (p. 21)

Her conclusion is the "40 percent solution":

This finding suggests to me that . . . 40 percent of the differences in our happiness levels are still left unexplained. What makes up this 40 percent? Besides our genes and the situations that we confront, there is one critical thing left: our behavior. Thus the key to happiness lies *not* in changing our genetic makeup . . . and *not* in changing our circumstances . . . but in our daily intentional activities. . . . The 40 percent . . . is within our ability to control . . . through what we *do* . . . and how we *think* [e.g., "expressing gratitude," "offer helping hands," "practice optimism"] . . .

A massive literature reveals what kinds of attributes, thoughts, and behaviors characterize the happiest people. In my laboratory and the laboratories of a few others, ways of harnessing the power of our own thoughts and behaviors—that is, our intentional activities—have been tested. We have conducted formal happiness-increasing intervention studies devised to increase and maintain a person's happiness level *over and above his or her set point*.[4] (pp. 22–23)

My own conclusion is that positive psychologists may be more in league with Tocqueville's (1840/1988) "indefinite perfectibility of man," about which he said, "man in general is endowed with an indefinite capacity for improvement" (p. 453), than I initially suggested. Calls for caution in drawing inferences that exceed the data in both the first (Snyder & Lopez, 2002, pp. 754–755) and second (Peterson, 2009, p. xxiii) editions of the *Handbook of Positive Psychology* are especially noteworthy in this regard, even though, recall, many positive psychologists do not deny the limitations and hardships we all inevitably face.

---

[4]See my note 6 for comparison of this statement with Seligman (2011) on the question of transcending one's set point.

But in making happiness a *personal or individual* matter of choice and effort, positive psychologists undermine the need for social, political, and economic change (see Becker & Marecek, 2008), even though some speak in national "economic" terms by way of an index that has been called "gross national happiness" or some variant thereof (e.g., Bok, 2010; Diener, 2000; Diener & Seligman, 2004; Ehrenreich, 2009, p. 151). Moreover, they proclaim various "routes" or "strategies" to achieve whatever amount of happiness we can each in principle attain, thereby *seeming* to profess the individual differences in coping for which critics of the movement, including me, have taken them to task: for example, Seligman's (2002) call to "identify your signature strengths" (p. 134), of the 24 he links to his six virtues; and Lyubomirsky's (2008) declaration that "you *can* . . . select just one strategy (or a few) ["of things that very happy people do every day"] that will work for you" (p. 23). Nonetheless, in my view positive psychologists may at least *implicitly* contribute to making the attainment of happiness a *moral categorical/ unconditional imperative that is by definition universalized—that is, regardless of individual circumstance.* It is in this implicit culturewide mandate that I find the happiness = virtue equation more ubiquitously and doggedly lodged than in any explicit statement made by any particular positive psychologist. The happiness = virtue equation, then, may be reduced to an implicit logical argument about happiness, which I now set forth.

THE CONTEMPORARY IMPLICIT LOGICAL ARGUMENT ABOUT HAPPINESS

The implicit logical argument comprises a set of premises and conclusions, and again it is not stated explicitly in any of the positive psychology literature that I have reviewed. Nonetheless, at the Second International Positive Psychology Summit in 2003, a woman in the audience expressed concern about "blame" in response to some of the media about positive psychology that I (Held, 2003; also see Held, 2005) presented there—for example, "Happier Means Healthier: Optimists Live Longer, and Optimism Can Be Cultivated" (by G. Condon, *Maine Sunday Telegram*, February 27, 2000), in which happiness is presented as a voluntary choice.[5] To his credit, Seligman agreed with the woman, conceding that the downside of something having voluntary choice attached to it is blame. He acknowledged that it's a real

---

[5]Other examples that I presented include "How to Make Yourself Happy: Cheer Up! New Science Says You Can Do Lots More to Inject Real Joy Into Your Life" (cover of *U.S. News & World Report*, September 3, 2001); "How to See the Glass Half Full" (by M. E. P. Seligman, *Newsweek*, September 16, 2002). And a few years later, "The Science of Happiness" (cover of *Time*, January 17, 2005).

problem.[6] Compare this to positive psychologists who reportedly "agree that the field's success has come with some pitfalls, including the dissemination by the mass media—though, they argue, not by the researchers themselves—of overly simplistic messages like the ones Held criticizes" (Azar, 2011, p. 36). In any case, here is my version of the implicit logical argument:

1. You *can* be happy, or at least happier, because positive psychology offers the scientifically validated tools (e.g., "happiness activities"[7]) by which to achieve greater happiness.
2. Therefore, you *should* be happy, or at least happier.
3. And so if you are not happy or happier, then it is your own personal choice/fault: You are a bad or unvirtuous person.
4. Conclusion: Feeling bad is being bad. That is, to be an unhappy person is to be a bad or unvirtuous person.

When the *can* of Statement 1 (whether it is empirically valid) becomes the *should* of Statement 2—that is, when a *descriptive* claim turns into a *prescription*[8]—we arrive at the moral imperative to be happy with which I began this argument by way of exemplary quotations. Here, then, we locate the essence of my term "the tyranny of the positive attitude," in which people are made to feel bad, unvirtuous, guilty, or defective about feeling bad (Held, 2001, 2002, 2004). As Seligman (2002) wrote, "Pessimism is maladaptive in most endeavors. . . . Thus, pessimists are losers on many fronts" (p. 178). He (Peterson & Seligman, 2004, p. 518) went further in explicitly linking various forms of positivity to "morally valued" "criteria" and negativity to what is "undesirable":

> Hope and optimism are highly valued characteristics. We admire those who can see the bright side; who can reach for the stars; who can keep their chins up, . . . who can find the silver lining; . . . who can see how it might all work out in the end—even if they are wrong. But often they are not wrong, because hope and optimism can be self-fulfilling. . . . The opposites of hope and optimism include *pessimism, hopelessness, gloom,*

---

[6]In his book *Flourish*, Seligman (2011) at first seemed to downplay the extent of voluntary choice in having a positive versus negative mentality by saying he takes a "more realistic approach to [the] dysphorias," because "most personality traits are highly heritable": "The negative personality traits have very strong biological limits, and the best a clinician can ever do with the cosmetic approach is to get patients to live in the best part of their set range of depression or anxiety or anger" (pp. 52–53). He advocated a "psychology of 'dealing with it.' . . . [i.e.,] 'to live heroically [by] functioning well even when you are very sad'" (p. 52). But he then, in line with Lyubomirsky, said that "unlike the skills of minimizing misery, ["the specific skills of positive psychology"] are self-sustaining" and thus not merely cosmetic, so "they likely treat depression and anxiety and they likely help prevent them as well" (pp. 54–55).
[7]See Lyubomirsky (2008, Chapters 4–9) for 12 "Happiness Activities" and Seligman (2011, Chapter 2) for "Creating Your Happiness: Positive Psychology Exercises That Work."
[8]See Held (2005, pp. 19–21) for discussion of Seligman's (2002, p. 303) claim that his "theory is not a morality or world-view [it is not a prescription]; it is a description."

and *helplessness*, none of them remotely desirable. (Peterson & Seligman, 2004, pp. 527–528)

Moreover, in their entry on "Optimism" in the *Encyclopedia of Positive Psychology*, in which they presented a table of "Differences in the Coping Tendencies of Optimists and Pessimists," Scheier and Carver (2009, p. 659) gave optimists the edge on all six points of morally infused comparison. And yet again there was no mention of Norem's prolific work on the positive coping value of "defensive pessimism," in either positive psychology's *Encyclopedia* or the second edition of its *Handbook*.

A third example can be found in Lyubomirsky's (2008, pp. 24–26) implicit happiness = virtue equation, the "can therefore should" logic I have explicated, in a book section titled "Why Be Happy?" This logic is especially evident in her inclusion of such "moral virtues" as charitableness and cooperativeness.

> Why *should* [italics added] we put forth all this effort in order to be happier? In case anyone needed convincing, the scientific evidence reveals many compelling reasons to aspire for greater happiness and fulfillment. My collaborators Ed Diener and Laura King and I have documented a large and growing psychological literature showing that becoming happier doesn't just make you *feel good*. It turns out that happiness brings with it multiple fringe benefits. Compared with their less happy peers, happier people are more sociable and energetic, more charitable and cooperative, and better liked by others. . . . They are better leaders and negotiators and earn more money. They are more resilient in the face of hardship, have stronger immune systems, and are physically healthier. Happy people even live longer.[9] (pp. 24–25)

This last quotation especially interests me because it also hits all the "high" notes of the first of what I consider two inverse "stages" of the positive psychology movement (Held, 2005, p. 29; cf. Kristjánsson, 2010, p. 298). Prior to his 2002 book, in which he propounded what I called his "old 'new positive psychology,'" Seligman proclaimed the virtues of being happy: Being happy, or at least optimistic/positive, is good for you—bringing with it health, wealth, and beyond (Seligman, 1990; Seligman & Csikszentmihalyi, 2000). With the publication of *Authentic Happiness* (2002) and *Character Strengths and Virtues* (Peterson & Seligman, 2004), in which he propounded his "new 'new positive psychology,'" Seligman proclaimed the virtues of being good:

---

[9]See, e.g., Coyne and Tennen (2010); Coyne, Tennen, and Ranchor (2010); and Stefanek, Palmer, Thombs, and Coyne (2009) for challenges to some of these claims. Also see Howard Friedman's (2010) "Get Stressed, Worry, Live Longer" and Friedman and Martin's (2011) book, *The Longevity Project: Surprising Discoveries for Health and Long Life from the Landmark Eight-Decade Study*, for extensive evidence about how more complete models, which study long-term processes, challenge some of the health claims made by positive psychologists.

being good/virtuous makes you *"authentically* happy." In *Flourish,* Seligman (2011) suggests an even newer version of positive psychology, by emphasizing flourishing.

THE BACKLASH

Movements often bring backlashes, and so too have the various positive thought movements that have permeated our culture. Ehrenreich's (2009) *Bright-Sided,* Eric Wilson's (2009) *Against Happiness,* and Allan Horwitz and Jerome Wakefield's (2007) *The Loss of Sadness* are particularly noteworthy examples, as are a special issue of *Theory & Psychology* (Christopher, Richardson, & Slife, 2008) and Coyne and Tennen's (2010) and Coyne et al.'s (2010) "Great Debate" with Lisa Aspinwall and Richard Tedeschi (2010a, 2010b). In that debate, held in 2008 at the Society of Behavioral Medicine Convention, Coyne and Tennen challenged positive psychology's claims about (a) the role of having a "'fighting spirit' in extending the life" of cancer patients; (b) the "effects of interventions cultivating positive psychological states on immune functioning and cancer progression and mortality"; and (c) "evidence concerning . . . benefit finding and . . . posttraumatic growth following serious illness such as cancer" (Abstract, p. 16).[10]

Apropos of the tyranny of the positive attitude, Coyne et al. (2010) quoted this personal plea for tolerance of diversity in coping styles, made by an Olympic athlete:

> Acceptance of diversity in human response to cancer allows room for the iconic image of Lance Armstrong as a heroic cancer survivor who declares that cancer made him a better person. But it also allows for the alternative image provided by Olympic gold medal winner Maarten Van de Weijden. The Dutch swimmer requests that no one confuse him with Lance Armstrong. And he adds "Armstrong describes his battle, how he was fighting, how he felt that he expelled the cancer cells from his body. What he basically says is that it is your own fault when you don't make it. That you didn't fight hard enough. . . . When my cancer was diagnosed, I laid down in the hospital and simply surrendered to the doctors. You always hear those stories that you have to think positively, that you have to fight to survive. This can be a great burden for patients. It has never been proven that you can cure from cancer by thinking positively or by fighting." (p. 40)

---

[10]See Kraemer, Kuchler, and Spiegel (2009) and Coyne, Thombs, Stefanek, and Palmer (2009) for an exchange regarding psychotherapy and cancer survival.

Though I do not suggest that we adopt Richard Bentall's (1992) "Proposal to Classify Happiness as a Psychiatric Disorder," I find in Van de Weijden's words a compelling case against the tyranny of positivity that can indeed blame the victim. So too with the findings of Smith, Loewenstein, Jankovic, and Ubel (2009), in their article "Happily Hopeless: Adaptation to a Permanent, But Not to a Temporary, Disability."

EVIL, VIRTUE, AND REALISM

The tyranny of the positive attitude can surely do harm, as can any tyranny, and so it can be rightly seen as a form of evil. Again, I do not see positive psychologists as embodying evil in any way whatsoever. Nonetheless, I do think that, as with all movements, unintended deleterious consequences can obtain (Held, 2005)—in this case lending the mantle of science to a happiness = virtue equation that lacks *logical* support, no matter how much positive psychologists profess the validity of their (probabilistic) scientific/empirical findings. Here we confront the important matter of realism.

Getting Reality Right

That some positive psychologists declare the realism of optimism (among other forms of positive thinking) is also not in itself a form or cause of evil. But it does contribute to what I have called positive psychology's "reality problems" in various ways that I will address in due course. Here note that as Maureen O'Hara (2009) so astutely pointed out, evil thrives, indeed depends, on a commitment to deny (or at least ignore) what is real (also see Schneider, 2009, pp. 12–15, on what amounts to "depressive realism"). To illustrate, psychologist Bruce Levine quoted Ehrenreich in his *Huffington Post* (posted online July 22, 2010) piece titled "Psychologists Profit on Unending U.S. Wars by Teaching Positive Thinking to Soldiers":

> It's easy to see positive thinking as a uniquely American form of naïveté, but it is neither uniquely American nor endearingly naïve. In vastly different settings, positive thinking has been a tool of political repression worldwide. . . . In the Soviet Union, as in the Eastern European states and North Korea, the censors required upbeat art, books, and films, meaning upbeat heroes, plots about fulfilling production quotas, and endings promising a glorious revolutionary future. . . . The penalties for negative thinking were real. Not to be positive and optimistic was to be "defeatist." . . . Accusing someone of spreading defeatism condemned him to several years in Stalinist camps. (Ehrenreich, 2009, pp. 201–202, as cited in Levine, 2010)

Regarding optimism and realism, consider these quotations: Suzanne Segerstrom, who won a Templeton Positive Psychology Prize in 2002, said, "[Some say] optimists are naïve and vulnerable to disappointment when they come face to face with reality. My evidence suggests that optimists are not naïve; they are however, wiser in expending their energies" ("Psychologists Receive," 2002). Aspinwall (in Snyder & Lopez, 2002, p. 754), who won a Templeton Positive Psychology Prize for her reformulation of optimism (Azar, 2000), said, "Happier and Wiser: Optimism and Positive Affect Promote Careful Realistic Thinking and Behavior." To their credit, in their "Great Debate" with Coyne and Tennen (2010), Aspinwall and Tedeschi (2010b, p. 10) emphasized "Avoiding the 'Tyranny of Optimism'"—a term, interestingly, coined (to my knowledge) by Seligman himself (1990, p. 292). Nonetheless, Aspinwall and Tedeschi (2010b) gave this standard definition: "Optimism is a generalized expectancy for positive outcomes that appears to be trait-like and predicts how people cope with stress" (p. 5). Scheier and Carver (2009) gave a similar definition in the *Encyclopedia*, although they also said that optimists "try to accept the reality of their situation," unlike pessimists' alleged denial (p. 659).

Of course, claiming that optimism *causes* realism is not the same as saying that optimism *is* realism, which it surely is not. After all, as the standard definitions quoted above suggest, optimism is a *biased* expectation about the future, as is pessimism. Accordingly, some positive psychologists have downplayed the extent to which optimism should be *too* biased/unrealistic: For example, Snyder, Rand, King, Feldman, and Woodward (2002, p. 1007) said, "Having high hope means that a person may have a slight positive self-referential bias, but not an extreme [positive] illusion that is counterproductive." By contrast, others, such as Taylor, Kemeny, Reed, Bower, and Gruenewald (2000, pp. 102–103), spoke with some approbation of *unrealistic* optimism. And Sandra Schneider (2001) even tried to resolve the legitimate logical problem of a "realistic optimism" philosophically, by arguing that reality *itself* is (ontologically) "fuzzy," thereby eroding our nonfuzzy (epistemic) access to it: This "solution" supposedly licensed the logic of a (nonbiased) "realistic optimism" (see Held, 2004). The point is, whether deemed more or less realistic, optimism remains an epistemic bias whose virtues positive psychologists extol repeatedly. And like pessimism, it stands in stark distinction to the epistemic realism or objectivism (diminishment of bias) that Seligman (2002; Peterson & Seligman, 2004) considers a route to the virtue of wisdom.

In Held (2004, 2005) I theorized that perhaps "positive" findings about optimism are rewarded within positive psychology, at least in part, because they permit two competing/incompatible "virtues" within that movement to be made compatible: (a) the virtue of holding an optimistic bias in *everyday knowing* and (b) the virtue of striving for objectivity, of striving to eliminate any and all bias as much as possible, in *both everyday knowing and in scientific knowing*. This amounts to a double epistemic standard *between* (a) everyday knowing and (b) scientific knowing, and a bona fide contradiction *within* everyday knowing. In Held (2005, pp. 26–27) I explained it this way:

> The double epistemic standard between scientific knowing and everyday knowing, and the contradiction within everyday knowing, can best be seen by contrasting Seligman's explicit statements about epistemology with his statements about positive illusions. He stands positive psychology on the rock of scientific objectivity; . . . it is the foundation he relies upon to distinguish his positive psychology movement from its allegedly unscientific and therefore less virtuous predecessors (especially humanistic psychology—e.g., see Peterson & Seligman, 2004, p. 4; Seligman & Csikszentmihalyi, 2001, pp. 89–90). Moreover, he finds *personal* virtue in holding a "reality orientation" in everyday knowing. In *Authentic Happiness* Seligman (2002) said, "Learned optimism . . . is about accuracy" (p. 96). There, in describing the routes to the virtue of "wisdom and knowledge," he wrote, "By judgment, I mean the exercise of sifting information objectively and rationally. . . . It [judgment] . . . embodies reality orientation. . . . This is a significant part of the healthy trait of not confusing your own wants and needs with the facts of the world" (p. 142).
>
> But Seligman (2002) happily—or at least readily—sacrifices the epistemic realism and the objective knowledge he generally exalts, when he turns his attention to the attainment of beneficial outcomes in the context of everyday knowing [where he also touts the virtues of holding an optimistic/nonobjective bias—hence the contradiction within everyday knowing].

Regarding that last sentence, consider this (antiprescriptive!) statement made by Seligman (2002), in which he accepts loss of realism in everyday knowing:

> It is not the job of Positive Psychology to tell you that you *should* be optimistic, or spiritual, or kind or good-humored; it is rather to *describe* the consequences of these traits (for example, that being optimistic brings about less depression, better physical health, and higher achievement, *at a cost perhaps of less realism*) [all italics added]. (p. 129)

Is the call to an optimistic bias by upholders of modern objective (positive) psychological science—of supporting positive illusion in the name of a happier, fuller, more liberated life—all that different (epistemically speaking) from the call by upholders of postmodern/narrative (i.e., antiobjectivist) therapists and theorists to rewrite or renarrate one's life in the name of freedom/emancipation (e.g., Baumgardner & Rappoport, 1996; Gergen & Kaye, 1992; Stancombe & White, 1998)? If not, we have in these two movements strange epistemic bedfellows indeed (see Held, 2002, pp. 972–976). Though both movements seek liberation from the inevitable pain of living, their scientific epistemologies could not differ more. In this we see the perils of movements, as Michael Katzko (2002a, 2002b) so astutely pointed out in distinguishing the epistemic values/missions of science (the "first-order analysis" of the "scientist explorer") from the social/political values/missions of scientific movements (the "second-order rhetoric" of the "scientist warrior"; see Held, 2005, pp. 14–15, 28–29, for elaboration).

Getting the Right Reality

In distinction to the *epistemic* virtue of getting reality right, of knowing the real conditions of human existence, there is the *ontological* virtue of existing in the "right" way, which for Seligman (2002) and his followers is the "authentically happy" way that allegedly constitutes virtue itself. Of course, the two types of virtues are interrelated: One's (epistemic) "take" on reality surely has implications for the life one experiences/lives (ontologically speaking; Held, 1995, 1998, 2007).

A century before Seligman launched the positive psychology movement, another famous American psychologist (and philosopher), William James (1902/1923), wrote of these matters in his classic book, *The Varieties of Religious Experience*. There James devoted two lectures to "The Religion of Healthy-Mindedness." This "religion" is surely a forerunner of the positive psychology movement and, by my lights, the tyranny of the positive attitude, which may be a side effect of both culturewide and professional "negativity about negativity" (Held, 2004, pp. 18–26). In *Bright-Sided* Ehrenreich (2009) quoted James from these two lectures:

> James enthused over the New Thought approach to healing. . . . To James, it did not matter that New Thought was a philosophical muddle; it *worked*. . . . James understood that New Thought offered much more than a new approach to healing; it was an entirely new way of seeing the world . . . : "One hears of the 'Gospel of Relaxation,' of the 'Don't Worry Movement.' . . . More and more people are recognizing it to be bad form to speak of disagreeable sensations." . . . As a scientist, he was repelled by much of the New Thought literature, finding it "so moonstruck with optimism and so vaguely expressed . . . ." Still, he blessed the new way of thinking as "healthy-mindedness." . . . [Thus] James . . . made positive thinking respectable, not because he found it intellectually convincing but because of its undeniable success in "curing" the poor invalid victims of Calvinism. (pp. 87–89)

Ehrenreich did not quote James (1902/1923) from his two lectures that followed the ones on "Healthy-Mindedness." These he titled "The Sick Soul," and near the end of them he, who himself struggled with agonizing depression, also struggled with a difficult question regarding what he called the "experience of evil":

We can see how great an antagonism may naturally arise between the healthy-minded way of viewing life and the way that takes all this experience of evil as something essential. To this latter way, the morbid-minded way, as we might call it, healthy-mindedness pure and simple seems unspeakably blind and shallow. To the healthy-minded way, on the other hand, the way of the sick soul seems unmanly and diseased. . . . What are we to say of this quarrel? It seems to me that we are bound to say that morbid-mindedness ranges over the wider scale of experience, and that its survey is the one that overlaps. The method of averting one's attention from evil, and living simply in the light of the good is splendid as long as it will work. It will work with many persons; it will work far more generally than most of us are ready to suppose; and within the sphere of its successful operation there is nothing to be said against it as a religious solution. But it breaks down impotently as soon as melancholy comes; and even though one be quite free from melancholy one's self, there is no doubt that *healthy-mindedness is inadequate as a philosophical doctrine, because the evil facts which it refuses positively to account for are a genuine portion of reality; and they may after all be the best key to life's significance, and possibly the only openers of our eyes to the deepest levels of truth* [italics added]. (James, 1902/1923, pp. 162–163)

I do not know whether evil is an essential feature of human nature or is cultivated by circumstance or depends on both for its existence. In any case, many positive psychologists (including Seligman) have come a long way from Seligman's initial pronouncements about the unvirtuousness (if not evil) of negativity. Nonetheless, in my view the mere *existence* of their movement contributes to the *implicit* logical argument/leap that I explicated earlier: You *can* be happy (owing to positive psychology's "technology"), therefore you *should* be happy, and if you're not happy or at least happier, then it is your *own* choice/fault. Despite all due credit for their concern about blaming the victim (e.g., Aspinwall & Tedeschi, 2010a, 2010b; Gable & Haidt, 2005; Seligman, 2011, see my note 6), this implicit logical leap may be an unavoidable consequence of the rhetoric of positivity that necessarily inheres in the positive psychology movement, the rhetoric that indeed constitutes the very name of the movement itself.

THE PERILS OF PERSONHOOD

William James captured the perils of personhood exquisitely in his understanding of the inevitable "evils" of existence. As original as his insights were, insights about the perils of personhood were expressed more than two millennia earlier, though in vastly different terms.

In *Greek Gods, Human Lives: What We Can Learn from Myths*, classical Greek scholar Mary Lefkowitz (2003) explained how the realism of ancient

Greek religion helped humans understand the causes of the hardships that we all inevitably face (see also Lloyd-Jones, 2001). About Zeus, the "top" God, she said, in referring to the *Iliad*, which she called "the most important ancient Greek religious text" (p. 53), "Zeus can give a man a combination of evil and good, or just evil (24.527-30)" (p. 82). That is, Zeus cannot give us only good. And in her concluding chapter Lefkowitz (2003) stated with all possible clarity,

> The myths, as the ancient authors relate them, do not offer hope so much as a means of understanding.[11] They enable us as onlookers to place ourselves in the world, and to get a sense of what we may reasonably expect in the course of our lives. Suffering and hardship cannot be avoided; death is inevitable; virtue is not always rewarded. Justice may not be done in the short run, although eventually wrongs will be righted, even if many innocent people will suffer. There is no hope of universal redemption, no sense that in the future the victims of the terrible action of the drama will receive any recompense for their suffering.
>
> Why should mortals worship gods who offer them so few benefits? Perhaps the most important reason is that they are powerful. . . . Mortals can also learn from the myths that they cannot control what happens to them. Certain events are determined by fate. . . . But even within the confines of their fate, mortals still have choices. (p. 235)

Although Lefkowitz (2003) said that not all ancient peoples accepted the myths, she gave a different reason for the final demise of the "traditional" myths:

> In the end, I believe, what caused people to abandon the traditional mythology was not the many fantasies it contains, but rather its ultimate realism: the myths show a world full of evil forces, unpredictable change, difficult conditions, and inevitable death and defeat. By contrast, other religions offered security, and a promise of redemption and reward both in this life and after death. (p. 236)

Here I offer no religious or nonreligious solutions to life's many hardships. Nonetheless, like James and Lefkowitz, I remain steadfast in the realism I have defended throughout my career. Whether humanity's "dark side" is innate, cultivated, or both, I believe we are morally obligated to strive to notice and understand it, as well as all aspects of our existence, as accurately as possible. This is for me the best chance we have for living more virtuous lives, no matter how happy we may feel as a result. Though I surely prefer that everyone feel good, feeling good is not the same as being good. And if I had to choose one, I would choose being good, beginning with the relentless search for truth.

---

[11]See Rollo May's (1991) *The Cry for Myth* for additional views about "the need for myth in our day" (p. 9). My thanks to Kirk Schneider for bringing this to my attention.

REFERENCES

Aspinwall, L. G., & Tedeschi, R. G. (2010a). Of babies and bathwater: A reply to Coyne and Tennen's views on positive psychology and health. *Annals of Behavioral Medicine, 39*, 27–34. doi:10.1007/s12160-010-9155-y

Aspinwall, L. G., & Tedeschi, R. G. (2010b). The value of positive psychology: Progress and pitfalls in examining the relation of positive phenomena to health. *Annals of Behavioral Medicine, 39*, 4–15. doi:10.1007/s12160-009-9153-0

Azar, B. (2000, July/August). Psychology's largest prize goes to four extraordinary scientists. *Monitor on Psychology, 31*, 38–40. Retrieved from http://www.apa.org/monitor/

Azar, B. (2011). Positive psychology advances, with growing pains. *Monitor on Psychology, 42*, 32–36.

Baumgardner, S. R., & Rappoport, L. (1996). Culture and self in postmodern perspective. *The Humanistic Psychologist, 24*, 116–139. doi:10.1080/08873267.1996.9986845

Becker, D., & Marecek, J. (2008). Positive psychology: History in the remaking? *Theory & Psychology, 18*, 591–604. doi:10.1177/0959354308093397

Bentall, R. P. (1992). A proposal to classify happiness as a psychiatric disorder. *Journal of Medical Ethics, 18*, 94–98. doi:10.1136/jme.18.2.94

Bok, D. (2010). *The politics of happiness: What government can learn from the new research on well-being.* Princeton, NJ: Princeton University Press.

Christopher, J. C., Richardson, F. C., & Slife, B. D. (2008). Thinking through positive psychology. *Theory & Psychology, 18*, 555–561. doi:10.1177/0959354308093395

Cook, J. (1993). *The book of positive quotations* (2nd ed.). Minneapolis, MN: Fairview Press.

Coyne, J. C., & Tennen, H. (2010). Positive psychology in cancer care: Bad Science, exaggerated claims, and unproven medicine. *Annals of Behavioral Medicine, 39*, 16–26. doi:10.1007/s12160-009-9154-z

Coyne, J. C., Tennen, H., & Ranchor, A. V. (2010). Psychology in cancer care: A story line resistant to evidence. *Annals of Behavioral Medicine, 39*, 35–42. doi:10.1007/s12160-010-9157-9

Coyne, J. C., Thombs, B. D., Stefanek, M., & Palmer, S. C. (2009). Time to let go of the illusion that psychotherapy extends the survival of cancer patients: Reply to Kraemer, Kuchler, & Spiegel (2009). *Psychological Bulletin, 135*, 179–182. doi:10.1037/a0014720

Diener, E. (2000). Subjective well-being: The science of happiness and a proposal for a national index. *American Psychologist, 55*, 34–43. doi:10.1037/0003-066X.55.1.34

Diener, E. (2009). Positive psychology: Past, present, future. In C. R. Snyder & S. J. Lopez (Eds.), *Oxford handbook of positive psychology* (2nd ed., pp. 7–11). New York, NY: Oxford University Press.

Diener, E., Lucas, R. E., & Scollon, C. N. (2006). Beyond the hedonic treadmill: Revising the adaptation theory of well-being. *American Psychologist, 61*, 305–314. doi:10.1037/0003-066X.61.4.305

Diener, E., Oishi, S., & Lucas, R. E. (2009). Subjective well-being: The science of happiness and life satisfaction. In C. R. Snyder & S. J. Lopez (Eds.), *Oxford handbook of positive psychology* (2nd ed., pp. 187–194). New York, NY: Oxford University Press.

Diener, E., & Seligman, M. E. P. (2004). Beyond money: Toward an economy of well-being. *Psychological Science in the Public Interest, 5*, 1–31. doi:10.1111/j.0963-7214.2004.00501001.x

Diener, E., Suh, E. M., Lucas, R. E., & Smith, H. L. (1999). Subjective well-being: Three decades of progress. *Psychological Bulletin, 125*, 276–302. doi:10.1037/0033-2909.125.2.276

Dunn, D. S., Uswatte, G., & Elliott, T. R. (2009). Happiness, resilience, and positive growth following physical disability: Issues for understanding, research, and therapeutic intervention. In C. R. Snyder & S. J. Lopez (Eds.), *Oxford handbook of positive psychology* (2nd ed., pp. 651–664). New York, NY: Oxford University Press.

Ehrenreich, B. (2009). *Bright-sided: How the relentless promotion of positive thinking has undermined America.* New York, NY: Metropolitan Books.

Fowers, B. J. (2005). *Virtue and psychology: Pursuing excellence in ordinary practices.* Washington, DC: American Psychological Association. doi:10.1037/11219-000

Fowers, B. J. (2008). From continence to virtue: Recovering goodness, character unity, and character types for positive psychology. *Theory & Psychology, 18*, 629–653. doi:10.1177/0959354308093399

Fowers, B. J. (2009). Virtue ethics. In S. Lopez (Ed.), *The encyclopedia of positive psychology* (Vol. II, pp. 1011–1016). West Sussex, England: Wiley-Blackwell.

Frederickson, B. L. (2009). *Positivity: Top-notch research reveals the 3-to-1 ratio that will change your life.* New York, NY: Three Rivers Press.

Friedman, H. S. (2010, August). *Get stressed, worry, live longer.* Invited address at the 118th Annual Convention of the American Psychological Association, San Diego, CA.

Friedman, H. S., & Martin, L. R. (2011). *The longevity project: Surprising discoveries for health and long life from the landmark eight-decade study.* New York, NY: Hudson Street Press.

Gable, S. L., & Haidt, J. (2005). What (and why) is positive psychology? *Review of General Psychology, 9*, 103–110. doi:10.1037/1089-2680.9.2.103

Gergen, K. J., & Kaye, J. (1992). Beyond narrative in the negotiation of therapeutic meaning. In S. McNamee & K. J. Gergen (Eds.), *Therapy as social construction* (pp. 166–185). London: Sage.

Held, B. S. (1995). *Back to reality: A critique of postmodern theory in psychotherapy.* New York, NY: Norton.

Held, B. S. (1998). The many truths of postmodernist discourse. *Journal of Theoretical and Philosophical Psychology, 18,* 193–217. doi:10.1037/h0091185

Held, B. S. (2001). *Stop smiling, start kvetching: A 5-step guide to creative complaining.* New York, NY: St Martin's Griffin.

Held, B. S. (2002). The tyranny of the positive attitude in America: Observation and speculation. *Journal of Clinical Psychology, 58,* 965–991. doi:10.1002/jclp.10093

Held, B. S. (2003, October). The "virtues" of positive psychology. In E. Diener (Chair), *Critiques and limitations of positive psychology.* Symposium conducted at the Second International Positive Psychology Summit, Washington, DC.

Held, B. S. (2004). The negative side of positive psychology. *Journal of Humanistic Psychology, 44,* 9–46. doi:10.1177/0022167803259645

Held, B. S. (2005). The "virtues" of positive psychology. *Journal of Theoretical and Philosophical Psychology, 25,* 1–34. doi:10.1037/h0091249

Held, B. S. (2007). *Psychology's interpretive turn: The search for truth and agency in theoretical and philosophical psychology.* Washington, DC: American Psychological Association. doi:10.1037/11588-000

Horwitz, A. V., & Wakefield, J. C. (2007). *The loss of sadness: How psychiatry transformed normal sadness into depressive disorder.* New York, NY: Oxford University Press.

Howell, R. T. (2009). Lyubomirsky, Sonja. In S. Lopez (Ed.), *The encyclopedia of positive psychology* (Vol. II, p. 592). West Sussex, England: Wiley-Blackwell.

James, W. (1902/1923). *The varieties of religious experience: A study in human nature.* New York, NY: Longmans, Green. doi:10.1037/10004-000

Katzko, M. W. (2002a). The construction of "social constructionism": A case study in the rhetoric of debate. *Theory & Psychology, 12,* 671–683. doi:10.1177/0959354302012005898

Katzko, M. W. (2002b). The rhetoric of psychological research and the problem of unification in psychology. *American Psychologist, 57,* 262–270. doi:10.1037/0003-066X.57.4.262

Kraemer, H. C., Kuchler, T., & Spiegel, D. (2009). Use and misuse of the consolidated standards of reporting trials (CONSORT) guidelines to assess research findings: Comment on Coyne, Stefanek, and Palmer (2007). *Psychological Bulletin, 135,* 173–178. doi:10.1037/0033-2909.135.2.173

Kristjánsson, K. (2010). Positive psychology, happiness, and virtue: The troublesome conceptual issues. *Review of General Psychology, 14,* 296–310. doi:10.1037/a0020781

Lefkowitz, M. (2003). *Greek gods, human lives: What we can learn from myths.* New Haven, CT: Yale University Press.

Levine, B. E. (2010). *Psychologists profit on unending U.S. wars by teaching positive thinking to soldiers.* Retrieved from http://www.huffingtonpost.com/bruce-e-levine/psychologists-profit-on-u_b_655400.html

Lloyd-Jones, H. (2001). Ancient Greek religion. *Proceedings of the American Philosophical Society, 145,* 456–464.

Lucas, R. E., & Donnellan, M. B. (2007). How stable is happiness? Using the STARTS model to estimate the stability of life satisfaction. *Journal of Research in Personality, 41*, 1091–1098. doi:10.1016/j.jrp.2006.11.005

Lyubomirsky, S. (2008). *The how of happiness: A scientific approach to getting the life you want.* New York, NY: Penguin Books.

May, R. (1991). *The cry for myth.* New York, NY: Norton.

Ng, W., & Diener, E. (2009). Feeling bad? The "power" of positive thinking may not apply to everyone. *Journal of Research in Personality, 43*, 455–463. doi:10.1016/j.jrp.2009.01.020

Norem, J. K. (2001). *The positive power of negative thinking: Using defensive pessimism to harness anxiety and perform at your peak.* New York, NY: Basic Books.

O'Hara, M. (2009, August). Humanistic visionaries reconsidered in the face of 21st century challenges. Paper presented in A. Bohart (Chair), *Carl Rogers, Rollo May, and humanity's dark side.* Symposium conducted at the 117th Annual Convention of the American Psychological Association, Toronto, Canada.

Peale, N. V. (1952). *The power of positive thinking.* New York, NY: Prentice Hall.

Peterson, C. (2009). Foreword. In C. R. Snyder & S. J. Lopez (Eds.), *Oxford handbook of positive psychology* (2nd ed., pp. xxiii–xxiv). Oxford, NY: Oxford University Press.

Peterson, C., & Seligman, M. E. P. (2004). *Character strengths and virtues: A handbook and classification.* Washington, DC, and New York, NY: American Psychological Association and Oxford University Press.

Psychologists receive profession's largest monetary prize for research on the effect positive traits such as optimism have on psychological and physical health. (2002, May 23). *APA Online.* Retrieved from http://www.apa.org/news/press/releases/2002/05/templeton.aspx

Robinson, D. N. (1989). *Aristotle's psychology.* New York, NY: Columbia University Press.

Scheier, M. F., & Carver, C. S. (2009). Optimism. In S. Lopez (Ed.), *The encyclopedia of positive psychology* (Vol. II, pp. 656–663). West Sussex, England: Wiley-Blackwell.

Schneider, K. J. (2009). *Awakening to awe: Personal stories of profound transformation.* Lanham, MD: Aronson.

Schneider, S. L. (2001). In search of realistic optimism: Meaning, knowledge, and warm fuzziness. *American Psychologist, 56*, 250–263. doi:10.1037/0003-066X.56.3.250

Seligman, M. E. P. (1990). *Learned optimism: How to change your mind and your life.* New York, NY: Pocket Books.

Seligman, M. E. P. (2002). *Authentic happiness: Using the new positive psychology to realize your potential for lasting fulfillment.* New York, NY: Free Press.

Seligman, M. E. P. (2004, May 3). Happiness interventions that work: The first results. *Authentic Happiness Coaching Newsletter, 2*(10). Retrieved from http://www.authentichappinesscoaching.com

Seligman, M. E. P. (2011). *Flourish: A visionary new understanding of happiness and well-being*. New York, NY: Free Press.

Seligman, M. E. P., & Csikszentmihalyi, M. (2000). Positive psychology: An introduction. *American Psychologist, 55*, 5–14. doi:10.1037/0003-066X.55.1.5

Seligman, M. E. P., & Csikszentmihalyi, M. (2001). Reply to comments. *American Psychologist, 56*, 89–90. doi:10.1037/0003-066X.56.1.89

Smith, D. M., Loewenstein, G., Jankovic, A., & Ubel, P. A. (2009). Happily hopeless: Adaptation to a permanent, but not to a temporary, disability. *Health Psychology, 28*, 787–791. doi:10.1037/a0016624

Snyder, C. R., & Lopez, S. J. (2002). The future of positive psychology: A declaration of independence. In C. R. Snyder & S. Lopez (Eds.), *Handbook of positive psychology* (pp. 751–767). New York, NY: Oxford University Press.

Snyder, C. R., Rand, K. L., King, E. A., Feldman, D. B., & Woodward, J. T. (2002). "False" hope. *Journal of Clinical Psychology, 58*, 1003–1022. doi:10.1002/jclp.10096

Stancombe, J., & White, S. (1998). Psychotherapy without foundations: Hermeneutics, discourse, and the end of certainty. *Theory & Psychology, 8*, 579–599. doi:10.1177/0959354398085001

Stefanek, M. E., Palmer, S. C., Thombs, B. D., & Coyne, J. C. (2009). Finding what is not there: Unwarranted claims of an effect of psychosocial intervention on recurrence and survival. *Cancer, 115*, 5612–5616. doi:10.1002/cncr.24671

Taylor, S. E., Kemeny, M. E., Reed, G. M., Bower, J. E., & Gruenewald, T. L. (2000). Psychological resources, positive illusions, and health. *American Psychologist, 55*, 99–109. doi:10.1037/0003-066X.55.1.99

Tocqueville, A. de. (1988). *Democracy in America, Vol. 2*. (G. Lawrence, Trans., J. P. Mayer, Ed.). New York, NY: Harper & Row, Perennial Library. (Original work published in 1840)

Wilson, E. (2009). *Against happiness: In praise of melancholy*. New York, NY: Farrar, Straus, & Giroux.

AFTERWORD

ARTHUR C. BOHART

In this afterword, I briefly summarize themes and questions that occur throughout the chapters and then comment on the relationship of theory to practice as evidenced in this volume.

DEFINING EVIL AND THE DARK SIDE

We broadly construe the dark side as those aspects of human nature that lead to destructive behavior, either directed toward others or directed toward the self. Several authors focus more specifically on the topic of evil. They discuss their views of evil and implications for the practice of psychotherapy.

Briere and Lazarus note that the perception of an act as evil depended on circumstances. For instance, behavior that is sanctioned by society in the form of a war might not be considered evil. This raises the issue of the intention underlying the behavior. Lazarus defines evil as a deliberate action that causes harm. Briere notes that the perception of the intention underlying an act makes a difference in how traumatic an action is for a victim. The more a victim attributes deliberate intent to someone who has done something "evil," the more traumatic it is likely to be. This also involves the issue of free will: The more the actor is seen as having had free will to choose or not choose what he or she did, the more likely it is to be experienced as traumatic. As a counterexample, Briere notes that although natural disasters can be traumatic, they are often not as traumatic as traumas inflicted by human beings.

For Briere this distinction matters in terms of treatment: A major focus of his treatment is to use the Buddhistic conception of "dependent origination" to help both victims and perpetrators of evil realize that evil behavior may arise from a whole set of factors, human and nonhuman alike. Using the concept of dependent origination moves perception of the behavior from that of "he is evil; he chose to hurt me" to "his behavior was determined by circumstances." This may make it easier for victims to recover from acts of evil visited upon them. Accordingly, Briere encourages forgiveness for the sake not of the perpetrators of evil but of the victims of evil.

There is some difference among authors over whether there exist evil persons. Briere and Leitner hold that while people may behave evilly because of dependent origination, we cannot rightly say that those exhibiting such behavior are evil persons per se if we understand the circumstances from which their evil behavior arose. Smith argues that from a Freudian perspective people do what they do owing to the "subpersonal" aspects of their personalities; therefore, it is not proper to make moral judgments about them. On the other hand, Lazarus notes that Albert Ellis also argued that there were no evil persons, only evil acts; yet Lazarus wonders if there were cases (e.g., Hitler) when the degree and frequency of evil acts were sufficiently extreme for us to warrant saying, "this person is evil, or at least bad."

THE NATURE OF EVIL AND THE DARK SIDE

Schmid and Hollis both appeal to philosophical and theological history to examine the nature of evil. Both note that there are two different historical conceptions of evil. One holds that evil exists in its own right. Hollis notes, for instance, that in some theologies there are multiple gods and not all of them are good. The other tradition holds that there is only one good and that evil is the absence of good, much like dark is the absence of light. These differing conceptions play out to some degree in modern psychological theories. Some theories claim that humans have an innate potential to act destructively. Lazarus, for example, thinks that humans are innately aggressive. He gives the example of Nazi prison guards, ordinary people who easily became brutal given the proper modeling and reinforcing circumstances. This conceptualization squares with Rollo May's conception of humans as well as with Schneider's. Rollo May thought that although humans are not innately evil, they have just as much potential to be evil as to be good, given the proper reinforcing circumstances. Hollis, too, falls into this camp, holding that humans have many different potentialities; for him the very idea of a unitary good is itself illusory and, moreover, can create its own dark side (see the section on virtue-driven organizations below).

By contrast, the view that there is only one good and that evil is the absence of the good is somewhat akin to the theory of Carl Rogers, as described by both Schmid and Bohart. Carl Rogers believed in an actualizing tendency that could turn in a negative direction if someone ran into circumstances that blocked movement in a positive direction. Superficially, this may appear similar to the Lazarus–May conception that circumstances can just as easily turn people in a negative as in a positive direction; however, the relevant difference is that Rogers believed that the actualizing tendency has a directional quality. That is, the actualizing tendency is "engineered" to go in a positive direction unless it becomes obstructed by circumstances, in which case it is channeled into a negative direction—evil and destructiveness could be conceptualized as the "blockage" of the good. Bohart adopts this conceptualization when he maintains that any blockage of humans' innate capacities for self-organizing wisdom may lead them to act destructively.

IMPLICATIONS FOR PSYCHOTHERAPY

These two differing conceptualizations bear some resemblance to two differing meanings of the metaphor of the dark side as well. On the one hand, the dark side can be construed as negative emotions, motives, and thoughts that have their own independent existence and can lead to destructive behavior, such as anger, despair, fear, and hostility. The other meaning suggests that no mental state or act is necessarily dark in and of itself. Mental states and acts *become* dark because they are avoided or unexamined, that is, they are cast into what Jung called the *shadow*. This can include even potentially positive mentation, such as one's creativity, which may have to be disowned if one lives in a family or context that actively discourages creativity. Or this may include, for a male, his "feminine" or "soft" side, which may be disowned because the culture wants him to be tough. By disowning these qualities, by pushing them into the shadow side out of awareness, the person cuts off some of his or her potential to live life more fully. Furthermore, by disowning, say, one's feminine side, a man might become rigidly judgmental and intolerant of other men whom he sees as "soft" or "emotional."

These two different conceptualizations of the dark side lead to different approaches to it in psychotherapy. If aspects of the personality, such as traits, emotions, motives, or thoughts, are intrinsically dark (a thirst for revenge; a selfish, egocentric side; a fear that produces harmful acts), then it may become important for the person to confront his or her dark side in therapy, particularly if these aspects are disowned or denied. This is emphasized by Hollis, who writes from a Jungian point of view, and Mendelowitz and Schneider, who write from an existential point of view. One has to "own up" to one's dark side in order to accept it and integrate it into one's whole being. In doing so one "de-potentizes" its potential to lead to destructive behavior.

By contrast, for those who maintain that there is an innate growth potential toward "the good," meaning a potential to become more fully human in the sense of becoming both more effectively autonomous and self-directed and more socially caring and responsible, the goal of therapy emphasizes the facilitation of growth through activating this potential. From this vantage point, confronting one's dark side is not intrinsically required. As part of the organismic growth process, the person herself may intuitively know she must confront her dark side in order to self-organize in more positive self-supportive and prosocial ways (see the chapter by Bohart). She may know she needs to face up to her dark side and integrate it to achieve effective organismic balance. In this case the impetus to self-confront comes from the client rather than the therapist.

This alternative view does not entail simply reinforcing the "good" in people. Rather, it promotes growth potential, mobilizing positive regenerative forces. An analogy might be having a deformed hand. If the deformed hand is not accepted as part of oneself, Hollis, Schneider, and Mendelowitz might wish to support the person's confronting and accepting it. By contrast, a Rogerian therapist, as portrayed by Bohart, would not insist on this. Instead, through empathic support and listening, the client would be supported to move out toward the world and do as much as possible. In so doing, she would likely become aware that she needs to accept the existence of the deformed hand as part of herself to work productively with it. However, the "confront" and "promote growth" points of view are not mutually exclusive.

ACCEPTING THE DARK SIDE AS A PART OF LIFE

Beyond psychotherapy, several authors implied that accepting the dark side as part of life is important in order to be fully human. Hollis goes so far as to argue that "we are all in the dark woods together," that life intrinsically includes suffering and other dark aspects, and that the idea of a "happy ego," fully in charge of the organism, is an illusion. He wonders if cognitive–behavioral points of view, which emphasize eliminating dysfunctional cognitions and training social skills, may create an illusion of ego self-control that may inadvertently cause people to be undermined when unconscious aspects of the personality surface or when we face experiences for which we are not prepared. For Hollis, life is an ongoing engagement with the dark side—with the shadow and the unconscious—which is needed for living a full life. Living a more full life is not top-down control, but rather the ability for constant dialogical engagement between conscious and unconscious. This view resonates with the views of Schneider and Mendelowitz as well. We never achieve full "mental health." We must always be engaged in a process of self-examination and resultant self-awareness.

Held examines this notion in the context of positive psychology. She observes that positive psychology's emphasis on happiness may lead those who have "darker" (so-called negative) emotions to feel that something is wrong with them. Those who suffer, those who are not happy, now not only have the problems associated with their suffering/unhappiness, they may also believe that something is wrong with them because they are suffering/unhappy. Rather than seeing suffering and unhappiness as (a) a normal part of life and (b) an acceptable way of being, they may be admonished about how they can be happy and therefore should be happy, if they only follow certain prescriptions. Thus, being unhappy is pathologized. Like the client Lazarus describes working with, who viewed *herself* as evil owing to the norms and ideas of those around her, individuals who may be more temperamentally prone to pessimism and other forms of alleged "negativity" are now pathologized. Held is concerned that a positive orthodoxy is being imposed on people, and if so, it could marginalize or even stigmatize those with a more negative, even tragic, outlook on life. At the intrapersonal level, Hollis, Schneider, and Mendelowitz fear that this orthodoxy could be dangerous, by encouraging people to split off the negative and so avoid facing the basic existential issues of life, namely, those that require dealing with angst, ambiguity, and despair. According to Hollis, such splitting causes people to lead timorous lives. Furthermore, it causes the projection of negativity onto others and thus creates some of the evil and suffering that it denies. According to Schneider, this splitting may literally block individuals from accessing their positive sides in a deep and meaningful way in the form of awe and wonder at life. According to Mendelowitz, it may also prevent individuals from mining their own depths, causing them to be alienated from a world that does not accept or understand them.

In conclusion, several authors suggest that rejecting or disowning the dark side, whether in psychotherapy or in life, can be deleterious. This implies a need for therapists to help clients confront their dark sides. In partial contrast, the person-centered tradition emphasizes the importance of trusting the client's capacities for creative self-organization. As clients' growth potential is unlocked, they can grow in a positive prosocial direction, with or without self-confrontation.

HOW PEOPLE TREAT ONE ANOTHER AND THE DARK SIDE

Held's belief that there can be a "tyranny of the positive attitude," which denies individuals the opportunity to be themselves (if they happen to have pessimistic personalities; Held, 2004, 2005), is compatible with a theme raised especially by Schmid but also by Leitner and Bohart. This theme is the importance of relating to persons *as* persons and the importance of prizing the unique individuality of each person—that is, respecting everyone's deepest personal meanings, as Leitner would put it. Schmid calls this *personalizing*, which entails treating others in a way that seriously acknowledges the other's personhood.

Although all the authors in this book would agree with the idea of deeply respecting the personhood of the client, there is a theoretical difference worth exploring. Schmid distinguishes his "person-centered" view from the "being-centered" view of Rollo May. May, coming out of an existential position, focuses on the nature of what it is to be a human "being-in-the-world," with all its attendant conflicts and contradictions. For instance, Schneider (2011), following on May's position, distinguishes various aspects of being human that all individuals wrestle with, such as a struggle over being free versus being constricted (i.e., by shrinking from the responsibility of freedom). Thus May and other existentialists are trying to describe something general about the human being. This may be used in therapy to help construe clients' conflicts. In contrast, Schmid's theoretical focus puts the personhood of the particular individual center stage as the main concept, before all other concepts, including such issues as freedom versus constriction. That is, the central theoretical concept is to enter therapy with the aim of understanding this particular individual prior to any conceptual schemes imported from any theoretical position. Schmid sees the process of recognizing and treating persons as unique individuals as the core "healing" process.

Regardless of whether deeply relating to and respecting the personhood of the client is one's central theoretical concept, the reason personalizing is important is that it (or its opposite) appears to be significantly related to acting in either prosocial or evil or destructive ways. When we "de-person-alize" others, we are more likely to treat them in dehumanizing ways (Bandura, 1986). In addition, when we are depersonalized, that is, when we lose a sense of our unique personhood and along with that our humanity, we are more likely to act in destructive ways either toward others or toward the self. Zimbardo's (2007) research demonstrated that once people become anonymous (i.e., exist in a more general, less uniquely personalized way), they are more likely to act in destructive, immoral, or evil ways. People can become depersonalized through social pressures toward uniformity or by other ways in which they lose track of their unique identities. Dehumanization as depersonalization, therefore, works in two ways: (a) it allows people to perpetrate violence and other forms of evil on those whom they have dehumanized, and (b) it increases the probability that those who have been dehumanized will react in evil ways themselves or, at least, in destructive ways toward others and themselves.

Other authors (e.g., Hollis, Mendelowitz, Briere, Lazarus) also emphasize responding in a respectful, compassionate, and interpersonally connected way to help people overcome whatever in them has promoted self- or other-destructive behavior. Empathy in particular has been held to be of importance in promoting growth (Elliott, Bohart, Watson, & Greenberg, 2011). This is compatible with the suggestion of others outside of the psychotherapy realm who have argued for the importance of empathy in promoting prosocial behavior. Baron-Cohen (2011), in particular, sees a lack of empathy at the center of a capacity for one person to treat another evilly or destructively. What is particularly important, or even new, about what the various authors in this volume are saying has to do with *why* empathy and compassion work. It is, in part, because these qualities convey a sense of recognizing and prizing the personhood of the other.

THE DARK SIDE AND "VIRTUE-DRIVEN ORGANIZATIONS"

It has often been noted that more evil has been done in the name of "the good" than for any other reason. For example, H. L. Mencken said, "The urge to save humanity is almost always a false front for the urge to rule" (Mencken, n.d.). And C. S. Lewis said, "Of all tyrannies, a tyranny sincerely exercised for the good of its victims may be the most oppressive" (Lewis, n.d.). O'Hara and Omer observe that organizations can perpetuate the same kind of destructive behavior as can individuals. Sure of their own virtue, members of virtue-driven organizations can be oblivious to their own dark sides and so may unwittingly treat people in dehumanizing ways—especially those individuals who threaten the organization and its virtuous self-image.

Relatedly, Miller, Hollis, Leitner, and Held all suggest, albeit in different ways, that psychology itself may be a virtue-driven organization, one which, in its zeal to do good, may inadvertently do harm by not (a) reflecting upon its actions and (b) considering alternatives to dominant ideologies (see the Lewis quotation). We have already discussed Held's concern with the possible stigmatization or at least diminution of those who are deemed to have "negative" personalities/coping styles by the positive psychology movement and the broader American culture in which it thrives. Miller and Hollis are also concerned that psychology's determination to be a natural science and to disown its philosophical roots may prompt its refusal to acknowledge its own seminal moral foundations, in trying, for example, to sanitize its mission by using terms like *disorder*. Leitner draws attention to examples in which psychologists and other mental health professionals refuse to attend carefully or closely to clients' needs, even when evidence indicates that close listening helps substantially. Instead, clients may be prescribed medication, even when there are legitimate questions about the efficacy of the medications in use (Whitaker, 2010). Leitner points out that instead of responding to schizophrenics as unique persons by way of an I–thou encounter, in which they are treated as individuals, therapists medicate them (see also the chapter by Bohart). Thus, again, well-meaning psychologists may inadvertently collude in harming the very people they are trying to help by their virtue-driven acts.

ROLE OF PHILOSOPHY AND MORALITY IN PSYCHOLOGY AND PSYCHOTHERAPY

One impetus for this book was to study the role of theory in practice. Practice is not merely a technological (i.e., technique-based) enterprise based on the mindless application of technique to disorder. If we take metapsychological considerations to be theoretical in that they deal with basic stances toward reality, then philosophical considerations follow or are entailed. Miller, Schmid, Hollis, Held, and Smith directly or indirectly raise philosophical issues. Hollis argues that philosophy should be a key part of clinical training. Schmid's discussion of evil is grounded in both philosophical and theological tradition, as is Hollis's.

Morality is the most prominently discussed philosophical issue. Miller argues that the practice of therapy is fundamentally a moral enterprise and that our moral beliefs and our language significantly influence what we do. He notes that by construing therapy as if it were merely a technological enterprise, we disown its profoundly moral dimension. This has serious implications for how we practice. For instance, how we construe practice allows us to be influenced by larger societal forces in terms of what comes to be defined as "good outcomes," which may not consist of or may not contain the deeply meaningful outcomes that many practitioners hope to attain.

Following up on Miller's claim that psychotherapy is an inherently moral enterprise is his observation that many of the concerns that clients bring to psychotherapy have moral components. In the famous film of Gloria (Burry, 2009) working with Carl Rogers, Gloria asks Rogers whether she should be honest about her sex life with her daughter and whether it is "okay" for her to have sex although she is not married. She also worries about how to trust her own judgment, in essence how to do the "right things" for herself in her life. Clients who suffer from anxiety disorders and depression often criticize themselves for being bad in various ways. Couples in therapy typically criticize one another for failing to live up to some standard of behavior. There is a moral component to the judgment that someone drinks too much, is too dependent, is too unstable in their interpersonal relationships (e.g., borderline personality disorder). The list could go on ad infinitum.

To be sure, the very idea of the dark side implies a moral judgment. When we label certain behaviors, thoughts, and feelings as *destructive* or *undesirable*, we are making judgments about their goodness or badness. But what we judge to be good or bad acts may not be inherently moral in and of themselves. That is, an act or attitude may be judged bad only because it is thought to lead to *something else* (e.g., self- or other-injurious behaviors) that *is inherently* destructive/bad and thus the real target of the moral judgment. For example, it may be bad for someone to despise another, but if that person does not act on that feeling, is having the feeling itself a moral matter? (See Tjeltveit, 1999, for the distinction between what is good and what is moral.)

What role does morality play in therapy? First, as noted, both Miller and Hollis argue that many psychological judgments are moral judgments in disguise. Both maintain that by using terms like *disorder* we sanitize, if not eliminate, the moral judgments we make, not least by seeming to excuse it. Many labels, such as *narcissistic personality disorder* or *borderline personality disorder*, have moralistic, judgmental connotations (it is bad to be too stuck on oneself, self-absorbed, impulsive, demanding of others, and flighty/inconsistent). Both Miller and Hollis argue that in using diagnostic labels we use language to obfuscate the moral judgments that we make implicitly, and thus we minimize the cruelty contained within the behaviors we are judging, above and beyond their dysfunctional nature. Others have made similar points. Dan Wile (1984, 1992), for example, has pointed out the moralistic and judgmental nature hidden by various diagnostic labels, as well as the accusatory quality of many of the kinds of "therapeutic" interpretations that are offered to clients. Miller has also noted that so-called dysfunctional cognitions (as they are labeled by cognitive–behaviorists) often have a moralistic connotation. Consider, for instance, the rejection by rational emotive behavior therapists (Ellis & Whiteley, 1979) of our "shoulds," as in "I am a bad person because I should have done X instead of Y."

Therapists could be seen as making moral judgments and provoking clients to act more morally, without acknowledging their moralizing. The idea of the (hidden) dark side, found in both psychodynamic and humanistic theories, has this quality. It is not good to disown an aspect of oneself, to be dishonest with oneself, and doing this has negative consequences. Thus, there is a "should" in therapy: We should face up to our whole selves in order to avoid evil and live fully.

The moral dimension also appears in therapy when clients experience their problems and thus themselves as bad or even evil. Not only do they morally condemn themselves, such as Lazarus's client, who saw herself as evil, but they may also experience what others have done to them in moral terms. Briere points out that people are not as bothered by traumas that are brought about by natural disasters as they are by traumas that are perpetrated by humans. People are more likely to recover from the loss of their home in a hurricane than from being harmed by another person. Humans harming humans seems to be most traumatic. Why is this? One possible explanation is that the behavior violates moral norms, especially norms of fairness. It is traumatic to realize that another person can *deliberately* inflict pain. After all, natural disasters are seen as the result of blind impersonal forces over which we have little, if any, control.

Thus, moral matters are a crucial part of why clients are troubled in the first place. People who condemn themselves (see Lazarus, this volume) do so in moral terms—by definition. What is allegedly bad about them is not merely that they are ineffective but rather that something is wrong with them, something about which they feel shame or guilt. People who have been traumatized by others have not merely been physically or emotionally assaulted; they have been morally violated.

A noteworthy contrast can be seen in the differing perspectives of Miller and Smith. Miller argues that it is inappropriate to sanitize psychology by removing moral concepts, as if the therapist were a natural scientist merely "reengineering" natural phenomena. Yet this is precisely what Smith argues that psychoanalysts do. For Smith, psychological problems arise from the *subpersonal* level, from events occurring unconsciously and "mechanistically," that is, events over which the client has no agentic control. The analyst is thus not in a warranted position to make moral judgments in regard to the client's acts. I think Miller might (ironically?) agree with that. I say "ironically" because although Miller sees therapy as a moral enterprise, which invokes human agency, he does not believe that therapists should morally judge their clients, nor does he see therapy as a form of moral education.

Thus, neither Miller nor Smith believes that therapists impose moral imperatives on their clients. Despite the absence of clear explication about this, here is my interpretation: It is important to recognize the moral nature of what the client is struggling with. Clients are not merely struggling with dysfunctional cognitions or repressed wishes or disowned emotions. The issues they are struggling with have moral connotations at the level of the "whole person." It may be important for therapists to be aware of this and be willing to help clients deal with their moral struggles without making moral judgments of the clients or trying to provide moral answers for them. Lazarus's case example provides a perfect illustration. His client saw her masturbation as "immoral" and believed that God would punish her for it. Lazarus acknowledged the implicit moral dimension, certainly the "frame" through which she was viewing the problem, namely, the frame of God, and offered her a counterargument: Would God really worry that much about such a trivial matter, given the scope of the universe with which He must cope? Lazarus did not insist that her thinking/ cognition was impaired or that nothing was morally wrong with masturbation. Instead, he provided her with a counterargument that helped her to think differently about her behavior. When she returned the next session, it was clear that *she* had reevaluated her thinking on her own. Thus, Lazarus had not tried to change her moral convictions; rather, he had presented an alternative perspective that made the client reevaluate herself. This intervention stands in stark contrast to that of Albert Ellis, who would have challenged the client's "should"—in this case, that she should not masturbate, which of course would have challenged the client's own moral position.

In conclusion, the role of morality in therapy is raised by the discussion of humanity's dark side and warrants more extensive consideration along the lines discussed in these chapters.

METHODS OF WORKING WITH THE DARK SIDE AND THE ROLE OF THEORY IN THERAPY

It is clear from the chapters that how therapists conceptualize the dark side theoretically influences how they work with clients. None of the therapists whose chapters appear in this book view therapy merely as technological application; rather, each practice is deeply informed by theory. Schneider, Mendelowitz, and Hollis, working within their holistic theoretical positions that emphasize personal growth via self-awareness, help clients to access and confront their dark sides. Bohart, Leitner, and Schmid, working within humanistic theoretical positions that emphasize positive, nurturing interpersonal relationships, with a particular emphasis on prizing the person (not that other positions do not also prize the person), advocate a constructive therapeutic relationship with each unique client. Moreover, Bohart and Schmid's person-centered point of view proclaims no need in therapy to confront or explore the dark side, as it assumes that clients naturally do this on their own as part of their self-healing process (if that was what was needed in order to grow). Briere similarly uses the Buddhist notion of dependent origination to frame how he helps clients understand either their own destructive/evil acts or the destructive/evil acts that others have inflicted on them, so that they may let go and move on.

Lazarus, working from his integrative multimodal position grounded in cognitive–behavioral and social learning theory, does not focus on exploring or confronting the nature of the dark side of the person. Instead, he focuses on the specific behaviors, emotions, and cognitions that clients must change so that (a) if they are perpetrators of destructive/evil acts, they will be able to meet their needs in more effective and prosocial ways, and (b) if they are victims of destructive/evil acts, they will be able to relinquish self-blame and self-criticism and thus open space for finding more effective ways of meeting their needs. In other words, for Lazarus, the philosophical questions of the nature of good and evil are not relevant for purposes of therapy. Of note, however, is how, in the case he presents, Lazarus uses a form of empathic joining with his client when he challenges her "dysfunctional" cognitions. They are challenged from within her frame of reference, in contrast to a previous therapist, who challenged them by challenging her frame of reference.

CONCLUSION

We could say that the major value of this volume is to motivate readers to think about their own theoretical notions and how their notions influence what they do. Therapists in this volume demonstrate that their theoretical notions about the dark side of human nature play a role in how they construe the nature of therapy. Therapy is not merely a matter of technological intervention. Various aspects of the human potential for destructivity are intrinsically related to therapy, including negative emotions that may or may not be destructive depending on how they are related to, beliefs that can lead to toxic behaviors, and self- or other-destructive behaviors.

In particular, it is important to think about the dark side. Is therapy a matter in part of morality, and have we, in the hope of practicing a natural science, pushed its moral nature into our "dark side"? Do some of our theories deny the nature of the dark side? Do some of our theories negatively stereotype those who are more likely to look on the dark side of life in such a way as to perhaps stigmatize them? And can we as individual therapists, as well as being members of "virtuous organizations," inadvertently deny our own dark sides when believing we are doing "good"? These are all questions about which we hope this volume will stimulate thought.

REFERENCES

Bandura, A. (1986). *Social foundations of thought and action: A social cognitive theory.* New York, NY: Prentice Hall.

Baron-Cohen, S. (2011). *The science of evil.* New York, NY: Basic Books.

Burry, P. J. (2009). *Living with "the Gloria films": A daughter's memory.* Ross-on-Wye, Wales: PCCS Books.

Ellis, A., & Whiteley, J. M. (Eds.). (1979). *Theoretical and empirical foundations of rational-emotive therapy.* Monterey, CA: Brooks/Cole.

Held, B. S. (2004). The negative side of positive psychology. *Journal of Humanistic Psychology, 44,* 9–46. doi:10.1177/0022167803259645

Held, B. S. (2005). The "virtues" of positive psychology. *Journal of Theoretical and Philosophical Psychology, 25,* 1–34. doi:10.1037/h0091249

Lewis, C. S. (n.d.). *C. S. Lewis quotes.* In BrainyQuote. Seattle, WA: BookRags Media Network. Retrieved from http://www.brainyquote.com/quotes/quotes/c/cslewis136296.html

Mencken, H. L. (n.d.). *H. L. Mencken quotes.* In BrainyQuote. Seattle, WA: BookRags Media Network. Retrieved from http://www.brainyquote.com/quotes/quotes/h/hlmencke143263.html

Schneider, K. J. (2011). Existential–humanistic psychotherapies. In S. B. Messer & A. S. Gurman (Eds.), *Essential psychotherapies: Theory and practice* (3rd ed., pp. 261–296). New York, NY: Guilford Press.

Tjeltveit, A. C. (1999). *Ethics and values in psychotherapy.* London, England: Routledge. doi:10.4324/9780203360453

Whitaker, R. (2010). *Anatomy of an epidemic: Magic bullets, psychiatric drugs, and the astonishing rise of mental illness in America.* New York, NY: Crown Publishing Group.

Wile, D. B. (1984). Kohut, Kernberg, and accusatory interpretations. *Psychotherapy: Theory, Research, Practice, Training, 21,* 353–364. doi:10.1037/h0086097

Wile, D. B. (1992). *Couples therapy.* New York, NY: Wiley.

Zimbardo, P. (2007). *The Lucifer effect: Understanding how good people turn evil.* New York, NY: Random House.

INDEX

Freudian perspective, *continued*
  nihilism in, 195–197
  regression and moral responsibility
      in, 199–203
  subpersonal perspective in, 203–209
  the unconscious in, 198–199
Fromm, Erich, 39
Fromm-Reichmann, Frieda, 101, 103,
      106, 112
Functionalism, 205–206

Gable, S. L., 238
Galactic Empire, 57–58
Galvin, J., 23–24
Gatekeeping, 183
Gautama, 90
Gendlin, E. T., 58, 62–64
Genetic fallacy, 199
Genocide, 123, 233–234
Gergen, K., 225
Gilbert, P., 153
Gloria case study, 266–267
Goffman, 173
Golden mean, 238
Goodness
  in Darth Vader, 60
  in evil, 40–41
  in human nature, 158
  religious beliefs about, 90–91
Greaves, A. L., 64
Greece, ancient, 251–252
Greek Gods, Human Lives (M.
      Lefkowitz), 251–252
Green, H., 101–103
Greening, T., 24, 26
Groups
  cohesiveness of, 179–180
  defensive strategies of, 175
  identity of, 174
  misbehavior in, 170–171
Growth potential
  and actualization, 42–43
  as innate, 262
  in therapeutic change, 60–61
Gruenewald, T. L., 248
Guantanamo Bay, 114
Guilt
  feelings of, in perpetrator, 133–134
  by innuendo, 176

and introspection, 125
from organizational activities, 175

Haidt, J., 238
Handbook of Positive Psychology, 242
Hanh, Thich Nhat, 173n3
Happiness
  as delusory ideology, 96
  and emotions, 237–238
  in set-point theory, 241–242
  and suffering, 263
  and virtue, 243–247
Hard determinism, 197
Harmful acts, 174–178
Harmony, 23
Hate, 150
Healing, 129–130
Healing professions, 86
Hedonistic desires, 207–208
Held, B. S., 9–10, 244, 248–249,
      263–266
Heraklit, 38
Herman, E., 216
Herman, J., 171
Hinduism, 85
Hirigoyen, M.-F., 123, 124
Historical perspective. *See also* Western
      historical/religious perspective
  innocence American identity in,
      174–175
  mind–body relationship in, 203–209
  on psychology's denial of evil,
      218–220
  virtue in, 237–243
Hitler, Adolf, 44, 160, 202
Hollingdale, R. J., 114
Hollis, J., 96, 260, 262–263, 265–267,
      269
The Holocaust, 106, 172, 233–234
Homuncular functionalism, 205, 206
Horwitz, A. V., 246
The How of Happiness (S. Lyubomirsky),
      239, 241–242
Human connection, 119, 120
Human existence
  in daimonic model, 26–27
  the dark side as part of, 262–263
  human potential, 21–22
  inherent trauma of, 88–91

Optimistic bias, 247–249
Order, 23
Organismic growth process, 60–61, 262
Organizations. *See* Virtue-driven
    organizations
Origination, dependent, 143–144
Ormuz, 38
Others
    objectification of, 122–124
    one's own evil toward, 126–128
    one's treatment of, 264–265
Overgeneralization, 87–88
Oxford Handbook of Positive Psychology,
    240

Palpatine, 57–58, 60, 65
Parents, 94, 135
Parker, R., 124
Pascal, B., 91
Paul (apostle), 93
Peale, Norman Vincent, 241
Peck, M. S., 125, 129–130, 216
Perils of personhood, 240, 251–252
Perls, Fritz, 45
Permanence, self–other, 121–122
Perpetrators
    blame of, 230–231
    of child abuse, 159
    forgiveness of, 136–137
    guilt feelings in, 133–134
    intentionality of, 149–150
    treatment of, 129–133
Personal anthropology, 47–50
Personal choice, 243
Personal construct theory, 119
Personal–dialogic position, 47–51
Personality
    disorders of, 228, 266, 267
    in psychotherapeutic approach,
        261–262
Personalization
    avoidance of, 49–50
    in person-centered approach, 48–49
    process of, 69–71
    in treatment of others, 264–265
Personal level, 204–205, 208
Person-centered perspective, 35–51
    client in, 67
    the dark side in, 269

    and dualistic view of evil, 38–40
    and evil as minor good, 40–44
    evil in, 36–37
    freedom in, 44–45
    listening in, 70–71
    and personal–dialogic position,
        47–51
    for psychotherapeutic practice,
        45–47
    relational depth in, 26
    self-organizing wisdom in, 63–64,
        68–69
Personhood
    and evil, 49–50
    perils of, 240, 251–252
    in Rogerian approach, 68–69
    theoretical differences on, 264–265
Pessimism, 240, 248
Pfenninger, D. T., 133
The Phantom Menace (film), 57
Pharmaceutical agents, 223–224
Phillip case study, 27–31
Philosophical perspective
    anthropology in, 47–48
    being-centered, 46–47
    evil in, 171–172
    of May, 19–21
    morality in, 198–199, 215–218
    normalcy and madness in, 113–114
    psychology and psychotherapy in,
        266–269
    of Rogers, 41–42
    scientific worldview in, 198–199
    shadow concept in, 87–88
Physical evil, 37
Physicalism, 203–204
Physiological reactions, 227
Plato, 37
Pleasure principle, 200
Political ideology, 219–220, 231–232
Polytheism, 85, 90
Positive psychology movement
    backlash against, 246–247
    the dark side in, 263
    happiness in, 237–240
    implicit logical argument of,
        243–247
    and prior positive thought
        movements, 240–243

with denial of shadow by, 176
ego in, 90, 92–93
in Jungian perspective, 85–88,
91–95, 261
in organizations, 174
in psychotherapeutic practice, 261
Shadows on the Hudson (I. B. Singer),
106, 107
Shame, 175, 180–181
Sheila case study, 160–165
Sherif, M., 171
Shifting, of blame, 176–177
Silencing of victims, 175–176
Singer, I. B., 106, 107
Skinner, B. F., 232
Skywalker, Anakin, 57–58, 60, 65
Skywalker, Luke, 58
Smear campaigns, 175
Smith, D. L., 260, 266, 268
Smith, D. M., 247
Snyder, C. R., 248
Social change, 170, 243
Social conditioning, 44–45
Social interventions, 147–148
Social psychological factors, 5
Societal transformation, 170
Sociopath, 160
Socrates, 39
Spiritual change, 148
Stafford, W., 167, 184
Stanford Prison experiment, 7, 72, 171
Star Wars (film), 3, 57
Staub, I., 216
Staudinger, U. M., 64, 65, 72
Steinbeck, John, 90
Sternberg, R. J., 71
Stevenson, Robert Louis, 241
Stewart, Potter, 158
Storr, A., 158
Strawson, P., 202–203
Structural arrests, 120–122
Subpersonal perspective
agency in, 208, 268
as Freudian theme, 203–209
Substantial–relational beings, 48
Subtle victimizations, 135–136
Suffering. *See also* Dependent
origination
in bad behavior, 148

cognitive–behavioral view on,
262–263
in Jungian perspective, 95–97
and mental illness, 233
of perpetrator, 152
in positive psychology movement, 263
Sugarman, J., 225
Sukin, L., 107
Sullivan, H. S., 101
Superego, 208
Support, 151
Suppression of evidence, 175–176
Suspension, 122
Swamplands of the Soul (J. Hollis), 96
Szasz, Thomas, 222

"Table of Virtues," 238–240
Tabular form, 238
Tallman, Karen, 61
The Talmud, 99
Taylor, S. E., 248
Technique
focusing, 62, 64
in May–Rogers debate, 213
role of, 6–7
in therapeutic change, 6, 25
Tedeschi, R. G., 246, 248
Ten Commandments, 111
Tennen, H., 246, 248
Terence, 93
Terminal psychological ambivalence,
215–217
Terminology
in clinical judgments, 221
descriptive, 222
for diagnostic labels, 267
meaning conveyed by, 225
of moral judgment, 228–229
prescriptive, 222
Thanatos, 38
Theodicy, 85
Theoretical perspective
in conceptualizing evil, 5
on the dark side, 4
depth psychology as, 8
in psychotherapeutic practice, 266,
269–270
of self-organizing wisdom, 67
in therapeutic practice, 6–11

ABOUT THE EDITORS

Arthur C. Bohart, PhD, is Professor Emeritus at California State University, Dominguez Hills. He is best known for his work on the client's role as an active self-healing agent in psychotherapy. He has published a number of chapters and articles on this theme, including the book *How Clients Make Therapy Work: The Process of Active Self-Healing* (with Karen Tallman; 1999). His earlier work focused on the role of empathy in psychotherapy (e.g., *Empathy Reconsidered: New Directions in Psychotherapy*, coedited with Leslie S. Greenberg; 1997). He coedited *Constructive and Destructive Behavior: Implications for Family, School, and Society* (with Deborah J. Stipek; 2001). He has also published a number of papers and chapters on psychotherapy integration.

Barbara S. Held, PhD, is the Barry N. Wish Professor of Psychology and Social Studies at Bowdoin College in Brunswick, Maine. Her work focuses on the theoretical, philosophical, and practical aspects of movements in psychology and psychotherapy and the epistemology and ontology of human/mental kinds. She is the author of *Back to Reality: A Critique of Postmodern Theory in Psychotherapy* (1995), in which she provides theoretical and philosophical analysis of the postmodern linguistic turn in psychotherapy, and of

Psychology's Interpretive Turn: The Search for Truth and Agency in Theoretical and Philosophical Psychology (2007), in which she examines recent hermeneutic, neopragmatic, and constructionist trends in the ontological and epistemological underpinnings of psychological inquiry. She was the 2008–2009 president of the Society for Theoretical and Philosophical Psychology (Division 24 of the American Psychological Association), of which she is a fellow. She is also the author of numerous scholarly articles and chapters and has served on the editorial board of several journals. Trained as a clinical psychologist, she practiced therapy for 15 years. In her popular book *Stop Smiling, Start Kvetching: A 5-Step Guide to Creative Complaining* (2001) and in subsequent scholarly articles, she challenges what she calls the "tyranny of the positive attitude in America" and as a result has become a leading critic of the positive psychology movement. This work has led to extensive national and worldwide media attention, including features in *The New York Times*, *People* magazine, and *Smithsonian* magazine, as well as appearances on NBC's *Today* show, ABC's *World News*, National Public Radio's *Talk of the Nation* and *All Things Considered*, the BBC, and the CBC. She lives with her husband on the coast of Maine.

Edward Mendelowitz, PhD, completed his doctoral studies at the California School of Professional Psychology, where he worked closely with Rollo May. He is on the board of editors for the *Journal of Humanistic Psychology* and is a contributor to some of the major compendiums of existential/humanistic/depth psychotherapy. He has presented numerous papers on psychology, psychotherapy, and their respective interrelations with the humanities in the United States, Europe, and, most recently, East Asia. His work resides on the gnostic frontiers of psychology in its eloquent blending of art, literature, music, cinema, religion, philosophy, and clinical narrative with the more recognizable fare of theory and scholarship. His collage-like *Ethics and Lao-tzu* was called "an extraordinary moral narrative" by Robert Coles and "a remarkable book, a compendium of wisdom from an astonishing variety of sources" by the late psychoanalyst Allen Wheelis. Dr. Mendelowitz is on the faculty of Saybrook Graduate School, is a lecturer at Tufts Medical Center, and Distinguished Visiting Professor at the University of the Rockies. He writes a quarterly online column, *Humanitas*, for the Society of Humanistic Psychology and lives and works in Boston.

Kirk J. Schneider, PhD, is a leading spokesperson for contemporary existential–humanistic psychology. Dr. Schneider is current editor of the *Journal of Humanistic Psychology*, vice president of the Existential–Humanistic Institute, and adjunct faculty at Saybrook University and Teachers College of Columbia University. Dr. Schneider has published more than 100 articles and chapters and has authored or edited eight books, including *The Paradoxical Self: Toward an Understanding of Our Contradictory Nature* (1999); *Horror and the Holy: Wisdom-Teachings of the Monster Tale* (1993); *The Psychology of Existence: An Integrative, Clinical Perspective* (with Rollo May; 1994); *The Handbook of Humanistic Psychology: Leading Edges in Theory, Research, and Practice* (with James F. T. Bugental and J. Fraser Pierson; 2002); *Rediscovery of Awe: Splendor, Mystery and the Fluid Center of Life* (2004); *Existential–Integrative Psychotherapy: Guideposts to the Core of Practice* (2007); *Existential–Humanistic Therapy* (with Orah T. Krug; 2009; accompanying APA video also available); and *Awakening to Awe: Personal Stories of Profound Transformation* (2009). In April 2010, Dr. Schneider delivered the opening keynote address at the First International (East–West) Existential Psychology Conference in Nanjing, China.